THE GRASS of ANOTHER COUNTRY

Other Books by Christopher Merrill

Workbook
(poems)

Outcroppings: John McPhee in the West
(editor)

Fevers & Tides
(poems)

The Forgotten Language: Contemporary Poets and Nature
(editor)

From the Faraway Nearby: Georgia O'Keeffe as Icon
(editor, with Ellen Bradbury)

Christopher Merrill

THE GRASS
of ANOTHER
COUNTRY

· · · · · · ·

*A Journey Through
the World of
Soccer*

HENRY HOLT AND COMPANY
New York

Henry Holt and Company, Inc.
Publishers since 1866
115 West 18th Street
New York, New York 10011

Grateful acknowledgment is made for permission to reprint
the following: "Platko" by Rafael Alberti, from *The Owl's Insomnia:
Poems by Rafael Alberti Selected and Translated by Mark Strand*
(New York: Atheneum, 1972, 1973), reprinted by permission of the translator;
excerpt from *The Journey* by James Wright, copyright © 1977, 1978, 1979,
1980, 1981, 1982 by Anne Wright, Executrix of the Estate of James Wright,
reprinted by permission of Random House, Inc.; lines from "The *Kama Sutra*
According to Fiat," © 1987, 1991 by David St. John, reprinted by permission
of the author; excerpts from "Readings" and "Elegy for N.N.," © 1988 by
Czeslaw Milosz Royalties, Inc., from *The Collected Poems, 1931–1987* by
Czeslaw Milosz, published by The Ecco Press, reprinted by permission.

Library of Congress Cataloging-in-Publication Data
Merrill, Christopher
The grass of another country : a journey through
the world of soccer / Christopher Merrill. — 1st ed.
p.   cm.
Includes bibliographical references
1. Soccer.   2. Soccer—United States.
3. World Cup (Soccer)   I. Title.
GV943.M475   1993   93-4022
796.334—dc20   CIP

ISBN 0-8050-2771-8
ISBN 0-8050-3591-5 (An Owl Book: pbk.)

First published in hardcover in 1993
by Henry Holt and Company, Inc.

First Owl Book Edition—1994

Designed by Francesca Belanger

Printed in the United States of America
All first editions are printed on acid-free paper.∞

1   3   5   7   9   10   8   6   4   2
1   3   5   7   9   10   8   6   4   2   (pbk.)

for Leslie Norris

CONTENTS

• • • • • • •

PREFACE

Miracles abound in New Mexico—wonders and visions and inexplicable occurrences. UFO sightings are common in the desert, and in villages ghosts and gods make regular appearances, walking the hills, etched into adobe, wrapped in tortillas. I know a photographer in Santa Fe, a skeptical man who was surprised one winter morning by a visitation he could neither dismiss nor quite believe. The ice on his bathroom window, he discovered while shaving, had melted and refrozen into a perfect likeness of Christ. An apparition with bad timing: the previous occupants of the house, a devout Catholic couple, had prayed fervently for such a sign from above. My friend photographed the sign vouchsafed to him, resolving not to exhibit it while he lived there. The influx of pilgrims hoping for another miracle might overwhelm him. Travelers in the Land of Enchantment, as New Mexico's license plates read, are as attracted to the strangeness of stories like my friend's as to the sheer beauty of the landscape.

The soccer world is as exotic as anything in New Mexico. What follows is a travel book through the enchanted lands of soccer: a record of encounters with, and enthusiasms about, the world's most popular game. It was a miracle of sorts—the U.S. National Team's success in the qualifying rounds of the 1990 World Cup soccer championship—that inspired my travels. This journey began in

Santa Fe and ended in Rome, at the final match of the fourteenth World Cup, what *Time* magazine called "one sweet dream"—the last major international sporting event before the conclusion of the Cold War plunged the world into its present "time of uncertainties." What was certain at Italia 90, or Mondiale, as Italians referred to their version of the World Cup, was that for millions upon millions of people soccer is a way of life. I wanted to describe that way of life, one foreign to most Americans. *The Grass of Another Country* is a chronicle of exploration into soccer, and the stories I collected will, I hope, make the game understandable and interesting to readers who may join the rest of the world in watching the 1994 World Cup, which will be held for the first time in the United States.

The game had changed since I last put on my cleats to run around a field. Although I grew up in northern New Jersey (a center of American soccer), played through college, then coached in soccer camps and at my alma mater, I discovered that I no longer understood the game's nuances and tactics. It was as if I had to learn a new language in which to appreciate soccer. "The things that unite a society like ours in the late twentieth century seem to be few and far between," Dr. Richard Crepeau, an expert in sports history, said recently. "Sport seems to be a place where we can come together and communicate in some kind of common vocabulary and common sense of values." I traveled here and abroad to learn soccer's vocabulary and values, in hopes of learning something about our common destiny. More speak this language fluently than, say, the languages of Christianity or Islam, Marxism or free market economics. No sport rivals soccer in the number of people it brings together.

Fortunately, I had a wonderful guide and interpreter in Ron McEachen, my college coach and dear friend, who accompanied me to Europe; whatever is intelligent in this book is due in large part to his careful explanations of soccer's changing ways. Our hosts in Italy, Jackie and Enrico Benini, taught us how to appreciate their beautiful country; their hospitality, generosity, and good humor made our stay idyllic. Francisco Elisalde provided me with tickets and good stories all the way through the World Cup final. Sean and Mimi O'Donnell, Roy and Sheila Hodgson, Claudio and Maressa

De Vecchio, Ann Snodgrass, U.S. Ambassador Peter Secchia and his family, all offered me more in the way of friendship and kindness than any acknowledgement can ever match. To Brewster and Olive Ghiselin I owe a special debt: a gift from them made it possible for my wife, Lisa, to share their love of Italy. And Paula and William Merwin invited me to stay in their house in Maui, where I wrote the final draft of this book. I cannot imagine more pleasing surroundings for creative work.

I am grateful to my parents, to Sally Guard, Miller Bugliari, Anne Moore and Greg Beltrane, Ellen Bradbury, John Davis, Cliff and Rosie Gowdy, Bob and Nancy Maynard, Hank White, Helen Whybrow, Andy and Melissa Woolford, and others mentioned in this narrative for their help and good cheer. Agha Shahid Ali, Norman Dubie, Pattiann Rogers, and Brooke and Terry Tempest Williams suffered through long telephone conversations in which I tried out ideas central to my writing. I wish to thank them for their patience. Thanks, too, to Linda Asher, Jeanne McCulloch, Bob Reiss, and Frederick Turner, who read all or part of an early draft of this book. Leslie Norris encouraged me from the outset, read the manuscript with care, and saved me many errors; dedicating *The Grass of Another Country* to him is at best a partial expression of gratitude for the lessons, literary and otherwise, he has taught me through the years.

Jim Schley, truest friend, coaxed a better book out of my first fumbling drafts. Lizzie Grossman, my literary agent, steered *The Grass of Another Country* into the hands of my editor, William Strachan, whose faith in this work sustained me. A timely grant from the Ingram Merrill Foundation freed me to write without fear of the bill collector. And my wife was there from the beginning: my thanks to her for her constant love and support.

Santa Fe, New Mexico

Blue and white shirts, in the air,
royal shirts,
rival shirts, against you, flying and dragging you
     with them,
Platko, far-off Platko,
blond Platko beheaded,
tiger burning in the grass of another country.
                    Rafael Alberti, "Platko"

1
. . . .
RED VEGETABLES

*T*he most important religious holiday in northern New Mexico is Good Friday. On that day hundreds and thousands of pilgrims arrive at the Santuario de Chimayo, an adobe church nestled in the village of Chimayo, a forty-minute drive north of Santa Fe. They come, on foot, from around the state, some marching a hundred miles or more, often dragging large wooden crosses as a form of penance. They make this pilgrimage partly to commemorate the crucifixion of Christ, partly to take home a handful of dirt—blessed dirt from the shrine in the small anteroom to the side of the altar. This Catholic church is built on sacred earth, a burial ground of the local, long-departed Indians. The dirt in the shrine, which every night is reputed to refill a hole in the stone floor, possesses miraculous healing powers: in the room next to the shrine are scores of crutches and testimonials left by the cured. Here the pilgrims light candles for their loved ones, say prayers for the sick and infirm, gather dirt for the journey home.

The pilgrims are usually Hispanic, though in recent years Anglos from Santa Fe have begun to make the trek as well. The newcomers call this a rite of spring or passage—it hardly matters which, for the event is as much a tourist attraction now as it is a religious spectacle. The irreverent tourists, it is true, lend a more festive air to the march, like the happy pilgrims of Chaucer's *Canterbury Tales,* for whom April's "shoures soote" were a call to ribaldry and the road. Yet it is also certain that others find in this ritual a crucial link to the Old World, to the deeper currents running through traditional ways of life, to lives in which faith continues to play a prominent role. I know a poet who visits this shrine before she begins a new book, and rubs the holy dirt in her palm for luck. That she is Jewish seems not to matter in the curious workings of luck: she is one of the most esteemed writers in America.

On Good Friday 1990 I made my own pilgrimage in search of a link to the Old World—away from Chimayo. I traveled south from my home in Santa Fe toward Albuquerque, where the newest franchises in the American Professional Soccer League (APSL), the New Mexico Chiles and the Salt Lake Sting, were making their debut. Since soccer is *the* game of the Old World, the most popular sport —both for players and spectators—on the face of the earth, I wanted to see how it was faring in this part of the New World. Only six months before, the United States had qualified, for the first time in forty years, for the World Cup soccer final—the *crème de la crème* of international sporting events, which in 1990 would take place in Italy. Several members of the U.S. World Cup team were on loan from clubs in the APSL, a principal training ground for our national program.

Founded in 1985, the APSL was a scaled-down version of the North American Soccer League (NASL), the most celebrated (and now bankrupt) attempt to professionalize the game in this country. The NASL had recruited such international stars as Pelé, Franz Beckenbauer, Giorgio Chinaglia, George Best, and Johan Cruyff; created first-class organizations like the New York Cosmos and Los Angeles Aztecs; attracted a measure of support from the public and the media; then abruptly failed in the early 1980s. The APSL had no foreign stars, nor did the media show much interest in the league. Nevertheless, scattered up and down both coasts, as well as in Arizona, Colorado, Utah, and New Mexico, were twenty-two clubs with knowledgeable coaches, talented players who had honed their skills on college and university teams, and enough committed owners to make the league a going concern (at least in the short run).

What does it mean to be a professional soccer player in the United States? What is our audience for the game that four hundred million people around the world play and more than a billion follow, often with what amounts to a kind of religious fervor? And the level of play here—is it world-class? What will it tell me about our chances in the Mondiale, Italy's World Cup? These were the questions I asked myself as I drove down Interstate 25, speeding by Indian reservations and dried river beds. I passed arroyos and mesas covered with piñons and junipers, sagebrush and sand the color of the sky now streaked with the setting sun, tall mountains on either side of the Rio Grande valley. I thought of some of the importations, religious and political, architectural and agricultural, social and aesthetic, thrust upon the Southwest beginning with the arrival of the Spaniards: horses, cattle, *acequias* (an irrigation system modeled on the watering plans of the Moors), churches, beans, and banks. Soccer was only the latest in a long line of exotic introductions.

I considered the strange fate of the Penitentes, the secretive religious brotherhood whose *moradas* or churches dotted northern New Mexico. In the absence of priests, the Spanish settlers had created their own brand of Catholicism, a mysterious sect complete with rituals like flagellation and annual reenactments of the Crucifixion, which sometimes resulted in the deaths of the young men chosen to play the part of the Savior. After hundreds of years of relative neglect, the Penitentes were now objects of interest to religious and lay people alike. The new Archbishop in Santa Fe was making efforts to draw the faithful into the Church's fold. Tourists traveled to villages to photograph the *moradas*. Dennis Hopper, it was rumored, wanted to make a feature film about the Penitentes. Soon even their hymns and prayers might be revealed to the outside world. Here was an untutored form of Catholicism, which for that very reason allowed its believers to retain a depth of faith unfamiliar to a secular age. A religious distortion? Certainly. But what translation ever maintains absolute fidelity to the original? The trick, in religion as in literature, is not to violate the spirit of the primary text. The Penitentes had taken liberties with the original, fashioning for themselves a raw, eccentric vision of religious life in the New World. They had transformed an ancient faith to suit their local needs.

Soccer has been subject to the same kinds of transformation and distortion. I wondered how the game would translate into American; if it could occupy the central place in our lives that it does for so much of the world's population; or if it would remain simply a colorful addition to our sporting landscape. I drove by a band of pilgrims hopelessly late for the services in Chimayo, a low-rider broken down in the highway median, a billboard proclaiming one Tommy Macaione — an aging landscape painter of dubious gifts — to be the latest star in the firmament of artists. I could not imagine a suitable role for soccer here.

The sign advising Picasso, Monet, and van Gogh to make room for one of Santa Fe's lesser artistic lights led me to wonder if the boosterism endemic to the local art world was not also typical of the national soccer scene. Despite the excitement generated by the U.S. team's success, I knew enough to be suspicious about our true standing in the international soccer community. After all, a high-ranking official at the U.S. Soccer Federation (USSF) had told me, in confidence, that our team was made up of little more than "college kids": a squad of Davids on its way to meet Goliaths who were not only faster, tougher, better skilled, and considerably more prepared but who also "knew the game in their blood and bones." Although soccer is one of our fastest-growing participatory sports, no doubt it will take us years to establish a national program capable of competing with traditional soccer powers like Italy, Germany, England, Brazil, and Argentina. For much of the world, soccer — or football, as it is called everywhere but here — is a way of life. For many Americans it is a foreign, boring game.

Yet boys and girls, and growing numbers of men and women, are now playing soccer in this country — more than fifteen million, according to the USSF, which in its promotional literature declares that "America's youth soccer program [is] one of the most sophisticated in the world today." There are good reasons for this mounting interest. It is a game anyone can play, anywhere (indoors and out), at any time of year. Outfitting a soccer club is much less expensive than fielding a football team: a soccer player needs only a good pair of cleats (youngsters can get by with sneakers), shin pads, shorts, a jersey, and a ball. The game can be played on a regulation soccer pitch, a football field, a vacant lot, a street, or in a gymnasium— almost any space will do. And there are positions for everyone in this game, regardless of his or her size or athletic prowess. Soccer is a democratic sport that favors players of average size and build. Diego Maradona, once the greatest player in the world, stands only five feet five inches tall and weighs just 150 pounds.

Soccer's other notable democratic feature is that it attracts play- ers and supporters from a wide range of backgrounds. Maradona, for example, the son of a factory worker, grew up in a barrio of Buenos Aires, not an unusual beginning for international stars. Indeed, a complaint about our soccer players is that because they often come from the middle class they lack the hunger and drive necessary to be truly great. Even Werner Fricker, the former president of the USSF, would use the 1990 World Cup as an occasion to say that soccer in the United States would never reach its potential so long as it was unpopular in our inner cities. Some pundits believe our soccer future lies in places like Albuquerque, a sprawling city of half a million people, with a rich ethnic mix of Hispanics, Native Americans, and Anglos; a strong youth soccer program; and thousands of potential fans. This I kept in mind as I entered the city limits, then drove east along a cement arroyo, up into the foothills of the Sandia Mountains, one of the southernmost incarnations of the Rockies. "There is a rough vigor to Albuquerque," Frederick Turner writes, "that results whenever a railroad town sprawls into a city." I followed that vigor, that sprawl, until I came to Manzano High School, the unlikely home of the New Mexico APSL franchise.

The Chiles were the brainchild of Alan Stopper, an entrepre- neur who with his wife had built what he called "a kitchen-table job" —a mail-order children's clothing business named After the Stork— into a company worth more than $12 million in 1989. In 1990 he sold the business, retaining the presidency for the next five years, then devoted himself to making professional soccer happen in Al- buquerque. A tall order, considering the difficulties involved in mounting any large-scale operation, to say nothing of those integral to unpopular sports like soccer. Duke Keith, a local sportswriter, observed that "pro franchises have found Albuquerque to be a sports desert, absorbing teams faster than rain." Few gave the Chiles much chance of surviving. This is a city in love with the University of New Mexico basketball team, the Lobos (the football team is a perennial loser); a city whose NBC affiliate lets its viewers call in each week to choose which NFL game it will broadcast that Sunday, uncertain whether to describe the Denver Broncos or Dallas Cowboys as "home teams"; a city with only one successful pro franchise, the Dukes of the Pacific Coast League, a Triple-A baseball club grooming young players for the Los Angeles Dodgers. Yet Stopper and his partners, former Albuquerque mayor David Rusk and local CPA Dennis Burt, were determined to bring professional soccer to the Southwest.

"I see my life in decades," Stopper told a reporter, "and I've made a commitment to stick with the Chiles for ten years."

He brought to this undertaking his entrepreneurial spirit, love of the game, and sound business sense. To break even, he estimated he needed to average 3,000 fans a game—a figure that for financial reasons would later be revised upward; he *hoped* to attract 2,000. Thus he created an ambitious advertising campaign, targeting the sizable Hispanic market, offering low-priced tickets and discounts to youth teams and clubs from the senior leagues. He worked out a television deal to present matches with a Spanish station, on a tape-delayed basis. And before the season started, when the rest of the media showed little interest in his team, he took out weekly advertisements in the Albuquerque *Journal,* notices in the form of press releases designed to keep potential supporters abreast of the Chiles' progress: which players had been signed, who was in town, how training sessions were going. The dirt parking lot adjacent to Manzano High School, crowded with cars, vans, and buses, provided clear evidence that Stopper's marketing gambit had paid off: more than 5,000 fans streamed into F. M. Wilson Stadium, an arena with seating for 7,000. Over the course of the season the Chiles would average better than 4,800 fans a game.

In the stadium that night there was a festive air, as if this were the homecoming game at a small college: the crowd gathered for the sake of gathering. The stands were lined with families and teams, of all ages, in their respective uniforms; a surprising number of teenagers—boys *and* girls—shuffled about on crutches, presumably injured in soccer matches. It was a players' crowd. Everyone—Hispanic and Anglo, youngster and adult—seemed to know everyone else. Over the public address system music crackled, a tape of Glenn Frey singing "The Heat Is On," the Chiles' theme song. The announcer kept breaking in to welcome us to the "Chile Bowl," as the stadium was now to be called. Catchin' Fire was the Chiles' motto; the team colors were red and green, the colors of the hot peppers that give northern New Mexico cuisine its special flavor. "Go Red Vegetables!" chanted a group of boys near me, waving at the players down on the field. The crowd was in a fine mood on this warm spring evening. The sky was clear, and the Sandia Mountains rising starkly behind the stands on the opposite side of the field gave off a reddish tinge, a blush the color of watermelon pulp, a glow that held long after sunset. A carnival atmosphere prevailed, not unlike what I might find across town at a Dukes' game. These were the minor leagues: nothing was on the line, as far as this crowd was concerned.

Surely the players concluding their warm-ups had different ideas about the stakes involved in this match. They were beginning their professional careers, the average age of the Chiles being twenty-four; several had only recently completed college. Starting pay? Decidedly minor-league for the Chiles: $70 for a win, $50 for a loss or a tie, plus travel expenses. Most if not all of the players took second jobs to make ends meet, waiting tables, substitute teaching, or working at Sandia National Laboratories—a major defense research center. In this they resembled young artists more than sports figures, choosing to labor in obscurity for the love of their craft instead of for wealth and glory, though each one must have entertained dreams of landing a spot on the next World Cup team, of playing abroad, of discovering fame and fortune. Theirs was a noble cause, like poetry. As they took their last shots on goal, and the keepers practiced long throws and dropkicks, and one or two midfielders ran short sprints to stretch their legs, I admired their spirit and tenacity. They were determined, against all odds, to make their mark in a sport still ignored by most Americans.

Shortly before game time, both teams returned to their locker rooms to hear their coaches' final words of advice. During the match itself, the coaches would offer encouragement and, except for what they might say in their brief half-time meetings, only minimal instructions; the rules prohibit active coaching from the sidelines. Unlike the cat-and-mouse moves a baseball manager makes pitch by pitch; or the carefully programmed play a football coach (backed by a battery of scouts, trainers, and coordinators of the offensive, defensive, and specialty teams) sends in before each snap of the pigskin; or the time outs a basketball coach calls to disrupt the momentum of the opposing team, give his players a breather, and diagram another variation on a set play—most of a soccer coach's work takes place before the match begins.

Once the referee blows the whistle to signal the start of play, the soccer coach becomes a spectator who must hope his team will perform according to his wishes, ideas, and training methods—a choreographer, if you will, of a ballet conditioned by chance, by the way the ball bounces, spins, and flies. Even the option of making substitutions is severely restricted. Eighteen players suit up for the match, eleven of whom start, but the coach is allowed to substitute only twice. Those are decisions he cannot afford to take lightly. If, for example, he makes both substitutions and then another player goes down with an injury, his team must play the rest of the match one short. Likewise, there are no substitutions for players ejected for misconduct. Soccer is a brutally simple sport.

The stadium lights came on, and the teams filed out together behind the referee and two linesmen. The public address system sputtered again; then the announcer introduced the players, the coach of the Sting, and dignitaries from the APSL. Unaccountably, he forgot to mention Dave Carr, the coach and general manager of the Chiles. Carr was wearing the same uniform as his players—his counterpart, Laurie Calloway, a dapper Englishman who had played and coached in the NASL, was dressed in a gray suit—and I wondered if the announcer had mistaken him for a player. Although I had only spoken with Carr over the phone, I felt as if I knew him. Had my life worked out differently, I realized with a start, I might now find myself coaching a team like the Chiles. Stranger things have happened. Carr and I had both grown up playing soccer in New Jersey, discovered our respective vocations while coaching the B soccer team at Middlebury College in Vermont, and were now working in the Southwest. I had decided to be a writer rather than a full-time coach. Yet I believed I shared with Dave Carr, my successor at Middlebury, a vital connection.

But my soccer career—if you could call it that—had ended almost a decade ago. I had played for three years at Middlebury, skipping my last year of eligibility to go to graduate school. When I returned to my alma mater—with another degree, a head full of ideas about literature, and the woman who would be my wife—to work for my old friend, head coach Ron McEachen, I imagined I had something to finish, soccer-wise. Often I had regretted passing up my final year of play; perhaps coaching would provide some closure. But I lasted only one season: my real interests lay in books. Besides, I lacked the knowledge, experience, and vision of good coaches like McEachen—the talent and drive to mold a winning team. Musicians complain about conductors stumbling for the first time through a piece members of the orchestra may have played at a dozen concerts or more. "He's green," violinists say among themselves, nodding at a conductor sweating on the podium. The same holds for soccer coaches, who in this country frequently cannot or refuse to gain the experience necessary for success. In the hills of Vermont, gazing at the brilliant colors of the changing leaves, I knew I would always be that kind of coach.

Thus after my last game at Middlebury, I returned to the literary world, where I was more comfortable with the notion of learning my craft in public—that is, in the pages of the little magazines and journals that offered to publish my first poems and stories. "A writer can be seen clumsily learning to walk," the late John Cheever wrote of his own literary apprenticeship, "to tie his necktie, to make love, and to eat his peas off his fork. He appears much alone and determined to instruct himself." That regimen seemed to suit me better than the coaching profession.

Dave Carr had had other ideas about his own future. He had used his experience at Middlebury as a springboard to a professional coaching career. His next stop was the University of Charleston (West Virginia), where he built from scratch a respectable program and won the attention of Alan Stopper, who hired him to do the same with his APSL franchise. As coach and general manager, Carr had to scramble to put the Chiles together: he had to recruit, coach, and find second jobs for his players; arrange team travel; enlist corporate sponsors; set up soccer camps throughout the state. Eighty-hour work weeks were not unusual.

"In October it was an idea," he said of his team, "and in April it was a reality."

What I saw on the field was his creation, his vision of soccer. Although the Chiles would end up with a losing record and miss the play-offs, that night I admired what he had created. He had signed players from colleges and clubs around the country, including Kevin Wiley, one of Ron McEachen's standouts at the University of Vermont, where Ron was now coaching. He had trained them to play together as a team and generated enthusiasm in the community. Now he had a stadium almost filled with spectators anxious to see what his Chiles could do. Yes, I was envious.

How many times had I gone for a run on the mesa behind my house, daydreaming about playing or coaching on the professional level! I thought of all the hours I had devoted to reliving certain moments in my own career: a ball rolling through the penalty area in a match against Connecticut College, a ball needing nothing more than the side of my foot to put it into the net and send Middlebury into the next round of the Eastern College Athletic Conference (ECAC) tournament—a ball I would never reach. But if I had, I would tell myself, running among the piñons and squawking magpies, then maybe . . . No. Now I was covering soccer. "Write about what you know," young writers are advised. And here I was, taking notes on the game I had spent so much of my life playing, and dreaming about.

The smell of smoke woke me from my reverie.

Someone had placed a flare at the top of the penalty area to my right, and the thick plume of smoke issuing from it drifted over the field. Around me fans craned their necks and stared up at the sky, as if searching for a sign from the heavens. Here was a remarkable sight: four sky divers plummeting into the Chile Bowl, using the smoke's trail to gauge the direction of the wind. Perhaps equally amazing was what the parachutists saw. Their target, the circle at midfield, where they were supposed to land and deliver the game ball, was studded with players, coaches, officials, and dignitaries. The timing of the pregame activities was off. The sky divers had nowhere to land, and so they scattered toward the four corners of the stadium, twisting in the light wind. For a startling moment it looked as if one might even plunge into our section of the stands. Then he veered away and dropped onto the track separating us from the field. Another landed on the track in front of the stands across the way, his chute settling over the first few rows of seats. While he reeled in his cloth and cords, the crowd clapped and laughed. In the end the field was cleared, the ball handed over to the referee. A fuzzy rendition of our national anthem echoed around the stadium, the scratches in the record audible in the public address system, and then the match began.

Any illusions the players may have harbored about the APSL's professionalism must have been dispelled by the sky-diving debacle. In like manner, the field itself left something to be desired. It was, of course, a football field, complete with yardage signs, hash marks, and end zones, and it was narrower than most soccer pitches. "In International Matches," the rule book states, "the length shall be not more than 120 yards nor less than 110 yards and the breadth not more than 80 yards nor less than 70 yards." The field in the Chile Bowl seemed smaller by far. What is more, the concrete border dividing the track from the field was covered on one side by 150 burlap sacks filled with cotton husks—a safety measure made possible by a local feed company and a fruit dealer. But their largess did not extend all the way around the border, for the other side was bare. And because the surface of this field was artificial turf instead of grass (the only surface allowed in international play), for drainage purposes its pitch sloped downward toward both sidelines; players centering the ball from either wing would have to strike it slightly uphill, like a golfer using a wedge to clear a bunker.

Artificial turf makes for a faster game, since the ball skids instead of rolls across the carpet. From the outset both teams moved the ball quickly, building up attacks with short, crisp passes, then switching the ball from one side of the field to the other, looking for openings in the defense, guarding against swift counterattacks. "We have to be able to play on this stuff," Carr had said in a pregame interview. "Movement, player position, hitting the ball, speed of play, narrowness—it's more direct." The rhythm of the match was also direct, and constant. An earmark of American soccer: the inability to shift tempos, to slow the action down or speed it up. Like poetry and jazz, soccer is a subtle art, a game of nuances, and rhythm is one of its essential elements. Sophisticated players can play in a bewildering variety of rhythms, changing speeds smoothly, imaginatively, improvising from one moment to the next. Yet many American soccer players, like many American poets and rock musicians, seem to know only one rhythm—high tempo. Foreign coaches and players like to attribute that to our innocence, our inexperience. In the Chile Bowl it meant the ball skimmed over and skipped across the artificial turf, picking up speed. The pace of the match never let up.

If part of soccer's artistry lies in its rhythmic possibilities—the ability of stars like Pelé and Beckenbauer, Best and Maradona to dictate the changing tempos of a match—another part resides in its fluidity. Unlike those of baseball, football, and basketball, sports in which stoppages of play are the norm rather than the exception, the rules of soccer are designed to keep the game moving. When the referee signals an infraction, the ball is usually back in play within seconds. Only when a player is injured; when a major foul is called near one goal or the other; or when the referee must book (that is, warn) or eject a player for excessive roughness, unsportsmanlike conduct, using foul or abusive language, or for committing a "professional foul" (for example, tripping a player who has a breakaway attempt on goal), does play stop for more than a moment. A sixty-minute football game takes about three hours to complete, a ninety-minute soccer match less than two.

Like a play marching inexorably toward its climax and conclusion, a soccer match occurs in a dramatic context, which depends for its effects on an uninterrupted flow of action and lull, give and take, attack and counterattack. Each of its forty-five-minute halves creates an arc of rising and falling intensity—an arc as yet incompatible with the advertising demands of commercial television networks in this country. While many goals are scored in the first or last ten minutes of a half, when one or the other team may be either caught off-balance or tiring, the dynamics of a match are often most interesting during the first twenty or twenty-five minutes, when each team has had a chance to test the other. Then the game's rhythms become apparent. What the arc of the match between the Chiles and Sting revealed was a mixture of skillful play and mistakes arising from inexperience or innocence, nerves, and lack of training. Yet even to the unsophisticated eye the spectacle of two teams passing and dribbling and chasing down the ball, creating patterns of movement on the spur of the moment, was exciting.

"Go Red Vegetables!" cried another group of boys in green Chiles' T-shirts. "Go Melman! Go!"

The "Melman" was Mel Williams, a twenty-two-year-old forward for the Chiles. A sturdy player, fast and talented and dangerous with the ball, Williams had been a member of the Far West Regional Team. Tonight he was the crowd favorite. His advice to the youngsters who idolized him was plainspoken: "Practice a lot of touch by yourself." And he had touch, the kind of ball control that separates good players from bad. In other sports and art forms touch is what distinguishes genius from journeyman—a Magic Johnson from a Mark Eaton, a Woody Allen from an Andrew Dice Clay, a John Updike from a Stephen King. The same is true in soccer. Good players can trap any ball, with any part of their bodies—except, of course, their hands and arms—and quickly bring it under control. They can dribble at full speed or slow, faking and feinting past defenders. They can use spins to pass and can shoot around and over their opponents. In short, touch is the key element of soccer's craft.

Juggling a soccer ball—or an orange, or a sock filled with wadded newspapers or, harder yet, a tennis ball—is one way to acquire touch and technique. Keeping a ball aloft with the inside, outside, and instep of both feet, thighs, and head; tapping it from side to side and up into the air, making certain it does not hit the ground: that is how many players learn to control the ball in flight or on the run. Touch is a function of imagination and inventiveness; soccer players praised for their artistry have devoted their lives to developing "ball sense," often juggling a ball for hours at a time, bouncing it from "right foot to left foot," as I wrote in my first published poem, "A Boy Juggling a Soccer Ball":

> stepping forward and back,
> to right foot and left foot,
> and left foot up to his thigh, holding
> it on his thigh as he twists
> around in a circle until it rolls
> down the inside of his leg,
> like a tickle of sweat,

and so on. Indeed, in my childhood I considered juggling a soccer ball a perfect way to spend a summer afternoon, a passion shared with players all over the world.

One of soccer's origins lies in ball juggling, an activity and art with roots deep in memory. Legend has it that five thousand years ago, during the reign of the Yellow Emperor in China, young men performed juggling tricks with a ball similar to the leather soccer ball used today. In the Han Dynasty three thousand years later, in an epoch marked by the introduction of Buddhism and elsewhere by the birth of Christ, artists carved reliefs of juggling footballers. The early Greeks passed ball juggling on to the Romans, who invented what historians agree was a precursor to the modern game. To this day monks in Shinto temples, in small groups and dressed in ritual attire, juggle a wicker ball for ceremonial purpose, passing it among themselves like American college students playing hacky-sack between classes. And the religious ball games of North American Indians, which are still performed in many places, may once have involved juggling tricks. Defying gravity with a ball, whether for athletic, aesthetic, or religious purposes, has always delighted people.

This is what had first drawn the youngsters near me to the Melman. In the warm-up he had amazed them with his juggling skills, heading the ball into the air, then catching it with his foot and balancing it on his instep. Now he took a well-struck ball on his chest and, holding it there as he made a half-turn to shield it from a defender, he brought the ball down to his feet and exploded past the other player, dribbling toward the penalty area—a brilliant move and run cut short by another defender, who stripped the ball from the Melman with a vicious tackle that earned him a verbal warning from the referee.

Williams rose slowly to his feet, clutching his shin. Touch, I reminded myself, only carries you so far.

Soccer may be a brutally simple sport, but for much of its history it was simply brutal. From the beginning, it seems, humans have loved to kick things—balls, doors, skulls; in the records of every civilization there is evidence of kicking games like soccer. Chinese court games, Japanese *kemari,* Pueblo kickball, the ball games of the ancient Egyptians, the *calcio storico* still played in Italy, village football—"the mob game for ruffians" the English invented or imported from the Continent, codified into the modern game of soccer in 1863, then exported around the world—in almost every culture humans have relaxed from the tedium of daily life by kicking something round over plains and fields, through streets and cities, in courts and stadiums.

A few hundred miles south of Albuquerque, travelers may come across some of the dozens of ball court ruins scattered throughout Mexico and Central America, legacies from the Mayan and Aztec cultures, dating back to the ninth century. While the game played or performed in these elaborate temple complexes did not develop into modern soccer, nevertheless the central place it held in Mesoamerican society is hauntingly familiar. Certainly the conquering Spaniards understood the importance of "ballgame": in 1528 Cortez brought a pair of Aztec ballplayers back to the court of Charles V, showed them off, then outlawed the game, ostensibly because of its violent, bloody nature. This was, in the Spanish view (and in fact), another religious ritual to eradicate. Doomed though ballgame was, scholars have pieced together a picture of it, a sport and ceremony at once sacred and profane, beautiful and savage.

The game was played in arenas whose walls were covered with moonscapes and the precession of equinoxes. "Some [of the costumed] performers represented the sun, the moon, or other celestial forms," Richard Mandell writes in his cultural history of sport:

> If parts of the contest were left to skill or chance, the process and results were interpreted oracularly and provided the priests with hints as to which deities should be satisfied in order to guarantee the orderly progress of the seasons, to secure good harvests, and forestall the ineradicable terror of social chaos.

The object of the game was to knock a small hard ball made of gum or rubber through stone rings jutting from the walls. The performers, helmeted and padded like U.S. football players, passed and shot the ball with their hips; there are reports of the ball moving so fast it whistled in the air, sometimes killing those it struck in the head. Violent forearm smashes and body checks were offset by stylized and balletlike movements. The price of defeat was high: decapitation. "The scenes of the costumed losers recall the festive executions of gladiators" in Rome, Mandell suggests, then adds a macabre caution against mourning for the losers: "We cannot be sure they were losers. In the light of the prestige accorded to some victims slated for ritual execution and cannibalism, perhaps they were winners."

Ballgame's beheadings may remind us of another possible origin of soccer: warriors kicking the heads of their vanquished foes over a battlefield. Just as an evolving language retains on some level of memory the root meaning of each of its words, so modern soccer contains memories of its barbaric origins, ball juggling and beheadings, religious rituals and battle scars. The defender who had knocked the Melman down, for instance, was called—not without justification—"a hatchetman," a player charged with the responsibility of taking out the opposing team's star. It does not require a great leap of imagination to picture a hatchetman on a Mayan ball court or an ordinary soccer fan at a gladiator's execution in the Colosseum. Many sports began in blood and beauty.

There was more blood than beauty in the village football played throughout medieval Europe. This early form of soccer, reserved for feast days and often waged between neighboring villages, was closer in spirit to battle than sport. Richard Mandell describes it:

> There were few rules and they were never written. Old men and women and children were not excluded. Spectators might join in and people could change sides. Injuries and deaths were most frequent when the teams (which could easily number a hundred to a side) were rival villages with ancient enmities—which were perpetuated by injuries during the football games. In such contests the intervening distance—which could be more than two miles—provided the area over which a stuffed pig's bladder was pulled to and fro. There were no referees or time outs. The game could last a whole day. The melee was more important than a victory. With darkness contestants and spectators abandoned themselves to riotous drinking.

No wonder English authorities and moralists condemned the game. Their opposition, Mandell writes, explains why we have "more archival documentation testifying to village football's popularity in England" than anywhere else, and yet their efforts to halt the spread of the game were futile.

Modern soccer derives from sports played in the English public schools of the nineteenth century. In 1863 a group of headmasters met in London to draw up rules insuring that village football would give way to the tamer "dribbling game" their students played, the game British sailors in the coming years would leave, like illegitimate children, in every port of call. Soccer would become the most popular (and perhaps benign) export of Queen Victoria's empire, though not until the headmasters settled a thorny problem: whether or not to allow the use of hands. In one meeting an argument erupted over this issue, and those who favored the use of hands seceded from the association to codify the game of rugby, which in turn spawned American football. (Reeling from the effects of a different kind of secession, and suspicious of anything British, especially in light of Great Britain's support of the Confederacy in the Civil War, Americans were reluctant to take up soccer. That Abner Doubleday's game was already sweeping the countryside did not help matters: baseball was well on its way to becoming our national pastime.) The remaining headmasters—by far the majority—formed Association football, and soccer (the word comes from *Assoc,* short for *Association*) was born.

The Scottish invention of the forward pass in 1870 restored to soccer some of the style missing since the days of ball juggling. Tactics became an element of the game; touch acquired a degree of importance; *creativity* worked its way into the vocabulary of those describing the sport. Thenceforth, soccer would be a balancing act between our animal and angelic impulses, brute force and grace. Founded on physical contact, the modern game would depend on touch and technique for its effects, artistry, and excitement. The decision to forbid the use of hands proved to be a stroke of genius. Since manual dexterity is one of our distinguishing human features, sports that undercut this "advantage" may allow for purer expressions of our kinship with the animal kingdom. Soccer players, except goalkeepers and those throwing the ball inbounds, must compensate for the loss of that which makes them tool-bearing individuals, and that is a limitation conducive to creativity, a necessity that fosters invention—bicycle kicks, spins on the ball, dribbling displays.

The object of the game, of course, has changed little since medieval times: scoring goals. In recent years it has become more difficult to put the ball in the net, defensive schemes and strategies having grown so expert that the eight-by-twenty-four-foot goals now seem altogether too small. Just the same, the best moments of a match

usually occur near one or the other goal. And it was the Salt Lake
Sting that offered the most excitement in the Chile Bowl, creating
many more chances to score than the home team. By now it was full
dark; the desert night was cooling quickly. Again and again the
Sting's two forwards and striker broke through the Chiles' disorganized defenses to take good shots on goal. Jimmy De Rose, the Chiles'
goalkeeper and a former New England NAIA (National Association
of Intercollegiate Athletics) Collegiate Player of the Year, made several fine saves, leaping across the goal mouth, fisting the ball away,
breaking up plays in the penalty area. Often he cleared the ball past
midfield, his booming left-footed dropkicks drawing applause from
the crowd, only soon to face another onslaught.

One sure goal was deflected by a New Mexico defender standing
in front of an open net, and the Chiles' efforts to catch the attacking
Sting offside — one player shouting "Get the hell up!" to the other
Chiles, moving the whole defense upfield to trap the Sting on the
wrong side of the ball (that is, between the last Chiles' defender and
the goalkeeper) — failed repeatedly. Three minutes before the end of
the first half, Sting forward Dominic Militello took advantage of
another Chiles' defensive lapse to score. Two minutes later he scored
again, this time on a hard shot to the lower right-hand corner of the
goal. The referee's whistle moments later to signal the end of the first
half was a welcome relief. The Chiles had been outplayed, outshot
13−2, and frustrated at every turn; the 2−0 score could have been
much worse. The crowd's initial excitement was gone. The youngsters near me were more interested in the half-time activities — a
penalty shoot-out, sponsored by a local soccer merchant, for "five
lucky fans" — than in the fate of their professional team.

It may have been Good Friday, but it was also Friday the 13th.
If I were more superstitious, I might have found in that coincidence
an omen or warning. The Chiles' poor showing on the field was only
the beginning of what would seem an endless string of bad news,
including injuries to key players, more losses than wins, disciplinary
problems. Worst of all, despite good crowds and solid community
support, before Christmas the Chiles would be out of business. The
team would lose several hundred thousand dollars, its aggressive

marketing campaign costing much more than it could recoup at the gate, and it would lack the money required to stay in the league — a $1.5 million fee payable to the USSF, according to a source close to the team. Before the end of the year, the APSL franchises in Colorado, Portland, and Arizona would be bankrupt, other teams would be planning mergers, and even the Sting, whose owners included comic actor Bill Murray, would be looking for new investors. Professional soccer in this country would be in disarray, in spite of the USSF's assurances that a viable league would be in place long before the next World Cup.

Perhaps I sensed some of these impending problems. I was depressed by the circus atmosphere in the Chile Bowl — first the sad spectacle of the sky divers, then the constant jabber of the public address announcer, who kept listing names and birthdays and discounts and upcoming attractions, like a barker in the big top. Here was soccer dressed up for an American audience, and the effect bordered on the comic. Everyone — players, coaches, dignitaries, vendors, ushers, fans — was trying too hard, though it was plain to see that neither team was much better than a good college side. Hence even the TV cameras sweeping over the crowd, amusing children and adults, upset me: I knew they would not be back. This was a one-shot affair, a human-interest angle, not an ongoing story.

The second half began much as the first half had ended, with the Chiles on the defensive. Seven minutes into play, the Melman decked one of his defenders, knocking him right off his feet. Williams's frustration netted him a yellow card from the referee; it could have resulted in a red card and ejection from the match. A more prescient observer might have discerned in his behavior hints of future trouble. This crowd-pleaser's luck would change. Although the Melman would lead the Chiles in scoring early in the season, he would suffer a knee injury serious enough to sideline him for several weeks; soon after returning to the team, he would be dismissed for "disciplinary reasons." Now he created two good scoring chances; and midway through the half, on a free kick from Osian Roberts, Williams headed home the Chiles' first goal, bringing the spectators to their feet.

But the euphoria was short-lived. Less than a minute after the Melman's goal, Militello completed a hat trick—surrounded by Chiles. His goal deflated whatever hopes the Chiles and their fans had mustered. The Sting were faster, had more skill, more touch, than the Chiles, and the final score—3 – 1—would have been more lopsided if not for De Rose's fine play in the goal. Indeed, his efforts earned him Player of the Game honors: $100—twice the amount he made for turning aside almost twenty shots—would be donated in his name to the New Mexico Coalition for Children.

Dave Carr had invited me to a postgame reception at the Hilton, an invitation the public address announcer extended to the crowd, over and over again. I left the Chile Bowl and drove downtown, expecting to see hundreds of fans milling around the hotel. For the first hour or so, fewer than a dozen of us were there to greet the players shuffling into the bar. The young men carried their own bags, bought beers, stood to one side of the bar, talking quietly to their friends. They reminded me of a traveling theater company more than a professional sports team—struggling artists instead of athletes dreaming, perhaps, of contracts and endorsements.

Laurie Calloway, the coach of the Sting, wandered around the bar, greeting players and fans, a broad smile on his face. But there was no sign of his counterpart. On my way out of the stadium I had seen Dave Carr at midfield, surrounded by TV cameras, answering the sportscasters' questions. These were his fifteen minutes of fame, in Albuquerque. I waited another hour, hoping to meet him. More players trickled in, another fan or two arrived, and the noise level rose slightly. But the party had nothing in common with the "riotous drinking" of the medieval village footballers. In the end I gave up on waiting for Dave Carr. I had a long drive back to Santa Fe. I knew the roads were filled with drunk drivers. I did not want to take any chances on a night like this.

2
· · · · · · ·
DUSTLESS DIRT

*F*archer's Grove lies just north of Route 22 in Union, New Jersey. Surrounded by nondescript factories and plants, this social club for the local German-American population houses in one run-down building a bar, restaurant, lounge, and dance hall. Outside, beyond a rusting fence and a faded sign advertising car alarms, is one of the oldest lighted soccer fields in North America, a mecca of sorts for soccer players in this country. This is where the Union Lancers, Elizabeth Sport Club, and dozens of soccer teams — youth, adult, and senior; amateur, semiprofessional, and professional — have in this century trained and played, including the Newark Sport Club, on whose youth team I had played half a lifetime ago. It was here that I made the next stop on my journey into the world of soccer — an excursion guided as much by my own memories of the game as by a documentary interest in revisiting a soccer shrine.

On a warm Friday night in May, I met two old friends, Sean and Mimi O'Donnell, to watch the Lancers play an exhibition match against the Fort Lauderdale Strikers, a leading club from the Eastern Division of the APSL. In the rickety wooden stands near the club-house there were about 150 people, almost all of whom knew Sean, a local soccer legend. He is a short, strong Scotsman, with curly blond hair and blue eyes that light up repeatedly in conversation. A high-spirited man, Sean has a mischievous grin, a certain puckishness. There is more than a little of the elf in him, as anyone who has ever played against him will tell you, especially those given the unhappy task of trying to keep him from scoring. I had not seen him in fifteen years, yet I vividly remembered the times I had counted myself fortunate to be playing with Sean instead of against him. He was, my friends and I had agreed, a wizard on the field.

Sean and I had met as sophomores at Pingry, a boys' day school on the verge of dramatic change: first it would become a coeducational institution, then move, after our graduation, from its urban setting in Hillside to a new campus out in the country, among the horse farms, estates, and suburban homes in the village of Martinsville, some twenty miles to the west. One constant in the midst of these changes was Pingry's long-standing tradition as a soccer power. Coached by Miller Bugliari, an eccentric and inspiring man who in thirty-odd years at his team's helm has racked up more than four hundred victories, including seven Union County championships, fifteen State Prep A titles, and a fifty-eight-game winning streak back in the late 1960s and early 1970s, Pingry has produced an astonishing number of fine players.

"Half of them go on to play in college," Bugliari had told me earlier in the week. "A few years ago we had three Pingry kids playing in the same NCAA [National Collegiate Athletic Association] Final Four."

A remarkable accomplishment, considering the small size of the school, and an achievement that has not gone unnoticed in soccer circles. In the first part of his career, Bugliari turned down several offers to become general manager of a professional team, preferring to stay at Pingry, where twice he has been awarded National Coach of the Year honors.

"My strength is talking to the kids," he had said in his office, which was chockablock with soccer memorabilia—photographs of every team, trophies and medals, uniforms, catalogs, deflated soccer balls, yellowing newspaper clippings, piles of soccer magazines. Even his metal file cabinets, pulled open and cluttered with files and notes on his players and teams, seemed devoted much more to soccer than to his nonathletic responsibilities, teaching biology and directing alumni affairs. "That's why I couldn't do the other things," he grinned, waving at a basket of student papers and correspondence destined, perhaps, never to be plumbed.

What he could do was take a player like Sean and give him a chance not only to excel on the soccer field but also to get a first-rate education. Sean had made the most of his opportunity, setting enough scoring records to attract the attention of college coaches everywhere. He may have been Pingry's greatest player. Certainly he was one of Bugliari's favorites.

"Here, look at this," the coach insisted, displaying a photograph of Sean on the cover of an old *Soccer World*. Then he recited some of his star player's honors: "All-County. All-State. Season scoring record. Most goals in a game. All-Ivy. National Teams. Olympic tryout. What a player!"

What a player, indeed. After graduating from Pingry, Sean had become the first player ever to start four straight years on the University of Pennsylvania soccer team, setting its modern scoring record. While still in college, he trained with the New York Cosmos' B Team —a weekend activity that came to an abrupt end once the front office discovered he had yet to graduate. "They didn't want to get in trouble with the colleges," Sean said. His professional career ended before it had even begun, he collected his degree in Civil Engineering and, while working toward an M.B.A. at Seton Hall, played for clubs in the metropolitan area—Eintrach of the German-American League, the Kearny Scots, the Lancers. Now he is with a club in the Italian-American League, because their Sunday matches take place near his home in Basking Ridge. As director of sales and marketing for Datacorp, a software designer in Madison, New Jersey, he travels too much to be able to practice with the Lancers.

"I never liked practicing anyway," he laughed. "And if you don't practice, you don't get paid. Not that you make much: fifty bucks for a win, twenty-five for a draw, nothing if you lose."

"If you didn't practice," I said, "then how did you learn to control the ball so well?"

"This field," he explained, nodding at the players finishing their warm-up. "I wasn't into juggling. It was too boring! But trying to do something with the ball in all these ruts—that gives you touch in a hurry."

The field, to put it plainly, was a mess. Bare as a vacant lot razed for a landscaping project, it got so much use that grass could not grow on it.

"They tried to plant grass here once," Sean recalled. "They closed everything down, trucked in topsoil, seeded the whole field. It didn't work. There's too much wind. Now the topsoil's all over the railroad tracks," he grinned, pointing at the power plant to our right. "They even tried some kind of dustless dirt! But that didn't work either."

What resulted was a dirt field capable of frustrating even the most skilled players. Bad bounces are the rule at Farcher's Grove. I remembered training here under the lights in midwinter: how the cleat marks, divots, and holes in the mud would freeze until the field was harder and rougher than a cobblestone street. Good players like Sean learned to run with short strides, moving their feet constantly, hoping not to turn an ankle. They learned to trap the ball with a minimum of effort, dribble it close to their feet so that it would not get away from them, adapt instantly to balls ricocheting off the ground, deliver to their teammates quick, accurate passes, and pray for the best.

Half an hour late, the match finally began (with, I might add, no fanfare, none of the hoopla I had witnessed at the New Mexico Chiles' opening game in Albuquerque). The public address announcer, a man with a thick German accent, read off the names of the players on both teams, and that was the last we heard from him until half time. Even the crowd was silent at first, except for two heavily made-up young women near us, who had designs on several Lancers. The women giggled, pointing at the players in the black-and-white striped Lancer jerseys that, unlike those of their opponents, bore no team insignia, only Prussak Electrical Contractor printed in large letters.

The women had little interest in the match itself. Many in the crowd felt the same way once they realized that the Strikers, fitter than the Lancers and match toughened after their road trip through the Northeast, would carry the day against the home club. Soon I felt as if I were at a social event instead of an athletic contest. The women comparing notes on the young men on the field, the retired players around us mixing stories of old soccer matches with family news, the older men dispensing drinks from a long table set up outside the clubhouse—everything here reminded me that Farcher's Grove was a social club. This match was a prelude to the night's activities, a kind of happy hour before some people settled down to more serious drinking in the bar, others went to dinner, and still others assembled for the weekly singles' dance. For Sean it was a homecoming. Because so many people asked after his father, uncle, and brothers, all of whom had been standout players, it took him more than twenty minutes to buy a six-pack of Coors.

"A buck and a quarter a beer," he said, passing me a cold can. "Where else can you drink so cheap?"

"At home," Mimi said playfully.

Sean smiled. "We used to play two-touch here as kids," he said. "The goals were empty kegs. Great days!"

Two-touch is a game that tests a player's skill and ball control. In each possession he may touch the ball no more than two times. Three touches—a trap, say, then a dribble and a pass—means the ball must be turned over to the other team. Such a demanding regimen can broaden a player's sense of possibilities. Because dribbling past an opponent is not allowed, you must make runs around defenders, "creating space," as coaches like to say, in which to receive a pass or provide an opening for another player running through. Teamwork and touch are the key ingredients in this game. You must be able to control any ball on the ground or in the air, pass it immediately to a teammate, then make what is called an "intelligent run" down either wing or across midfield, creating space for your team, or else you lose possession of the ball.

Like chess, two-touch is a game for those who can think several moves ahead. Like a Shakespearean sonnet or a sestina, intricate poetic forms that trip up even virtuoso writers, the rigid formal requirements of this exercise make it at once exasperating and potentially exhilarating to play. Good players find the limitations liberating, lesser players overwhelming. To watch a group of skilled players in a game of two-touch can be thrilling, and when the principles of one- and two-touch play are incorporated into a regular soccer match, the results are usually exciting. The ability to trap and distribute the ball without delay and then to make unselfish runs is what distinguishes the better players, including most of those on the field at Farcher's Grove.

The Union Lancers have a long, proud history. Formerly called the Elizabeth Sport Club, this is a team made of up ex-high school and college stars, which in 1972 won the National Amateur Cup. Sean played for the Lancers, like his father before him (who had played until the age of forty-three) and his Uncle Billy, a member of the cup-winning side. A roll call of all who had played either for or against this club might well read like a Who's Who of American soccer. The team, which has been around almost since the game's arrival in this country, is blessed by the fact that it is centered in one of soccer's traditional strongholds. Along with Baltimore and St. Louis, the industrial corridor of northeastern New Jersey has produced many of our finest players. In cities like Elizabeth, Newark, Union, Kearny, Harrison, and Bayonne, soccer is the sport of choice. Why? Because these are bastions of the Old World, ethnic havens where certain cultural traditions—contrary to popular assumptions—did not die out.

In the New York metropolitan area, social clubs for Scots, Italians, Greeks, Latinos, Ukrainians, and Germans helped keep Old World customs like soccer alive; there is a Farcher's Grove for almost every nationality. And if in recent years certain soccer officials, determined to broaden the game's appeal, have tried to wipe out all traces of ethnicity—the German-American League, for example, is now called the Cosmopolitan League—still the better players routinely come from working-class neighborhoods of cities like Harrison and Union. Three of the best players on the current U.S. National Team, Tab Ramos, Tony Meola, and John Harkes, are first-generation sons of, respectively, Uruguayan, Italian, and Scottish soccer-playing fathers. All three grew up in Kearny, where soccer remains a way of life. Perhaps our conventional notions about cultural assimilation have no bearing on sports, one of the media through which cultures express themselves. Soccer is a means by which immigrants to the New World preserve their identities, in the face of pressure to adopt the ways of their new countrymen.

"Once we rise above this ethnic thing, soccer will take off," Miller Bugliari had suggested, describing the changing makeup of his Pingry teams. "What I noticed when I was president of the National Soccer Coaches Association was how hard it was to attract the middle-income person: they don't like disrespect for the referee, and they don't like spitting." Then, recalling his own playing days in the rough-and-tumble Italian-American League: "It's such an emotional thing."

When Pingry moved out of the city, the school's demographics changed, and the same is true for soccer, which is becoming a middle-class pastime. Yet at Farcher's Grove I found it difficult to believe we would ever "rise above" our ethnic differences, which in many ways are what define us. The more I traveled through the world of soccer, the more I learned from players, coaches, and fans the importance of those very differences. A country's, a people's style of play is as identifiable as its geography, religion, politics, literature, art, music, and cuisine — in short, the whole of its cultural life. Italians, for instance, are considered artistic, pragmatic soccer players, while Germans are methodical, British physical and straight-ahead, Africans athletic; South Americans skillful and imaginative; and North Americans innocent and defensive. When Pelé complained about Brazil's tactics in the 1990 World Cup, the way the team abandoned the samba style it had made famous in favor of a more conservative European strategy, he was asserting the primacy of certain cultural values even as he condemned a coaching decision. "I do not like this Brazil," he wrote in his World Cup column. "It is possible to play beautiful soccer and win at the same time." Perhaps he was right: Argentina knocked Brazil out of the tournament in the second round. As Roberto Rivelino, a star on the last Brazilian team to win the World Cup, said in an interview: "The 'European' mentality, so admired by [Coach] Lazaroni, has to go, otherwise we shall not have Brazilian soccer anymore."

What would an American style of play entail? I kept asking myself and others I met during my travels. How might a pluralistic nation like ours express itself through soccer—assuming, that is, such an expression becomes meaningful for the average American?

The imaginary style I conjured up at Farcher's Grove, a version of the game that depends heavily on my own subjective reading of our cultural life, would be elastic enough to express the variable nature of our American character, our multiracial differences and desires, the simmering stew—political, religious, and aesthetic— that makes up our ongoing experiment in democracy. Imagine a style that would translate into soccer terms the native wisdom of William Carlos Williams and the traditional yearnings of T. S. Eliot, the craft of Ernest Hemingway and the extravagances of William Faulkner. A style embracing Jackson Pollock's risks, Georgia O'Keeffe's serene cool, Andy Warhol's flair, and the intelligence of Jasper Johns; blues, jazz, country and western music, and John Cage; Creole cooking and Pennsylvania Dutch meals; rivers and mountains, deserts and plains —in short, a style encompassing the diversity of American life.

Such a style, of course, does not exist here. It is possible that American soccer will never know anything close to what I imagined in the stands at Farcher's Grove, listening to a veritable potpourri of languages spoken near me. Only in America, I thought, wondering what, exactly, that might mean.

"Old Man Farcher built this field back in the thirties," Sean was saying now. "Back when Route 22 was one-way. He had the bar, and he wanted to attract people from Newark and Elizabeth. They'd drive out on Sunday afternoons, play a match, then stay for dinner. Some of them bought up land along the highway, and they made a lot of money: Route 22's prime real estate now. Those Germans, they were smart," he added, pausing long enough for me to think of the hundreds of businesses, car dealerships, furniture outlets, department stores, and fast-food restaurants lining what my friends and I used to call the deadliest road in the world. "And when the old man died, they turned this into a nonprofit social club. The wealthy members of the board sponsor the Lancers. They're the ones who say you have to practice if you want to get paid."

I asked Sean if his family had ever belonged to the club.

"No way!" he said with a chuckle. "I mean, I'm welcome here, but only because they remember me on the field."

What they must have remembered was his uncanny ability to put the ball in the net. He had "a nose for the goal," a knack for being in the right place at the right time. Smaller than most of his opponents, Sean was still a commanding presence on the field, because at every moment it seemed as if he might score. I once saw Wade Boggs, then the celebrated third baseman for the Boston Red Sox, slice a twisting pop fly safely between the opposing shortstop, third baseman, and left fielder, any one of whom should have caught the ball. The sportscaster calling the game remarked, "Good hitters always find a way to get their hits. You could say Boggs was lucky there, but I think good hitters create their own luck." The same holds for high-scoring soccer players like Sean. I remembered a number of occasions when he seemed to have appeared from nowhere, emerging from a pack of defenders perhaps or sneaking behind someone to receive a pass and shoot on goal. Even when he had no chance to score, sometimes he managed to slip the ball into the net. There was one goal in particular I recalled: with his back to the goal, standing outside the penalty area, more than twenty yards from the net, Sean kicked a soft looping ball—not unlike Wade Boggs's pop fly single —over the heads of half a dozen defenders, a spinning shot that arced over the outstretched fingers of the surprised goalkeeper, who must have thought no one would ever take such a crazy stab at scoring.

Yet goals often result from one player doing the unexpected: shooting at an odd angle or from far away, making a daring run or pass, bending the rules—and not getting caught. Maradona's most famous, or infamous, goal is a case in point. In Mexico City, during a quarterfinal match of the 1986 World Cup against England, he scored the winning goal with what he later called "the hand of God." Maradona and Peter Shilton, England's aging goalkeeper, jumped at the same time, vying for a ball centered in from the wing, and when the Argentine captain saw that he had no hope of besting his much-taller opponent, he punched the ball into the net, breaking the cardinal rule of the game, in plain sight of literally millions of fans glued to television sets around the world. The referee saw nothing. Argentina went on to win the World Cup, and Maradona's goal became a signal event in the history of soccer. As George Vecsey noted in the *New York Times:* "It was that moment of cunning, or deception, or outright cheating, that elevated Maradona from merely the best soccer player of his time to a legendary figure all over the world."

Vecsey went on to explain that "soccer is such a difficult game, its goals so precious, its fans so proprietary and passionate, that anybody who propels the ball into the net becomes a conquering hero, taking an ecstatic tour of the field, throwing kisses, leaping into the air, and falling to his knees as if in some ancient tribal ceremony." Those are the moments in which matches, indeed careers, crystallize, everything coming together in one burst of excitement. That goals are hard to come by makes them all the more interesting. Their rarity confers on them a measure of the miraculous.

But that is what has also doomed soccer in the United States, as far as the sporting public is concerned. We are a people hooked on instant gratification, sociologists tell us. If in the domain of sports that characteristic translates into a desire for more and more scoring, then it may be years before we learn to appreciate the subtleties of soccer: the long and patient buildup that ends in one good shot on goal, the lightning strike off a counterattack, the well-timed set play, the individual display of genius, the countless artistic moves on or away from the ball. We want more miracles: a steady supply of goals.

In a radio interview Gertrude Stein remarked, "To like a football game is to understand it in the football way." It was clear that the crowd at Farcher's Grove understood the match between the Lancers and the Strikers "in the soccer way." Except for the two women chattering near us (now they were trading stories from their respective offices, their interest in certain players having flagged), these fans applauded individual moves, admired selfless runs and risky passes, and waited patiently for the first score. Which was not long in coming. Fort Lauderdale dominated play, swinging the ball from one side of the field to the other, then distributing it with only one or two touches, mustering shot after shot on goal. Midway through the first half, the Strikers scored after a scramble in front of the net. Moments later they scored again, their striker taking a bouncing ball and converting it into a beautiful half-volley destined for the upper left-hand corner of the Lancer goal, a shot praised by almost everyone in the stands. Indeed, perhaps because this was an exhibition match, the crowd seemed more interested in good soccer and telling stories than in rooting for one side or the other. No one was spared their contempt for bad play. When a Lancer forward missed an easy shot, the crowd was quick to boo him, though it soon returned to storytelling, drinking, and gossip.

"Who're they mad at?" said one of the women, looking up.

"Who knows?" said the other, then lit a cigarette and resumed her story about an upcoming marriage.

The crowd's outburst reminded me of an embarrassing moment from my own days in the German-American League. One night the Newark Sport Club played an indoor match in the Elizabeth Armory, a dilapidated (and now boarded-up) building in the heart of the city. Ours was a warm-up game before the Men's League matches got under way, yet the stands in the balcony circling above the wooden playing surface were full. Down on the floor my teammates and I heard Latinos shouting from one side of the stands, Scotsmen and Irishmen from the other; the smell of beer, sangria, and a variety of fried foods mingled in the air. "Whatever you do," said one of my friends, "don't mess up." "What do you mean?" I asked. "You'll see," he replied.

And I did. Just before the end of the first half, I learned why good scoring chances should never be squandered. I was running down the court, veering in from the wing to take a ball rolling across the floor. The goalkeeper had been drawn out of position, and I had an open shot on an empty net. I struck the ball with the outside of my foot, determined to keep it low. But it sailed over the goal. Crestfallen, I ran back up the court, shaking my head—and then I was soaking wet. An old Scotsman was leaning over the railing of the balcony, waving an empty beer mug at me. "Keep your head down, laddie!" he roared. The crowd laughed and clapped. I smelled like a tavern for the rest of the game.

Now I sipped my beer and turned to Sean. "Remember that match you scored four goals?" I said.

He nodded slowly.

"Didn't Bugliari have a rule that no one could score more than three?" I continued. "You think he looked the other way to let you break the record?"

Sean's eyes twinkled. "If he did, he'll never let on!"

Soon the first half came to a close. Sean wandered off to talk to friends, and I had a chance to catch up with Mimi. A pretty, dark-haired woman, she is a preschool teacher in Basking Ridge and mother of a little girl named Caitlin. Unlike our other high school friends, Mimi and Sean have managed to turn a teenage romance into a working marriage—an achievement so rare in our time that it too seems to belong to the Old World. The single stumbling block to their marriage had been religion. "Sean's parents were scared I wouldn't be Catholic," she said, "even though I'm Scottish, too."

"Those differences die hard," I said. "In Glasgow the Rangers are the Protestant soccer team, the Celtics Catholic, and when they play each other sometimes there are riots."

"It's almost tribal," she said. "Sean's parents? Their friends are all Scottish. The rest are acquaintances. And they'd be the first to tell you that."

By now Sean had returned, and she turned to him: "When you played for the Kearny Scots—that's when I started to understand what this Old World stuff was all about. I mean, I didn't have four kids by the time I was eighteen. When I went into the club after your matches, I was in for a surprise. In there it was women on one side, men on the other, and never the twain shall meet. Once I made the mistake of sitting with Sean. That caused a real problem. One woman said to me, 'You sit over here.' 'Why?' I said, 'I don't know any of you. I want to be with my husband.' 'That's not the way it's done here,' she told me."

Mimi looked at Sean. "Right?" she said.

He smiled.

The second half began in the same haphazard fashion as the first. Now Fort Lauderdale's better conditioning took its toll on

Union. "Only five or six Lancers are really fit," said Sean, "as opposed to all the Strikers. That's the difference right there." The Strikers made more and more daring runs, sent the ball—almost at will—across the field or into the Lancers' goal area, and took several fine shots. Meanwhile, the Lancers chased their opponents, taking advantage of every stoppage of play to catch their breath, occasionally faking injuries to give themselves a rest. They played the ball back to their goalkeeper instead of building an attack. They watched his punts sail across midfield. They were exhausted.

Soccer is a grueling game. A player may run anywhere from five to fifteen miles during a match, covering most of that distance in short and long sprints, cutting this way and that, resting only when play stops or shifts to the other side of the field. Because substitutions are final, players learn to pace themselves so that they can last the whole match. Jumping into the air to head the ball, muscling for position, making sliding tackles—these add to the already taxing load a player carries. No wonder soccer is a young man's sport. Even the fittest players who manage to avoid crippling injuries rarely last far into their thirties; most peak in their midtwenties. Only goalkeepers and an occasional phenomenon like Cameroon's Roger Milla, who at the age of thirty-eight was to be one of the stars of the Mondiale, last as long as, say, baseball players. The legs go first, and no one can disguise that loss, not in a game that lasts as long as a soccer match.

"A Seeing Eye," a short story by the Welsh poet and writer Leslie Norris, begins with a marvelous description of an aging soccer player's realization that his career is over:

> About ten thirty in the morning of the third Sunday in March, 1964, I was standing in a corner of the garage. I stood near the grimy skeleton of the old lawn mower and I was crying. Nothing loud and dramatic, just gentle, elegiac tears—anything stronger would have hurt my ribs. The previous day I had played my last game of soccer and I was mourning the passing of great times. The scene of my last encounter had been as hard as ebony, the sky more

colourful than bruises, the wind a flying iceberg. I knew
that every muscle would be sore until Thursday. Moreover,
turning awkwardly on the flinty surface, I had dislocated
three toes on my left foot. Afterwards I had limped home
like Lord Byron.

"That's it," my wife had said when she saw me.
"You've played your last game of soccer. No more for you.
A grown man coming home with his toes in plaster!"

I had no defence. I slept badly, and in the morning,
coming downstairs on my butt, one step at a time, groaning,
I felt she was right. I edged on my one sound foot towards
my breakfast.

"You're too old," my wife said, pouring the coffee. She
was smiling, but we both knew she meant it. Breakfast was
a sad meal.

Afterwards I took my soccer boots out of the bag and
looked at them. They were good boots, very expensive.
They would last another hundred games, but I would never
wear them again. Meticulously I began to clean them. With
the greatest care, with affection, I took away the grains of
frozen mud from the seams of the leather, unwound the
threads and flakes of grass that clung about the studs, polished the open surfaces, sole and upper, until they glis-
tened. It was a serious ceremony. I was taking ritual
farewell of skills I had learned and practised until they
were habitual. From the age of ten I had played soccer
almost every week of my life, and now it was over. I was
finished. I was thirty-four years old.

Some of the Lancers were approaching the age of the narrator of
"A Seeing Eye," and perhaps a couple or more of the Strikers, too.
No doubt many had or were about to take full-time jobs, wives,
families, assuming the responsibilities we associate with adulthood.
Whatever dreams they may once have entertained about playing for
the national team or for a club in Europe were probably long gone.
This match, or another like it in the near future, would be the last for
them, and that knowledge lent a somber air to the action in the
second half. The Lancers' play was breaking down, the Strikers

scored another goal, and the women near us left well before the end of the match, presumably to get ready for the singles' dance that would begin within the hour.

Darkness fell, and with it came bats sweeping around the field. The referee blew his whistle to end the game, the thick-accented announcer proclaimed the 3 – 0 Striker victory (he never said who had scored the goals), and we filed back into the clubhouse. The bar was full of men, while in the adjacent dining room several families were eating dinner, their plates piled high with bratwurst and sauerkraut, steaming food we understood was not meant for us. We went up to a little window and ordered the fare available to nonclub members — hamburgers, hot dogs, french fries. Then, eating on our feet, we wandered around the room, studying the photographs and trophies in the display cases. We saw Sean at various ages, his father, and his Uncle Billy on the Amateur Cup – winning club, a string of sepia-tinted photographs depicting half a century's worth of soccer. Sean was now the same age as the narrator of Leslie Norris's story; family and business commitments left him time to play only once a week in the Italian-American League. I wondered if my friend found it sad to return to the site of his former glory, but I did not have the heart to ask him how he felt. Soon he went into the bar to talk to another old friend.

Mimi and I stood by the railing separating the bar from the dining room. We did not speak for several minutes. We watched Sean greet a number of men his age and older. Despite what he had said earlier, he seemed to belong to this soccer crowd, these ex-players shooting pool, plugging change into the pinball machines, or simply nursing beers.

"Come hell or high water," Mimi said suddenly, "I had to learn to love soccer, because it's Sean's life."

I nodded, sipped my beer, said nothing. Music drifted out of the room beyond the dining area where the dance was about to begin. I could not tell if the music I heard was a live band or taped, and I knew it was not my place to find out. It was time for us to leave. Mimi caught her husband's eye, and he sauntered over to us, beaming.

"I just agreed to play on the over-thirty team," Sean said. "It's only one night a week, and no practices!"

3
. . . .
THE FOURTH ESTATE

*D*ateline: Chocolatetown, U.S.A.!" a sportswriter called out from the other end of the press box, and a low rumble of laughter swept along the weather-beaten benches assigned to us. Twelve thousand soccer fans were filling Hershey Stadium in Hershey, Pennsylvania, the home of the famous chocolate factory, to see the U.S. National Team take on Poland's national squad. The converted football field was covered with players finishing their warm-up. All around me journalists were scrambling to find electrical outlets for their laptop computers. I opened my notebook and wrote: *This is one of the last chances before Italia 90 for Americans to see in person the players who stunned the international soccer community in the fall, qualifying for the World Cup final—after a hiatus of forty years.* This was also, I thought, the first time many journalists in the ramshackle press box would write about the U.S. team, or perhaps about soccer at all.

A month before the Mondiale, this series of tune-up games against Malta, Poland, and Holland's premier club Ajax attracted for the sport its first substantial American media coverage. Not all of it was well-informed, because many sportswriters had no experience covering the game. The young man to my left, for instance, was far more interested in what I knew about the Albuquerque *Journal*, where he hoped to land a job reporting on basketball games, than in the action on the field. (He would take no more than three lines of notes during the match, and since he did not strike me as a writer blessed with a prodigious memory, I could only imagine what kind of story he might file about the biggest local sporting event of the year.) To my right, however, was a passionate cub reporter for one of the soccer weeklies, a likable New Yorker who seemed to know everything about the game. Out of his shirt pocket he pulled a pen that had a plastic soccer ball attached to its top.

"Do everything in character," he said with a grin. "What's your deadline? Midnight?"

"December," I replied. "1992. I'm writing a book."

"A book," he repeated, nodding. "I tried to line up a book deal, but no one's into soccer. Football, basketball, baseball — no problem. But who wants to hear about the people's game?"

He paused to check the players' list in the media guide distributed by the USSF, then whispered to me, "Have you heard the stories about us greasing the wheel to get into the World Cup?"

No, I had not.

"You know about Mexico's death penalty," he went on.

I nodded. Mexico had been banned from international soccer competition for two years, receiving soccer's harshest punishment for fielding a team of overage players in the Boys Under-16 World Cup. Its elimination from the qualifying rounds of the Mondiale had given the United States a splendid opportunity to advance into the coveted final round.

"People in Central America think Henry Kissinger had something to do with it," said the reporter. "Mexicans don't always have birth certificates, especially in the villages some of their players come from. Rumor has it we paid one of their coaches to put a couple of ringers on their youth team, then tipped off FIFA [Fédération Internationale de Football Association, soccer's ruling body]. See, we *had* to make it into this World Cup if we wanted to be legitimate hosts of the final in '94. And here we are, a month away from Italy."

"Has anyone written about this?" I asked, incredulous.

He shook his head. "We can't," he muttered, waving at the other journalists. "The USSF would go crazy, and FIFA would ban us from reporting on the game. They have the power to silence us. No one can afford a lifetime ban."

"So Kissinger's disrupting soccer, too?" I said.

My new friend shrugged. "Maybe."

A press box is a fertile breeding ground for rumor and innuendo. In the coming weeks I would hear many such whispered stories, some centered on our place in the World Cup, others on potential coaching changes, and still others on the reasons behind soccer's lowly position in our public imagination. Surely the most interesting rumor I heard (apart from the constant talk of Franz Beckenbauer, West Germany's coach, assuming the reins of our national program) concerned the long-standing belief among certain soccer pundits that the National Football League had waged a successful media campaign against its sister sport, convincing print and electronic journalists to play down the world's most popular game. Every preseason, so the story went, the NFL would fly journalists to a resort for a weekend of entertainment and information about the upcoming season; sometime during the lavish proceedings the guests would be asked to steer away from covering soccer, reporting—if at all—only on its riots and tragedies. Fill your pages and airwaves with football stories, was the message delivered to the writers, editors, television producers, and announcers. American legends, not tales from abroad.

I was reluctant to believe that rumor. Evidence, it was true, might be gathered to support the belief that the NFL had lobbied against soccer. After all, how many columns of any American newspaper are devoted to the game? In the Hershey Stadium press box there must have been more than a few journalists who considered tonight's assignment an odious task. The young man to my left, for example, took more delight in the greasy hamburgers and diet sodas dispensed early in the contest than in the action between the two teams; the grumbling I heard among some of his peers led me to think he was not alone in his desire to be elsewhere. And why, I wondered, does soccer receive so little attention from the networks? Bobsledding and lugeing, rowing and water polo, archery and motocross racing—in any given year these sports may receive more air time than soccer. Like billiards, beach volleyball, and dressage, soccer is relegated to the cable television networks. Even the Mondiale would be broadcast in this country only on cable. While much of the world was watching nearly constant coverage of the World Cup on television sets in houses and bars, city squares and villages, from Africa to Asia, South America to Siberia, soccer fans in the United States would have to search—and pay—to see any of the games, with Spanish-speaking stations providing the best coverage.

Something was amiss.

But I knew there were other explanations for soccer's absence from our media. For one thing, network executives would argue that televising soccer was a losing proposition; it would never garner the ratings necessary to attract the major advertisers. A common refrain —"Low-scoring sports like soccer won't interest an American audience"—jangled in my mind, even as I acknowledged a certain truth to the network executives' complaints. The patience of uninformed viewers may be limited. With literally dozens of viewing options available, why would anyone waste time watching sports they do not appreciate? At the same time, a journalist trained to report on football, basketball, or baseball might want to ignore a fluid game like soccer, just as a reviewer of rock-and-roll concerts might try to avoid covering a performance of the Guarneri Quartet. No one likes to display his or her ignorance in print. It is, so often, a matter of numbers. In this country more fans and sportswriters were raised on football than on soccer, and although that is changing, it may still take another generation for soccer to develop an American audience and a circle of writers and commentators. The game's diminished stature in our media, then, may owe more to simple economics and popularity than to any concerted effort on the part of the NFL to dictate editorial policy.

It is also true that to the uninitiated, soccer can be a difficult subject to write about, as some of my first-time colleagues must have been discovering. The game was under way, and the Poles had already created good scoring chances, showing their strength in the air, winning almost every head ball. Despite a fine run by Mike Windischmann, the U.S. captain, and hard shots by both Eric

Wynalda and Peter Vermes, the Poles dominated the early stages of play. In the twenty-sixth minute there was a mix-up in front of the American goal, defender Steve Trittschuh teeing the ball up for his Polish counterpart, Jacek Ziober, who booted it in from one yard out. "Trittschuh with the assist," my new friend chuckled, typing rapidly on his laptop computer.

How would others describe that goal? I wondered. To write about soccer, a journalist might have to adopt a different approach to the craft, assuming a metaphorical way of thinking instead of the traditional statistics-bound mind-set. Soccer is a game of flux and action, of poetry and arcs of interest; there are no statistics with which to fill up a column. The line score reveals nothing more than the final tally, goals, players, substitutions, attendance, and the name of the referee; its very plainness may suggest worlds of possibilities to an imaginative writer, and frighten a reporter accustomed to a sheaf of figures. No wonder the young man who wanted to move to Albuquerque looked so disconcerted: he had no scaffolding of statistics on which to hang his reportage, nor did he seem to possess an instinct for poetry and analysis. He had no passion for the game — and no notes. He was not alone.

But my strongest reason for remaining skeptical about the NFL rumor was my impatience with conspiracy theories. Soccer is a marginal activity in America, and some of its followers are prone to uncovering elaborate plots to explain its exclusion from the center of our cultural life. I had already witnessed paranoia in the ranks of the USSF. Soon after signing my book contract, I learned from a friend privy to the inner workings of the organization that Bob Gansler, the head coach, was nervous about what I might write. "Don't worry," my friend had told him. "It'll be a positive book." What I hoped for was a book at once truthful and interesting, but I understood Gansler's apprehension. He must have felt soccer's future in this country was riding on his shoulders. The last thing he needed was another writer questioning his methods and decisions. As John Harkes, the midfielder from Kearny, New Jersey, said in an interview, "How we do in the World Cup could make or break soccer in the United States."

And the press had been hard on Gansler, criticizing him for a wide range of failings. His style of play was too defensive, too controlled, too . . . "bureaucratic," as one wag had put it; hence his players were afraid to take chances, afraid to be creative, which resulted in a dearth of goals. The newest joke circulating in the press box about our lackluster scoring went like this: "How many Americans does it take to score a goal? At least two: one to snap the ball, and one to hold it for the place-kicker!" Even Gansler's selection of players for his team was routinely questioned. Why, the press wondered, were our two most talented, experienced, and popular players —Ricky Davis and Hugo Perez—not given chances to try out once they had recovered from their respective leg injuries? The answer, according to the cub reporter, was that Gansler did not want players questioning his authority. Davis and Perez were too smart not to ask themselves, and perhaps others, why he had adopted such a conservative style of play.

"He's too German for us," the reporter said of the Hungarian-born Gansler. "He calls all the shots, so he doesn't need anyone— players, press, what have you—second-guessing him."

Yet it seemed that almost everyone entertained doubts about his coaching decisions, especially the one to leave Davis off the squad. "Davis—the most celebrated American soccer player of his generation, star of the Cosmos, teammate of Pelé and Chinaglia and Beckenbauer—[has] been cast aside," Paul Gardner wrote in the *New York Times,* declaring that "Gansler refused to be interviewed about the Davis situation outside of a public news conference."

"That tells me that I'm not being judged on ability," Davis had told Gardner, "that I intimidate Gansler, which is ludicrous, that I get too much publicity, that some of the players don't like me, that I'd be disruptive if I were brought in. I've never had problems with other players in all my life—why would it start now?

"I came through the Cosmos," Davis reminded the reporter, "where there were egos and personalities you wouldn't believe. It was a dog-eat-dog situation until game time, when we went out as pros and played. I don't feel that I deserve any special privileges. I wasn't looking for an automatic spot, or a token spot on the team. But everything I've done for the past two years has been with the 1990 World Cup in mind. What hurts," he admitted, "is that during all the time I've been recovering [from a series of knee operations], Bob Gansler never picked up the phone and called me. In over a year, all he did was return my calls. I don't think he ever planned to give me an opportunity. Now, after fifteen years' involvement [with the USSF], it has come down to this. To not make [the World Cup team] and to not even have the chance to prove myself, I think there's something wrong."

Others thought so, too. Many experts agreed that Davis might have provided a steadying influence, calming his younger teammates when the run of play turned against them. Like Roger Milla, Cameroon's aging star, Davis had the ability to make a difference on the field, spurring his teammates to play at a higher level. More important, as the symbol of American soccer, Davis would have been a natural media draw, a player youngsters could identify with, even idolize—the kind of personality the game needed to develop an audience in this country. But he would not get a chance to play that role, because the head coach had long since made up his mind about him. Gansler's skill as the central defender and captain of the U.S. Olympic Teams in 1964 and 1968 translated into a defensive style of coaching, which might bode ill for his team.

Nevertheless, his tactics were working tonight. Contrary to the expectations of several journalists here, his team did not collapse as soon as Poland scored. Instead, the Americans fought back, hustling after every ball. Tab Ramos generated scoring opportunities with a series of brilliant moves in the midfield. Only seven minutes after the Poles silenced the exuberant crowd, striker Bruce Murray brought them back to their feet, taking advantage of a mistake in the Polish defense to slot home his seventh international goal, tying him for third on the U.S. career scoring list. His goal ignited his teammates, and now Peter Vermes executed a perfect heel pass, dribbling upfield at full tilt, then flicking the ball back to Ramos, who was following close behind. His clever move completely fooled the Polish defenders, and Ramos quickly sent the ball across the penalty area, nearly connecting with Murray for another goal. This was the first of many skillful combinations worked by Vermes and Ramos, the two most creative American players. The tempo of the match picked up; a large contingent of youngsters chanted, "U.S.A.! U.S.A.!"; and even when Paul Caligiuri misplayed a ball back, offering the Poles a chance to change the run of play, the Americans battled on. When the first half ended in a 1–1 tie, the crowd was ecstatic.

"Oh, Caligiuri," sighed the cub reporter, typing rapidly. "Our only hero!" he added ruefully.

It was true. Notwithstanding the rumors of Henry Kissinger's machinations on our behalf, the United States had qualified for the World Cup final thanks in part to Caligiuri's heroic goal—the so-called shot-heard-round-the-world the defender had fired the previous November in Port of Spain, Trinidad—a crazy, looping, left-footed shot from almost thirty yards out, which clinched a 1–0 victory over Trinidad & Tobago. After ten qualifying CONCACAF (Confederación Norte-Centroamericana y del Caribe de Fútbol, which comprises the regional zone of the Caribbean, North America, and Central America) matches in Jamaica, Costa Rica, El Salvador, Guatemala, Trinidad, and at various sites in the United States, our national team made it into the Mondiale by the slimmest of margins. In the absence of Ricky Davis, Caligiuri became our new soccer hero, proving himself to be a player willing to take matters into his own hands, even if it meant occasionally abandoning Gansler's controlled style of play—anything to score. His goals, as Alessandro de Calo noted in *La Gazzetta Dello Sport,* would be "few but important."

None would ever be as important as what one writer called "the biggest goal in U.S. soccer history." On his return from Port of Spain, Caligiuri learned what instant fame entailed. "The phone's been ringing off the hook," he told an interviewer. "I have received phone calls from Italy, West Germany, Brazil, everywhere in the country from the press, from my family, all angles. The hype was amazing." More amazing was the fact that a crowd had waited for him at the Los Angeles International Airport, the kind of reception ordinarily reserved for politicians, celebrities, and star athletes from other sports. "There were TV cameras from every station. I've never spoken to any of them. Unbelievable. It's kind of like I have more pressure on me than before the game," he continued. "It's a situation I didn't expect. It came at me like a tidal wave. But I'm handling it all right."

No doubt he was experienced enough to cope with pressure, having been one of the first Americans to win a spot on a European professional team. After two years in West Germany's Second Division with SW Meppen, where he was named one of the top foreigners by *Kicker-Sportmagazin,* and a stint on the 1988 U.S. Olympic Team, the California-born and -raised Caligiuri had the right credentials to assume the hero's mantle, at least for the foreseeable future. If before his famous goal he had been known for clashing with his teammates — sportswriter Brian Trusdell suggested that "the players who had stayed stateside while Caligiuri played abroad felt Caligiuri's European experiences had given him a cocky attitude" — it was clear that his part in the victory over Trinidad & Tobago had gone a long way toward healing some of those wounds. "He stepped forward the week of training [before the historic match in Trinidad] and transformed his attitude," Bruce Murray told Trusdell. "We couldn't be happier if anyone else had scored." Indeed, it was the "U.S. Sonnyboy," as the West German press called the handsome American, who delivered in the clutch. "And when the all-important goal came," Paul Gardner wrote, "it came because Paul Caligiuri obeyed his own soccer instincts and did what *he* perceived to be the right thing, rather than obeying instructions. As he told George Vecsey of the *New York Times:* 'The game plan was to put the ball in the wings and funnel it towards the goal. I went against the game plan.' "

Gardner was not the only reporter who believed that the United States would have to ignore Gansler's game plan to succeed in the World Cup, though his denunciations in *Soccer America* of the USSF system of play were perhaps the most strident:

> In short, Gansler has molded a team in his own image of defensive, methodical, caution. The players know what they're supposed to do, they know their roles, and they know the game plans. It is a system that has managed to squeak us into the World Cup in Italy. It is also a system that made that process a lot more difficult

than it should have been. Because you are always going to be living precariously when your team averages less than a goal a game.

It is also a system that has shackled the U.S. players into a banally predictable style that has looked, at its worst moments, like total paralysis. Watching Gansler's team performing in [the qualifying rounds], I have seen caution carried to the point where it has changed, silently and nearly fatally, into fear. Fear of making a mistake, fear of giving up a goal, fear of committing wholeheartedly to the attack.

This is not a recipe for positive soccer. Nor is it an atmosphere that is likely to bring out the best in players. To start with, the player selection is always going to be slanted toward those who are willing simply to be role-players. And even when the creative people do make the team, they are rarely able to play with the freedom that they need.

Yet Gansler's methods prevailed against the Poles. The second half began, and his team kept pressing forward, relentlessly attacking. In the fiftieth minute, it was true, Roman Szewczyk nearly scored on a breakaway, testing U.S. backup goalkeeper Kasey Keller enough for him to shout to one of his defenders, "Get some cars out here: I need some lights!" But the young Americans commanded the field. Ramos had a hard shot from twenty-eight yards out, Murray made a fine run a minute later, and moments after that John Harkes had a breakaway—only to be tripped up with a wicked tackle. In the fifty-seventh minute Piotr Czachowski was called for a hand ball in the penalty area—that is, he deliberately touched the ball with his hand or arm, within the eighteen-by-forty-eight-yard rectangle marked off in front of the net—and Peter Vermes was awarded a penalty kick: an all-but-automatic goal.

Play came to a standstill. The ball was placed on the penalty mark, twelve yards from the Polish goal line. Players from both teams gathered around the penalty area, careful not to cross the lines until the ball was struck. Vermes took aim at the Polish goalkeeper, Jozef

Wandzik, who had to stand on his goal line without moving his feet until the American touched the ball. His only hope was to guess which side Vermes would shoot toward, then dive in that direction and try to block what would doubtless be a rifle shot. This the Polish keeper did, but Vermes' shot was too hard for him to handle. The United States took a 2–1 lead. The crowd went wild.

And when on the first play after the ensuing kickoff Murray connected with Harkes for another near goal, I began to think we might yet find success in the World Cup. What would define success for us in Italy? Certainly nothing more than a couple of victories and advancement into the second round of the tournament; no one was foolish enough to believe that the United States could do more than hold its own in the early going. Indeed, many observers hoped simply that the Americans would not embarrass themselves in the world's most prestigious sporting event. But with this second goal I could feel, even here in the press box, expectations rising.

"It'll only take five points to get us past the first round," the cub reporter reminded me—two points for a win, one for a tie, and nothing for a loss against our opening round of opponents—Czechoslovakia, Italy, and Austria. "And the Czechs should be a lot like the Poles: fast and aggressive. If we beat them and the Austrians, then draw with Italy—bingo: we're in!" He shook his head, smiled. "And if we beat Italy? In Rome? Unbelievable!"

"Like England," I said, "in 1950."

"Exactly," he said.

We were talking about what Clive Gammon of *Sports Illustrated* called "the biggest upset ever in the World Cup—possibly the biggest in the history of the sport." Forty years ago, in our last appearance in the World Cup, we had surprised everyone by defeating England 1–0. In Belo Horizonte, Brazil, a small band of determined Americans had achieved what until then the entire soccer community had considered impossible: victory over arguably the world's best team, which had not even bothered to qualify for earlier tournaments, so sure was it of its invincibility. "After all, as the birthplace of the sport," Gammon noted, "what did England have to prove?"

Especially against a squad whose players included an office clerk, a truck driver, a cannery worker, a schoolteacher, and a goalkeeper who worked in a brickyard! Gammon described them:

> Once assembled, the U.S. team was frankly, even humbly, willing to concede that it was in for a soccer lesson in Brazil. Qualifying for the World Cup was different then —in the aftermath of World War II, few countries had the means or the interest to sponsor teams. The U.S. qualified after losing twice to Mexico and tying and beating Cuba. There was no time for serious training. A club team from Istanbul shut out the Americans 5–0 five weeks before the U.S. team left for Brazil, and in New York City, on the eve of their departure, the Americans lost again, 1–0, to the English *third* squad, which had spent the previous night on a train from Windsor, Ontario.

The English were so confident against the Americans that their best player, Stanley Matthews, did not even go to the match, choosing to remain in Rio de Janiero "to rest." His seemed like the right decision for the first thirty minutes of play: the English peppered the American goal. "They were all over us," right fullback Harry Keough remembered, "hitting the bar, hitting the uprights. They had complete dominance, almost as if we were just watching them play." But they could not put the ball in the net.

"Suddenly, seemingly out of nowhere," Gammon wrote, "in the 37th minute of the first half, came the goal that shocked the soccer world.

> For once the Americans were inside England's half, and [Walter] Bahr struck an innocuous-looking shot from out on the right that the English goalkeeper, Bert Williams, had well covered.
>
> Then, just as suddenly, [Joe] Gaetjens was diving headlong for the ball, making contact and heading it into the net. It was U.S. 1, England 0, and 30,000 Brazilians

were wildly cheering. "Oh, my god," Keough recalled thinking, "we've awakened the sleeping lion."

But nothing of the sort happened, perhaps because the English were so stunned by Gaetjens's goal, a goal as improbable in its way as Caligiuri's "shot-heard-round-the-world."

"The English defense must have been thinking, 'What is this guy hoping for?' when Joe dove at the ball," Keough told Gammon. "Because if he had hit it square with his forehead, it was headed for the corner flag. To this day, I don't think anybody could tell you what made the ball travel as it did, because we all lost sight of it once it touched Joe's head, and both its timing and its trajectory would have changed. If Williams had seen it, he'd have saved it."

From then on the Americans played beyond their abilities, guarding their goal as if it were a beachhead they had gained by accident. The English could not score, heightening their anxiety and the crowd's fervor. The Brazilians, co-favorites (with England) to win the tournament, wanted to see their chief rival eliminated from the tournament. Eight minutes from the end, England's Stan Mortensen broke through the American defense and was on the verge of going one-on-one with our goalkeeper when he was brought down by what Gammon labeled "one of the most flagrant fouls in World Cup history"—Charlie Colombo's "crash tackle," which would have gotten him expelled from the match if not, so the story goes, for the fact that the referee was also Italian: he liked what the center fullback, who unaccountably always played in leather gloves, had done to the Englishman. Awarded a free kick just outside the penalty area, England almost scored the tying goal; and although some players believed that the ball had crossed the goal line, the score stayed as it was until the final whistle.

No one could believe what had happened. "Editors at the *New York Times* held off printing the score because they thought there had been a transmission error—the score must have been 10–1, England's favor," Gammon explained, while the "London *Daily Herald* came out bordered in black." The United States did not make it into the next round of the tournament, and the "heroes of Belo Horizonte slipped back to the States more or less unnoticed." Yet their remarkable achievement remains the touchstone for American soccer. In the stands in Hershey, among the friends and families of the current national team, you would surely find Walter Bahr and Harry Keough, two of the five surviving members of that famous World Cup squad, who now served as informal ambassadors for the USSF.

(You might even find one or both of Bahr's eminent sons, Matt and Chris, who were raised in nearby Boalsburg, Pennsylvania. Talented athletes, they gave up their father's sport to pursue more lucrative careers place-kicking in the NFL. With a number of soccer-playing foreigners, they revolutionized the kicking game in our version of football, replacing the straight-on, locked-hip style of kicking field goals and kickoffs Pat Summerall and others had popularized with a side-winding approach to the ball, perhaps planting in the minds of many Americans the notion that soccer is useful only insofar as it provides players for the least interesting parts of a football game.)

"Anything can happen in the World Cup," said the cub reporter. "There could be another surprise."

Ever since the victory over Trinidad & Tobago, American soccer people had held out the hope that a similar miracle might occur in Italy. A win over one of the world's soccer giants would insure credibility for our program, removing any doubts about our right to host the 1994 World Cup; with or without Kissinger's help, the USSF had to prove itself worthy of presiding over the sport's biggest tournament. It was time to correct the impression that the United States had been awarded the next Cup because of its money and expanding youth programs. Qualifying for the Mondiale was a good start; defeating a team like Italy would seal the USSF's case for legitimacy. But that was such a long shot that the cub reporter now seemed embarrassed to have even mentioned it. He changed the subject to American indifference to soccer.

"I have this theory," he said, "about politics."

"Politics," I repeated.

"The Civil War," he continued. "England supported the South. No one wanted anything to do with them and their sports after that. That's why it's so perfect we beat them in 1950."

I nodded. There were various explanations—ethnic, cultural, conspiratorial, political—for soccer's lack of success here, and for all I knew his was as good as any. Politics played a role in the makeup of our national team, as Ricky Davis and Hugo Perez had learned, as well as in the style of play the coaches insisted Caligiuri and his teammates adopt. Politics had effected the selection of the United States as the World Cup's next host country, and it would dictate which American cities would be among the eight to twelve sites chosen for the preliminary rounds. It steered the USSF's course through coaching, personnel, and development decisions. No doubt some of those decisions left a bad taste in many people's mouths.

Yet politics impinges on soccer in larger ways, especially in countries where the game is a central fact of life. In such places those involved in the art of the possible, whose skill or lack thereof can effect a government's success and failure, must consider soccer in the same light as taxes and birthrates. No statesman can afford to neglect anything essential to the body politic, including what Americans might call a simple sporting event, as the Polish journalist Ryszard Kapuscinski illustrates in his marvelous chronicle of the twenty-seven revolutions and coups he covered in the years between Sputnik's launching and the rise of the Solidarity movement. In the title piece of *The Soccer War* he writes:

> In Latin America, he [Luis Suarez, another journalist] said, the border between soccer and politics is vague. There is a long list of governments that have fallen or been over-thrown after the defeat of the national team. Players on the losing team are denounced in the press as traitors. When Brazil won the World Cup in Mexico, an exiled Brazilian colleague of mine was heartbroken: "The military right wing," he said, "can be assured of at least five more years of peaceful rule." On the way to the title, Brazil beat England. In an article with the headline "Jesus Defends Bra-

zil," the Rio de Janeiro paper *Jornal dos Sportes* explained the victory thus: "Whenever the ball flew toward our goal and a score seemed inevitable, Jesus reached his foot out of the clouds and cleared the ball.' Drawings accompanied the article, illustrating the supernatural intervention.

The outcome of a soccer match may have extreme consequences:

> Anyone at the stadium can lose his life. Take the match that Mexico lost to Peru, two—one. An embittered Mexican fan shouted in an ironic tone, *"Viva* Mexico!" A moment later he was dead, massacred by the crowd. But sometimes the heightened emotions find an outlet in other ways. After Mexico beat Belgium one—nil, Augusto Mariaga, the warden of a maximum-security prison in Chilpancingo (Guerrero State, Mexico), became delirious with joy and ran around firing a pistol into the air and shouting, *"Viva* Mexico!" He opened all the cells, releasing 142 dangerous criminals. A court acquitted him later, as, according to the verdict, he had "acted in patriotic exaltation."

Kapuscinski then fleshes out the story of the 1970 "soccer war" between Honduras and El Salvador—a war which, while fought over the very real issues of poverty and inadequate land reform, was occasioned by the World Cup qualifying matches between the two countries. The peasants' pent-up anger was released in the wake of the first match, which Honduras had taken 1–0. An eighteen-year-old girl from El Salvador shot herself in the heart because, as *El Nacional* reported the next day, she "could not bear to see her fatherland brought to its knees." Thus she became a martyr, and after El Salvador won the return match, 3–0, tension between the two countries rose to an unendurable level.

"The soccer war lasted one hundred hours," Kapuscinski writes. "Its victims: 6,000 dead, more than 12,000 wounded. Fifty thousand people lost their homes and fields. Many villages were destroyed." Other Latin American countries intervened to halt the hostilities, and the final game of the best-of-three series was held in Mexico, the Honduran fans on one side of the stadium, the Salvadorans on the other, "and down the middle sat 5,000 Mexican police armed with thick clubs." Twenty years later, in the qualifying rounds for the Mondiale the last two matches between El Salvador and Guatemala had to be canceled due to rising tension between the two countries.

I wondered what Kapuscinski would say about the lackluster performance of his countrymen here in Hershey. After spending most of his adult life covering revolutions in foreign countries, he must have relished the chance to stay home and write about the overthrow of communism in Eastern Europe. Perhaps the enormous changes in Poland—recorded, with any luck, by a battery of writers like Kapuscinski—weighed on the minds of the players. They had not qualified for the World Cup, their obligations to their respective clubs in Europe were finished for the season, and now on the field they seemed to be going through the motions: their hearts were elsewhere. It came as no surprise that in the seventy-eighth minute the Americans scored again. John Harkes played the ball out to Tab Ramos on the right wing, who then beat his man and delivered a perfect pass to Chris Sullivan. The twenty-four-year-old Californian took the ball at the edge of the goal area and, with the keeper pulled out of position, simply pushed it into the vacant net, making the score 3−1. Sullivan's second international goal further deflated Polish hopes. Although in the last two minutes of the game the Poles managed a breakaway and almost scored, it was obvious that for the first time in seventeen years they would lose to the United States.

The press box emptied even before the final whistle. As we made our way to the locker room for postgame interviews, the cub reporter said to me, "I want to ask Gansler what he thinks about his players having sex during the World Cup."

"What?" I said.

"I'm serious," he said.

I believed him.

"The Italian coach won't let his players see their wives or girlfriends," he explained. "He says it's too distracting, but his critics say that's dangerous, especially for Italians. They say his players will get overheated. He thinks that'll help them!"

"I see," I told him.

"The other night," he continued, "someone asked Dr. Ruth what she thought about sex and sports. She said it was fine to make love the night before a game, because it releases tension. But you shouldn't do it with someone new, someone you've just met, because then you might stay up all night and end up exhausted! That's why," he concluded, "you should only do it with your wife or girlfriend— then you can have a quickie and still get a good night's sleep."

I could not imagine how Gansler would respond. Indeed, it took my friend some time to work up the courage to pose his question to the head coach. Dressed in blue sweats and a white polo shirt, Gansler stood in a corner, nursing a Budweiser (a national team sponsor), castigating the journalists assembled in front of him. "If you guys would just do your homework," he kept saying, like an exasperated teacher. He prefaced answers with sighs, as if long ago he had run out of patience with the reporters scribbling in their notebooks or thrusting tape recorders at him. He was still smarting, it seemed, from criticism leveled at him in the press, and yet I could not feel sorry for him. Good criticism is vital to the health of any cultural activity—artistic, athletic, or political. Whether those questioning his coaching decisions were right or wrong, they raised issues the public could understand, educated readers, contributed to what might yet become an ongoing dialogue about the game. No one in the USSF could afford the luxury of press bashing. Soccer's case had to be pleaded in the media. Gansler's contempt for the fourth estate did not help his cause.

"Are you going to ban sex for your players, like the Italians?" the cub reporter finally asked.

"That's a stupid question," Gansler sneered.

"What about Hugo Perez?" said another reporter. "Will he get a chance to make the team?"

"I've already addressed that," said the head coach.

And so it went.

In Washington, D.C., three nights later, after drawing 1−1 with Ajax (which competed without seven of its best players, who were at home preparing for the World Cup), I watched Gansler ruin another splendid public relations opportunity. A television reporter asked the head coach if he could do a quick profile of him. "No," Gansler replied. "When I'm done here, that's it for the day." "It'll only take a minute," the reporter said. "All we have to do is go into the room next door." Gansler shook his head, and said, "I've had a long day." "We've all had long days," the frustrated reporter muttered, walking away. In that locker room of Robert F. Kennedy Stadium, and at subsequent press conferences in Switzerland and Italy, as in Hershey, Gansler acted as if the press were his enemy.

"We're capable of a surprise or two," he was saying now. "The United States has two decades of good growth in soccer, and these players are the product of that work."

He was right about that. Despite his sorry performance with the journalists, the rumors about the NFL and Henry Kissinger, and the youth of the players fielding questions in this locker room, I could believe soccer had a future here. "You never know what will happen in this game," John Harkes was telling another group of reporters. Although he spoke in sharply realistic terms, there was enough fire and innocence in his eyes to make me think that he and his teammates might yet astonish the soccer world.

The locker room started to empty. The cub reporter hurried off to file his story. The Albuquerque-bound reporter who had sat near me during the match was nowhere to be seen.

4

· · · · · · ·

IN THE COUNTRY
OF A THOUSAND YEARS
OF PEACE

S t. Gallen, a city of seventy thousand people located in the northeast corner of Switzerland, owes its founding to the travels and travail of an Irish monk. In A.D. 612 Gallus, wandering "through the wild valley of the Steinach," according to a brochure from the tourist office, fell into a brier, called his tumble a sign from God, and decided to stay. In a green landscape between Lake Constance and the Alps Gallus built a hermitage—with the help of a bear, which earned the beast a place on the city's standard. The monk's retreat developed into a monastery; by the Middle Ages textiles made in St. Gallen were famous throughout Europe. Now it is a city of gables and towers, turrets and bay windows: a popular tourist spot for Germans and Austrians. "Meetings in St. Gallen," my brochure revealed, "have a tradition dating back to the early monastery days." The meeting I had come for was a "friendly" match—that is, nonbinding —between the United States and Switzerland, the last game the Americans would play before the Mondiale.

On June 1, I arrived in St. Gallen with Ron McEachen, my friend and soccer guide for the first half of my journey abroad. After thirty-six hours of travel by plane, by taxi through the streets of Paris, by train, and finally on foot (with heavy bags: many times in the next six weeks I would curse my decision to bring a portable typewriter, a hardbound dictionary, and a large paperback selection of Yannis

Ritsos's poems), we felt as if we had fallen into a different kind of brier, whose brambles included exhaustion, hunger, thirst, and a lingering hangover from the party we had held for ourselves on the night flight from Boston to Paris. At 10 P.M. we found no obvious sign of God, only an open-air café where we feasted on bratwurst and potatoes and beer. It was almost midnight before we started searching for a hotel. Our housing options on a limited budget were few, so we ended up sharing a room in a flophouse above a bar. The other guests, lined up at the counter or trudging down the hall past our room, looked so seedy that when Ronnie woke up in the middle of the night to go to the bathroom, he chose to urinate in the sink rather than risk voyaging into the hall, where he did not know what he might find in the real water closet.

Ronnie is a practical man, a paragon of Yankee ingenuity. Present him with a problem, and he will solve it. Raised in the projects of West Hartford, Connecticut, at an early age he learned to fight or run; his legs became his best defense. In high school he excelled in football, basketball, and diving, and when he took up soccer at the age of sixteen, playing with Brazilians in Hartford's ethnic leagues, he acquired enough skill and experience to win a full scholarship to the University of West Virginia, where he became an All-American. From there he played for the Miami Toros in the NASL, the New York Cosmos' reserve team, a KLM Airline team, and as an all-star for the Connecticut Wildcats, Rhode Island Oceaneers, and Pittsburgh Miners — all in the American Soccer League. Along the way he earned his master's degree in physical education and began coaching — at West Point and Middlebury College (where I played for him a decade ago), at soccer camps, in the USSF youth program, and now at the University of Vermont. He hates to lose at anything he does.

"Mediocrity's my nemesis," he once said. "I can't stand being around people who aren't good at what they do."

He holds himself to the same standards. One summer he decided to become a golfer; by the end of August he had an eight handicap. Another year he took up squash and soon was an A-level player. Although he started soccer late, he has made it to the top of his profession in the United States, because he learns fast. An expert mimic, he masters new moves and fakes on the field as easily as the various accents and languages he picked up during our travels. Friends and rivals alike envy his uncanny ability to make the most of any situation. With limited resources and no scholarships, he uses his eye for talent to turn average squads into winners.

His gift for making things stretch serves him off the field, too. Ronnie and his wife, Karen, and their two young daughters live in a handsome frame house nestled in the Green Mountains and filled with valuable antiques. He and Karen know what to look for at the estate auctions they canvass in their spare time, an art my wife and I struggled in vain to learn the summer we took care of their place. It was not until they returned from Sweden, where Ronnie had trained with Malmö, a top First Division club, that we gleaned their secret: look in the corners, in the places least likely to yield anything worth salvaging—that is where discoveries are made, at auctions and in art, on the soccer field and in the marketplace. One sunlit autumn afternoon in Middlebury, Ronnie emerged from a tent behind an old house, clutching a stack of Elvis Presley 45s, fifteen with their original covers, a mischievous grin spreading across his face.

A powerfully built man of medium height, with dark hair and deep blue eyes, he is proud of his Scottish heritage and traits. Frugality. Humor. Self-sufficiency. I was not surprised to learn that he had found a way to relieve himself in the flophouse, while I suffered until daybreak when I was sure the other guests had gone to bed.

We overslept the next morning, waking after the 11 A.M. check-out. It was up to Ronnie to coax another hour out of our hung over proprietor. Speaking a mishmash of English and German to the bleary-eyed young man behind the bar, he soon secured grace time for us, though until his mouth opened I am sure he had no idea what he might say. He knew no German at all. It was a splendid performance, a necessary one, since we were moving slowly. We went for a short run through the rainy streets of St. Gallen, hoping to get our bearings. Nothing helped—not the run, nor the stretching, nor the cold shower, nor lunch and a beer, though as the old joke goes, the beer helped a little. Once we stored our luggage at the train station, it was time to go to the match and we plodded through the rain to a smallish stadium on the outskirts of town. Despite the wet, cold weather, the stands were filling with several thousand Swiss fans.

Here was a beautiful soccer field. The thick grass was immaculate, and in that weather I was reminded of a description in a letter the painter Georgia O'Keeffe had written of her family home in Charlottesville, Virginia: "cool—and rain—so that everything is wonderful heavy dark green—and the green is all so very clean." Hundreds of boys were juggling soccer balls with remarkable dexterity, calmly marching up and down the field without letting a ball touch the sodden turf. It was like watching the inner workings of a giant clock whose bells were the whistles the coaches blew to signal the end of this demonstration. The boys ran off the field, juggling all the way into the stands. The coaches followed, carrying large plastic bags full of new soccer balls. They stopped in front of the stands, emptied the bags, and kicked or threw the balls up to the spectators. Naturally, Ronnie ended up with one. "I'll give it to one of my girls," he said.

I must confess that when the U.S. team emerged from its locker room and took the field I felt something of a letdown. The young men running and stretching and taking their first shots on goal represented another incarnation of that band of hapless travelers immortalized in Mark Twain's *Innocents Abroad.* What chance did they have in a country where even the clumsiest youngsters could juggle a soccer ball hundreds of times? The rain stopped, and wisps of fog appeared on the hill beyond the stadium. But it was still cold. Roy Orbison traded songs over the public address system with a German balladeer, a small contingent of Swiss fans drummed up noise behind one of the goals, and scores of journalists filed into the press box. "This is about credibility for the U.S.," Ronnie told a Spanish interviewer, who may have wondered why *credibility* figured in so many statements issuing out of our country. "I think they'll fight hard," my friend added, "but I don't know if they have enough experience yet."

Just before the match began, an Austrian journalist turned to me and said, "Why is the United States the only country that hasn't adopted the metric system and soccer?"

I shrugged.

"Well," he continued, "wait till you get to Italy. They're the most soccer-mad people on the face of the earth. On Sunday they watch their match, all day Monday they talk only about the match, and on Tuesday they start talking about next Sunday's match—and that's all they talk about for the rest of the week!" He let out a hearty laugh, then abruptly hunched over his papers. He did not speak again. It was as if he had betrayed a secret and now felt ashamed to have spoken so openly to an American.

The Swiss team lacked seven of its best players, who were training for the country's club championship, which would be staged two days hence, in Bern. Yet for the first fifteen minutes the Swiss dominated the U.S. team, working clever combinations and sending several good crosses into the penalty area. Passing is the ligature that holds a team together, and although the Swiss were reduced to a makeshift lineup, still they controlled the tempo of the match because, unlike the Americans, they understood—in their bones—the principles of linking player to player, space to space. Even without a coach, they would know how to find passing lanes through which numerical advantages might be created.

The art of linking, according to Hubert Vogelsinger in *Winning Soccer Skills and Techniques,* is what develops teamwork. "The Hungarians, the outstanding postwar side in international soccer," he writes, "brought teamwork to its highest pitch by employing a chain-link technique. The man with the ball was like a stone thrown into water because around him, but not too near, were a cluster of players like outgoing ripples in a water splash. Each time the ball moved around the field," he concludes, "a new set of ripples was created." E. M. Forster's advice to young writers was "only connect," suggesting that the art of fiction lies in the exploitation of connections—hidden and overt, disparate and challenging—between various parts of a story. Good soccer teams exploit the same kinds of connections and possibilities, recognizing with Vogelsinger that "one good pass at the right time . . . can do more to develop team spirit and morale than reams of words."

It can excite a crowd, too, as the Swiss demonstrated time and again. Passes come in as many shades and varieties as players (the word *pass,* after all, takes up as much as a whole page in some dictionaries, among its meanings: "to extend; to circulate; to go, change, or be conveyed from one place, form, condition, circumstance, possession, etc., to another; to happen; to come to an end" — all of which bear on the soccer senses of the word), and passing is what melds individual brilliance into ensemble, stray notes into chords. This is one reason why the game evolved from kicking skulls across a battlefield or punting a pig bladder from one town square to another into a highly sophisticated sport closer to ballet than battle. Much of soccer's artistry resides in the links created by what at first glance may appear to be an ordinary pass. A knowledgeable crowd can take as much pleasure from deft passing as from the finishing goal, as this crowd illustrated, cheering good passes on either side of the field.

Passes can be used to mount an attack, probe an opponent's defenses, defuse the other team's attack, stall for time, lull defenders into false positions, reverse the direction of play, or set up a goal. They can be executed with the inside or outside of the foot, instep, toe, heel, chest, or head, delivered hard or soft, high or low, with or without spin, from five to fifty yards away, and sent directly to a teammate, into open space, or into a crowd of players. Every situation demands a different response, another improvisation. "Soccer," Gordon Bradley and Clive Toye write, "is like traditional jazz in that the players know the tune that is to be played, know there are an infinite number of varieties as to how to strike a note or a chord — or a play." Nowhere is their analogy more apt than when a player begins dribbling upfield, head raised so that he can see everything around him: anything can happen during his "solo."

If, for example, he is a brilliant dribbler, like Italy's Roberto Baggio or, to a lesser extent, Tab Ramos, he may try to penetrate as far as possible into his opponent's defenses before taking a shot or passing the ball to a teammate on either wing, to his side, in front or behind him. Or he may elect to widen his team's attack with a square pass, a ball pushed sideways across the field—except in front of his own goal, where it might be intercepted—to a teammate moving forward. Once the defense is spread apart, there may be an opening for a quick through ball, a short pass that springs an attacker free behind the defenders for a shot on goal. This is the most exciting, and most difficult, pass to deliver, because it demands perfect accuracy and timing. A quick jab with the toe, a ball rolling onto the foot of a striker who has slipped behind the defense, and a shot on goal: a good through pass can bring a crowd to its feet.

Likewise, so can a masterful cross into the penalty area, which draws the goalkeeper away from the net and gives the attackers a chance to shoot, volley, or head the ball into the undefended goal. Say a player feeds the ball to one of his wings or a back making a run down the sideline, who then dribbles around his defender and sprints to the corner as his teammates run into the penalty area. The winger has three centering choices, provided he can get free long enough to kick the ball: "He can chip the ball towards the far post," Vogelsinger explains, "high enough to beat the keeper's outstretched hands, possibly on to the head of an attacker rushing in." (As a child I spent hundreds of hours learning to "loft the ball," as we used to say, chipping it over trees and onto the roof of our garage, anything to get the ball up into the air, where in the penalty area it could cause confusion and create chances to score.) Or the winger "may drive the ball hard and low across the face of the goal, or sometimes even drive it low to the near post," hoping one of his teammates can get a foot on it, a half- or full-volley, or that it will deflect off a defender and into the goal. Most spectacular of all, the winger can run to the goal line and "pull the ball back at a really oblique angle placing it around the edge of the penalty area, which is usually vacated because defenders tend to run into the goalmouth to guard the area around the six-yard box." This is where a trailing player may have an excellent chance to score, reverse the play, or . . . The possibilities arising from a simple cross seem endless.

There are many kinds of passes, including—to name just a few of the ones Vogelsinger describes in his book—the push pass, lob volley pass (with the inside or outside of the foot), flick pass, flick-jab, back-heel, crossover back-heel, crossover instep, sole-of-the-foot, heel-volley flick pass, overhead volley lob pass, swerving pass, diagonal pass, wall pass (which resembles basketball's give-and-go), reverse pass, various passes off head balls, and many, many more. If in football the burden of passing falls squarely on the shoulder pads of the quarterback, who inaugurates each diagramed and practiced play with a set of signals timed as rigorously as the drumbeat anchoring a heavy-metal rock song, in soccer everyone on the field must know how to distribute the ball in a myriad of different ways, in ceaseless action unfolding like a jazz composition. When a play "breaks down" on the football field, and the quarterback scrambles outside his "pocket of protection," searching for an open receiver (one of the game's most exciting moments), evading tacklers in the hope of finding an outlet, he faces what every soccer player faces scores of times in a match.

William Matthews suggests that poets study a history of jazz if they want to understand some of the countless formal, rhetorical, and prosodic possibilities available to them in free verse. The same might hold for soccer aficionados who want to appreciate the intricacies, athletic and artistic, of the game. The musical discoveries that John Coltrane made at the height of his powers, exploring chordal and melodic structures so that he might take his listeners (and himself) to places they had never been, are analogous to the moves that Pelé once invented on the soccer field, creating openings in his opponents' defenses, thrilling his fans. How strange that the country that was home to the invention of jazz has almost successfully resisted falling for the most improvisatory of sports. Perhaps soccer, like jazz, is an acquired taste for most Americans?

Certainly touch, which is integral to passing and receiving, is an acquired skill that the Swiss had in abundance. Less nervous than the young Americans, in the opening minutes of play they put on an exhibition of ball control, trapping difficult passes with apparent ease. Trapping or receiving a ball is a matter of learning to cushion its impact against any part of the body, except the hands and arms.

If kicking applies pace to the ball, trapping takes it away; it is, Vogelsinger explains, like playing in reverse "a slow-motion film of a kicking action." A ball can be trapped with the inside, outside, or instep of either foot, thighs, chest, and even the head. The key is to caress the ball, as it were, making it part of your body. A head trap, for example, demands a jump into the air timed to "catch" the ball on the player's forehead, on his way *down:* an extraordinarily difficult way to settle the ball. In a pinch every player on this field could make such a trap.

To complicate matters, a player usually has to trap a pass with one or more defenders nearby. Thus he must learn how to shield the ball from his opponents, receiving it in the midst of moving and turning, faking and feinting, using his body to screen the ball. Even before the ball arrives, the player must know what he will do with the ball, which means he must jockey for position, survey the field, and make a series of decisions about whether to trap and protect the ball, pass it, dribble, shoot, or let it go through to a teammate, all while the ball speeds toward him. "Pelé's ability," Vogelsinger writes, "when receiving a high-cross is particularly fascinating to watch. He lets it ride off his chest, pivots, and takes a thunderous shot at the goal. Or the next time, he may deflect the ball behind the oncoming defender and follow up at top speed to create a split-second opening for himself." Pelé, of course, was in a class by himself, yet good players everywhere can make even the simplest sole-of-the-foot trap interesting and effective.

Then again, sometimes a player will choose not to trap the ball but rather pass it off or shoot it "first-time"—that is, strike it without first attempting to settle it. Such a strategy speeds up play, surprises defenders and goalkeepers, and adds excitement to the game. It is difficult to manage, however, because it demands from every player a sure sense of the ball, ideas about what to do with it, excellent timing, courage, and the skill to redirect even the hardest passes. Ronnie's teams, like many good squads, devote part of each practice to one-touch play, emphasizing what he calls "good first touches on the ball," an exercise as exacting and potentially liberating—for the skilled, that is—as an exercise the poet Richard Howard gives his students: writing a poem using only the keys on one side of the typewriter.

Nineteen minutes into the match, Peter Vermes drew a bead on a ball rolling toward him just outside the Swiss penalty area, struck it first-time, and fired a rocket off the post, rousing his teammates from their stupor.

One player taking a chance was all the Americans needed to find their bearings. The Swiss countered with a good shot, but wide of the goal. Then Tab Ramos made a clever run and fed Vermes for another fine shot. One minute later, Bruce Murray scored on a breakaway, and the sun came out, as if to manifest in its briefest of appearances one of those hackneyed epiphanies Hollywood producers love to slip into their movies. The crowd fell silent until the match and the rain resumed. When the Swiss nearly scored a few minutes later—Tony Meola, the American goalkeeper, made a splendid save off a head ball—the fans at one end of the stadium began the timeless chant I was to hear throughout the World Cup, a string of syllables—*olé, olé, olé*—resembling the Native American songs I heard at feast dances and celebrations in pueblos near my home in New Mexico. It was an eerie, ancient sound, a primal hymn of solidarity, a tribal call: a sign of nationalism. Before Murray's goal, his eighth in international competition, the crowd had cheered good play on both sides of the field. Now that spirit of fellowship, that charity toward the underdogs from the New World, dissolved. The chanting mounted with each advance the Americans made, both Ramos and Murray springing free for breakaway attempts on goal, their teammates more than holding their own against what everyone around me agreed was the better side. The Swiss created a number of scoring chances, including an easy one-on-one with Meola, yet they could not catch up with the Americans before the first half ended. Their fans were not happy. One Swiss journalist said to me, "Why do you Americans want to be so good at soccer? You already have baseball and football." I could not answer him.

In the second half, the Swiss made a tactical change that caught the Americans off-guard. Although Bob Gansler's coaching philosophy was founded on a defensive strategy in which each player "marked"—guarded or shadowed—one opponent all over the field, as in basketball's pressurized defense, it seemed that the Swiss always had a player free. The U.S. team, Ronnie explained, could not respond quickly enough to the changes the Swiss had made, because the American players relied, as we were to hear again and again, too much on principles, not enough on knowledge and instinct. "See, they've gone from a 4-4-2," he said, describing the Swiss system of play—four defenders or fullbacks, four midfielders or halfbacks, and two forwards—"to a 3-5-2, and the extra midfielder confuses us. We need another midfielder to mark him, and we don't know how to find him."

The Swiss dominated play. Twenty-one minutes into the second half, they tied the match on Peter Schepull's unremarkable goal; moments later, they almost scored again on what would have been a remarkable goal, a perfectly executed bicycle kick. What happened was this: the ball was centered from the wing, and a forward leaping into the air, as if to perform a back flip, volleyed the ball first-time over his head and toward the goal. It was a spectacular move, which drew from the crowd a burst of applause, and though the Swiss were stopped on that shot, it seemed only a matter of time before they would take the lead. Eight minutes later, Adrian Knup got the go-ahead goal on another breakaway.

Was he offside? Had he slipped behind the last American defender before receiving the ball from his teammate? Tony Meola, who had faced Knup one-on-one, thought so, and he ran all the way over to the linesman on the far side of the field to tell him he had missed the call.

Nothing changed.

Nothing ever changes once the call is made or missed. In soccer the referee is assisted by two linesmen on either side of the pitch, and they are obliged to keep the game moving. Except for flagrant fouls and the ball going out of bounds, much of what occurs in a match is subject to the referee's discretionary powers: Was that hand ball intentional? Did this foul slow a team's attack, or was the team able to retain its advantage, in which case no call should be made? Has that player's conduct crossed the shifting line between hard, clean play and dangerous behavior? Is this player injured, or is he simply stalling to give himself and his teammates a chance to rest, change the tempo of the match, or draw a call because he was going to lose the ball anyway? These are just some of the kinds of decisions the referee must make, moment by moment, recognizing that his chief responsibility is to keep the action flowing. Bruce Murray, for example, repeatedly fell to the turf, pretending to have been pushed or tripped when a defender had stripped him of the ball. But his acting was too dramatic, his falls too theatrical, his name and reputation insufficiently large to gain him any advantage. He rarely got the call he wanted. "It's worth a try," Ronnie said each time Murray went down. "You never know what'll happen." Indeed, there is no way of knowing exactly what the referee will do — or not do.

The arbitrary nature of officiating sporting events is both fascinating and exasperating: the players', coaches', and fans' helplessness in the wake of a bad call cuts to the heart of the human condition. The ruddy baseball manager, cheeks bulging with chewing tobacco, who argues with the umpire at home plate, screaming and kicking dirt across the batter's box, is not unlike Joseph K., the hapless hero of *The Trial,* Kafka's novel about a man who must defend himself against the accusation of a capital offense that he cannot fathom: both rail against judgments that will never be reversed. There is as much comedy as tragedy in the spectacle of a tennis player dressing down a linesman, a basketball star ejected from a game for mouthing off at an official, the knight in Bergman's film *The Seventh Seal* who tries to bargain with Death at the chess table only to discover that his opponent is in fact the arbiter of his fate. When Troy, the hero of August Wilson's *Fences,* struts across the stage, equating death with being called out on strikes, he articulates what we dimly understand to be the providential, even dictatorial, nature of the referee's role in sports, which mirrors both the unpredictability and finality of events within our lives. By the end of the play, the baseball tied to a string and hanging from a dead tree next to Troy's house has become a symbol of the innate connection between baseball and fate, games and life.

In soccer the referee is the incarnation of the sport's laws and limits. (There are only seventeen rules in the game. American football's rule book, on the other hand, is as thick as a telephone directory.) He is also occasionally a perfect illustration of chance, of the spirit of capriciousness hidden everywhere, reminding us of the subjective nature of even our most "objective" enterprises. Only a litigious society like ours could invent and sanction football's short-lived instant replay rule: the practice of reviewing an official's call with the help of a television monitor, yards of film displaying the event in question from a variety of camera angles, and a two-minute halt in the game. Because on any given play in football a host of infractions may be committed, the referee's decision to isolate one call and turn for confirmation or refutation to the replay official was akin to a district attorney's impaneling of a grand jury to charge a notorious gangster with illegal parking. Where do you start?

How I loved those moments when the replay official, stymied by the evidence presented him, had to let the play stand as it was called on the field—and how I hope soccer never succumbs to the pressure mounting in some quarters to adopt instant replay. Such a technological intrusion would mar the game's simplicity, upset the balances established by soccer's fluid give-and-take, destroy the autonomy of the action on the pitch. Unsettling as it is to see a well-played match turn on a bad call, a deserving team go down to defeat, or fortune override merit, still there is in that outcome something quintessentially human: a reflection of our experience in the world at large, an expression of life's tragicomic nature. No wonder the referee so easily becomes the focus of a crowd's frustration. Who else possesses such arbitrary power? Officials have often had to be escorted by police from stadiums in which the home team came out on the losing end. In Colombia in 1989 a referee lost his life after a match, apparently a victim of the drug wars, as well as of his precarious position in the soccer world. In our time we have an uncertain relationship to judgment and authority, which may explain why that Colombian was not the first man in black to be murdered.

The United States did not deserve to win its match against Switzerland, whether Meola was right or wrong about the linesman missing a crucial offside call; and the Americans' sluggish play after the disputed goal only reinforced that impression. The match ended, mercifully, by the margin of that single score. "We played a solid first half," Ronnie said, "then fell apart. What we have to do is put together a full ninety minutes of good play. We have to learn how to hold onto a lead. And we're running out of time." Yet the promise of that first half left him in good spirits, quickening his gait and what he called "the process of recovery" from our trans-Atlantic flight. His mood improved even more when, quite by chance, we met up with his old friend, Roy Hodgson, former coach of Malmö, the Swedish club Ronnie had trained with years ago. Roy and his wife Sheila were driving to Lake Constance for a short vacation before the Swiss Cup final and the Mondiale, and they invited us along. Our schedule was open for the next several days, and we were happy to postpone our long train ride to Florence; our approach to travel was to depend on spur-of-the-moment decisions.

On our way out of the stadium Roy stopped to talk to the referee.

"The Yanks looked good," said the English referee. "At least for a half."

Roy nodded. "They're honest players," he said. "Hard-working. But they lack pace, don't they?" he added in a lilting voice, his question more rhetorical than interrogatory. "They didn't have the ball enough, did they?"

"Not once the Swiss flooded the midfield," said the referee. "I understand you're moving here?"

"Neuchâtel," said Roy. Then, with a chuckle: "I've got my work cut out for me, don't I?"

"Best of luck to you," said the referee, turning to leave.

"And you," said Roy, then steered us toward the parking lot. When we were out of earshot, he paused and looked around the empty stadium. "Always a good idea to say hello to a referee," he told us, "because you never know when there will be a fifty-fifty call. If he has a friendly feeling about you, the call just might go your way." He winked and walked on.

That was only the first of many interesting notions I would glean from him in the next two days. A handsome, husky, well-read Englishman, sandy haired and natty in a brown leather jacket and scarf,

Roy was himself a study in what he prized in the writings of his favorite authors, J. P. Donleavy, John Updike, William Trevor, and Gabriel García Márquez: the juxtaposition of "high" and "low" aspects of cultural life. Here was a soccer coach who at the dinner table preferred to talk about books, a former professional player with an extensive knowledge of fine wines, a man who could describe—in English, German, French, or Swedish—the merits of any style of play or cuisine. Rumor had it, he had just signed a million-dollar contract to manage Neuchâtel Xamax, one of the two clubs in the Swiss Cup final.

His own playing career had come to an end, after stints with clubs in England and South Africa, when at the age of twenty-eight he had realized he would be "a better coach than player." After twelve years in Sweden ("A good jumping-off place," he said, "for travel"), where he had worked with several champions, Roy was happy to be back in central Europe. He and Sheila, a striking woman with auburn hair, stylishly dressed in blue jeans, a white blouse, and a jacket like her husband's, were now learning their way around Switzerland. We climbed into their Mercedes—a gift from Xamax's owner who, Roy explained, paid him "whenever he felt like it"—and drove to the train station to retrieve our luggage. Then, speeding under clearing skies through the Swiss countryside, among rolling hills and orchards, dairy farms, tidy woodlots, and churches with steeple clocks, music blaring from the tape deck (Roy's tastes ranged from Tracy Chapman to Italian opera, the Blues Brothers to art song), we talked about everything from Bernard Malamud's *Dubin's Lives* to the behavior of the American players. "They complain too much," Roy said. "They're all big fish in little ponds and come here to find they won't be babied the way they're used to, which is why they cry foul so much."

The ins and outs of coaching professional soccer fascinated him.

"On Xamax I have a Swede, a Pole, a Brazilian, an American born in Switzerland who knows nothing about his so-called homeland," said Roy, "as well as Swiss players from the German, French, and Italian parts of the country."

"How do you communicate?" I asked.

"French," he said. "Or with my hands. There's every style of play in Switzerland. We'll be a little closer to the British now. Oh, my shoulders hurt," he winced, shrugging. "I worked out a new keeper two days ago, and I'm still sore."

"That's because you're out of shape," Sheila teased.

"I've got to get back to work, don't I?" he said. "Observing talent"—which is what he had done at the United States–Switzerland match and what he would do at the Mondiale, traveling to Palermo to watch an Egyptian player he was considering signing for Xamax—"isn't good for the waistline, is it?" he said with a laugh.

Talent was what we discussed, in both literary and soccer terms, at dinner in an Italian restaurant on the German side of Constance, then the next day among the crowds of tourists in Meersburg, a prosperous town built around a fortress dating back to A.D. 628. To get to Meersburg, we took a ferry across the lake. Surrounded by blue-shirted boy scouts on bicycles, Roy pointed out the island of Mainau to the north, a vestige of the old Swedish empire. I wondered if he felt out of place in Switzerland, having left a secure coaching position to assume the reins of a club already basking in success? He was not as isolated as the ancestral monarchs on that distant island, but he may have been as nervous as they might once have been this far from their home. His mandate was to remake Xamax in his own fashion, and he had no time to lose. Hence he was looking for players everywhere, even among the Americans. Whatever he felt about his newest challenge, though, he kept to himself, choosing instead to talk about the novels of Philip Roth and Isaac Bashevis Singer, or the transfer fees—that is, the trading prices—certain players would command for their respective soccer federations.

Meersburg from the water was a wide hill with grapevines. And when we docked, we found stone steps leading down into the water. Palm trees. Cropped maples along the waterfront. Gardens with twenty-foot-high climbing roses, hosta lilies, foxgloves, impatiens, dusty miller, begonias, and boxwood hedges. Irises blooming in the middle of a shingle roof. Window boxes filled with geraniums and fuchsias brightening the facades of brown-shuttered houses. We came upon a water mill and water fountains. We saw the Alps glittering in the distance. Here were Americans with backpacks, motorcyclists in black, an old man wearing a *Lethal Weapon II* hat, pushing a rusted bicycle down a cobblestone street thick with vendors. Crowds of tourists from East Germany and Poland, the first waves of visitors from the crumbling world of communism, wandered about: families without money. Roy picked out an elegant restaurant along the shore, ordered two bottles of the local white wine, then suggested some dishes we might like. We ate fish caught in the lake. We gazed out the window at whitecaps rumpling the water.

"The Eastern European clubs are wising up to what they can get in transfer fees for their players," Roy said. "But that's still where all the bargains are. The governments own the clubs, and since they need cash they're willing to let their players go, sometimes for less than you might think."

"You can bet the World Cup will be a showcase for a lot of these players," said Ronnie.

"It's their big chance, isn't it?" said Roy. "The only ones not to get are Yugoslavs. If they had good characters, they'd be world champions every year. But they're not champions, talented as they are. Everyone knows not to get Yugoslavs. If they'd stop fighting among themselves," he continued, "you'd have a different result, wouldn't you?" He raised his glass, paused, then drained it in one gulp. "The Italians, though, are another story," he said.

"How do you mean?" I asked.

"They're a pragmatic soccer people," he explained, refilling our glasses.

"Artistic, too," Ronnie added.

"Aye," said Roy, nodding. "But pragmatic more than anything else. They'll do just what's necessary to win. Nothing more. And they'll irritate you with all their pressurizing. But I don't imagine they'll beat the U.S. badly. They'll do what they have to. Maybe one –nil, two–one."

We were in high spirits by the time we returned to the car. Roy took Sheila's hand, saying "I shan't need any nooky tonight!" She gave him a playful shove. The drive south to Bern passed in a blur of music and laughter. We sang along with the Temptations and the Righteous Brothers, listened to Roy's arias from *Aida,* and sped down the road. The Hodgsons dropped us off at a youth hostel near the center of the Swiss capital and made plans to meet the next day at the Cup final. On our way to dinner Ronnie and I chanced upon a small crowd assembled in front of a store window, watching on more than a dozen television screens a replay of a famous match between West Germany and Italy, a World Cup classic from 1974 in which seven goals were scored in overtime; these die-hard fans cheered each tally as if it had just occurred. Switzerland had not qualified for the Mondiale; nevertheless, here in Bern soccer was the only subject anyone wanted to talk about.

Monday, the day of the cup final, was a national holiday in Switzerland—Pentecost. We began it at the Swiss Football Federation headquarters, where the president gave us press passes for the afternoon match. We were surprised to see on his office wall a photograph of Henry Kissinger, and as we headed out into the rain to catch a bus back into town, Ronnie said, "Kissinger's written an article about soccer being a way of life." I nodded, wondering if soccer had influenced his understanding of foreign policy. An interesting thought: diplomacy in the form of a soccer match! Imagine if statesmanship had just seventeen rules and a running clock. I carried that line of reasoning no further once the bus let us out at the bear pit, a sunken, circular enclosure near a bridge overlooking the Aare River.

In the cold drizzle a crowd of soccer fans waited impatiently for the hours to pass before the match would start, hordes of young and middle-aged men and women waving flags, dressed in their respective team uniforms, their faces painted in stripes of their particular team's colors—black and red for Xamax, blue and white for Zurich's Grasshopper-Club. They were throwing pieces of bread, coins, and pebbles at the bears scampering around the rocks below them, chanting *olé, olé, olé:* a modern version of the medieval sport of bearbaiting. If in other parts of the city the devout were commemorating the Holy Spirit's descent upon his Apostles, these devoted soccer fans were working themselves into a frenzy not unlike the ecstasies experienced by believers in the Pentecostal tradition. In the capital of a country known for its peaceableness, restraint, clocks, and a clockwork approach to life hundreds of people were chanting nonsense syllables, as if speaking in tongues.

"Don't let them catch your eye," Ronnie warned. "You never know what'll set them off."

"Hooligans?" I said.

"They're like a pack of dogs," he said.

"I thought they were only in England," I said.

He shook his head. "They're all over Europe now," he muttered. "Wherever the economy's off, or people are bored, or who knows why. And this won't be the last we see of them. Come on, let's get out of here."

On the bridge we met an American couple unhappily studying a map of Switzerland. They had not expected to find that on their only day in Bern all the shops would be closed. Now they were trying to figure out another place to go—a town, city, or country where the observance of Pentecost might not be so strict as here in the capital.

"Why don't you come to the soccer match?" Ronnie offered. "You'll never see anything like it again."

"No," said the man. The woman added, "We didn't come to Europe to watch a soccer game. We came to see the Jungfrau"—a 13,642-foot-high peak in the Bernese Alps—"and we can't even see that with all this rain and fog." She threw up her hands and led the man toward the bear pit.

By game time the rain had let up, though the Jungfrau remained hidden behind clouds and mist. In the Bern stadium it seemed that all of the twenty-seven thousand fans were on their feet, screaming. Because Grasshopper-Club is based in the German-speaking part of Switzerland and Xamax in the French, announcements over the public address system were made in both languages. But no one could make out a word of what little was said. It was like attending an early Beatles' concert. After the players exchanged gifts at midfield—pennants, sweat shirts, club sweaters, and the like—the match began, and the noise was deafening. Horns, drums, and constant cheering, clapping, booing, or hissing. The winner of the match would earn the right to participate in the next year's European Club Championship, and for these fans it was an article of faith that they raise as much noise as possible to support their team.

The rain began again. The ball skidded across the wet turf. Touch, under these conditions, was essential. Both sides delighted the crowd with flick, back-heel, and behind-the-back passes, quick restarts after fouls, volleys, and a bicycle shot. When Thomas Wyss scored at the twenty-five-minute mark, the Grasshopper-Club supporters burst into shrieks of delirium, firing bottle rockets and flares at the field, singing "Amazing Grace" and "Yankee Doodle Dandy." The Xamax fans replied in kind sixteen minutes later as Didier Gigon tied the match. The score at the half was 1–1, and if Xamax had had the run of play in the first forty-five minutes, in the second half Grasshopper-Club dominated the action. Adrian De Vincente scored their winning goal twenty-three minutes into play.

At that point I took notice of Gilbert Gress, the man Roy would replace as soon as the match was over. After a professional playing career with First Division clubs in Strasbourg, Stuttgart, and Marseilles, a two-year stint as player-coach for Xamax, and coaching positions at Strasbourg and FC Burges, he had spent the last decade at Neuchâtel, where his teams had twice won the Swiss Championship. But he would not close out his tenure at the helm of Xamax as a winner, which did not sit well with him. This forty-eight-year-old man with his shoulder-length blond hair and fur coat cut quite a figure stomping up and down the sideline, flagrantly violating the no-coaching rule. He was almost ejected from the match, an all but unheard-of event in professional soccer. And he was still angry when the referee signaled the end of play, though few paid any attention to his histrionics, with smoke bombs and flares burning among the Grasshopper-Club fans, the winning team taking a victory lap around the field, the dejected Xamax players sprawled on the ground, and the noise level rising to a nearly intolerable pitch.

We met up with the Hodgsons, who had watched the match with Xamax's owner, and accompanied them to a local restaurant. Roy and Ronnie traded notes on Neuchâtel's play and on Gilbert

Gress's behavior. "He's an obnoxious sort, isn't he?" Roy said, ordering another delicious meal and wine for us all. "A man of his age with hair like that!" he snorted. "No one wears a mink coat to a match. I don't care how cold it is!" Then, when the wine had been delivered, approved, and poured, he raised a glass. "Personal victory for me, though, isn't it?" he said in a soft voice, his mind seemingly miles away. "It'll be hard enough for me as it is—without having to repeat as the Cup winner."

5

· · · · · · ·

WORLD CUPISM

*T*he new graffiti in Florence had taken on a sinister air: "Il Mondialismo Ti Uccide." (World Cupism Kills You.) It was true that a number of workers had lost their lives in construction accidents at the various stadiums in Italy, but these urban scrawlers had more in mind than the calamities that had marred preparations for the Mondiale. In their fatalistic pronouncements on the tournament about to unfold in twelve different cities, a month-long event that would attract legions of criminals and hooligans, they articulated a presentiment common to Italians and visitors alike: something, somewhere, was going to go tragically wrong. Stories of security problems, threatened strikes, and structural flaws in the newly remodeled stadiums circulated. In Rome, for example, emergency vehicles could not drive into Stadio Olimpico because the architects had designed the doorways six inches too low; a falling girder or a riot among the fans might have disastrous consequences. Everyone in Italy, it seemed, was expecting something to happen.

Ronnie and I had already experienced a certain amount of foreboding about our World Cup adventure. On the overnight train ride from Bern to Florence, a trip through the starkly beautiful Swiss Alps, we had been joined in our compartment by a scruffy Italian, a stocky youth who liked to play with a sharp knife. He had no interest in answering our questions, which we put to him in every language we knew—English, French, faltering Italian, and a crude version of sign. Nor could we convince him to take one of the vacant compartments on either side of ours. He was content, all the way from Switzerland, to watch us watching him. Occasionally he would walk out into the corridor to smoke a cigarette and meet with an equally ominous-looking young man. During those breaks Ronnie and I would make our plans: one of us would sleep while the other kept watch, ready to kick the dozing one awake at the first sign of trouble. "What an asshole," Ronnie muttered over and over again. We had heard enough tales of train robberies in Italy, hoods gassing compartments or knocking travelers out with clubs in order to steal their wallets and luggage. What sleep we got was fitful.

When we arrived in Florence a little after daybreak, we were exhausted, but our spirits lifted once we left the station to find a bus. It was bright and warm in what Mary McCarthy has called "a city of endurance, a city of stone," and we had survived our strange journey. Now we were in the birthplace of the Renaissance, the home of Dante, Petrarch, and Boccaccio; of Michelangelo, Donatello, Leonardo, and Fra Angelico; Machiavelli, Galileo, and the Medicis. The city in which the double-entry bookkeeping system was invented and Dostoevski finished *The Idiot;* the magnet that for generations has attracted English and American writers. Once I asked the poet Mark Strand whether on his visits to Italy he found it easy to write. "No," he said. "I just look. It's so beautiful all I can do is look." Now I would see what he meant. Boarding a bus for Antella, a village twenty minutes southeast of Florence, I thought of the ending to one of James Wright's last poems, a hymn of sorts to a spider he had discovered near here:

> Many men
> Have searched all over Tuscany and never found
> What I found there, the heart of the light
> Itself shelled and leaved, balancing
> On filaments themselves falling. The secret
> Of this journey is to let the wind

Blow its dust all over your body,
To let it go on blowing, to step lightly, lightly
All the way through your ruins, and not to lose
Any sleep over the dead, who surely
Will bury their own, don't worry.

If Wright could find "the secret / Of this journey," which is the secret of any journey, including the one we begin at birth, in a Tuscan spider, I hoped I could learn something in Italy: how to see, how to live.

We had arrived in time for what Enrico Benini, our host for the next several weeks, called "the moment of Italian soccer." Italy's First Division clubs were the best in the world. AC Milan had won the Intercontinental Cup, European Champions Cup, and the European Super Cup, while Juventus had taken the UEFA (Union of European Football Associations) Cup and Sampdoria the European Cup Winners' Cup. It was a clean sweep for Italy, which as the host country for the World Cup was the odds-on favorite to win it all. (The odds against the United States winning the tournament were 500−1.) In Florence there were signs of the Mondiale in every window we drove past. An adult theater featured a poster of a naked woman whose private parts were covered with soccer balls the colors of the country's flag—red, white, and green. The trademark of the Mondiale—the ubiquitous *Ciao!*—was affixed to pennants, mugs, T-shirts, maps, signs, and programs. Hello!

The bus let us off at its last stop, in the center of Antella, which even at this early hour was filled with old men leaning on canes in front of the open-air café, aging women hobbling out of the church, young mothers pushing strollers from the bread shop to the butcher's to the pharmacy. A phone call to Enrico Benini brought him to the square minutes later. A lawyer from an old Florentine family, a slim, dark-haired man with a chiseled profile and a well-deserved reputation for absentmindedness, Enrico was reluctant to return immediately to his house, insisting we first have a coffee in the café. What he ordered were thimble-sized cups of a drink so strong and bitter it burned my stomach, jolting me awake. Like Ronnie, I poured enough sugar into my coffee to make a batch of cookies and listened to Enrico describe the changes the Mondiale had visited upon Italy.

"In forty years," he sighed, "our Parliament couldn't pass a law limiting the length of a strike. Seven days before the World Cup starts, they pass such a law. Stupid!" he muttered, an expression he used repeatedly to characterize Italian politics, rising taxes, soccer players, coaches and tactics, telephones and fax machines, other drivers and the weather, even his job, though he was his own boss. "Now we have a new bridge," he continued in faultless English, "and the turnpike from Ponte Ema to Florence—we've been waiting twenty years for them to finish it. Now they're finally doing it. All because of the Mondiale. Stupid!"

Soon we were driving up a steep, winding road, a narrow lane that at each of its switchbacks demanded from Enrico a honk of the horn—a demand he obeyed in a haphazard fashion, eliciting from each driver coming down the mountain a flurry of curses, blasts from the horn, and shaking fists. Those who lived in the ancient houses dotting the mountain overlooking Antella could hear us coming for miles. We passed laborers clearing brush around grapevines, scything grass and broom slowly and deliberately. Near the top Enrico eased his compact Toyota through a narrow stone gate, coasted down the rutted driveway, and came to a stop at a refurbished farmhouse, where he lived with Jackie Roser-Benini—my high school girlfriend —and their two-year-old son, Federico.

Jackie, a small, olive-skinned, athletic woman with long dark hair and an almost Oriental regard, eyes narrow above her high cheekbones, had a kind of beauty enhanced by four months of pregnancy. Born into wealth and privilege, she was utterly unpretentious in her mien and dealings with others. Dressed casually in a plaid shift, she presided over her household in the same casual fashion with which her mother had managed their estate in Bedminster, New Jersey. Jackie came from a line of Quaker matriarchs, and she had assumed her familial role—albeit in the Old World—with what seemed like ease, though she had suffered more than a little on her way to this picture of domestic bliss. She had been a high school star in field hockey, track, and gymnastics until a series of injuries had cut her career short. In dressage she had competed on the national level only to find, in her early twenties, that the horse she had trained and ridden for years was lame and would have to be destroyed, ending her equestrian hopes. Now, after Federico's difficult birth (which had nearly cost her her life), warnings not to get pregnant again (medical advice she had no interest in following), and a miscarriage, Jackie was giving herself daily injections of hormones, facing the possibility of surgery just to bring her next child to term. She was every bit as stubborn as I remembered her. She would, I suspected, deliver against all odds a healthy baby.

She had met Enrico at her cousin's wedding to his brother, Lorenzo, and subsequently Jackie, too, had married into the Benini family. After living in an apartment in the city, she had decided that Florentine life was not for her. Thus she had found and bought this two-story stucco house, which during World War II had served as a Resistance hideout. Buried behind one of the walls, according to the farmer who used to live there and now took care of Jackie's gardens, vineyard, and orchard, was a machine gun. No one had found it yet, though Enrico searched the house from time to time. He was more suited to urban living, yet he had learned to love this estate—La Ragnaia 1839, as the Italian inscription read above the wrought-iron gate leading to the front door. The Spider House.

Here were thirty acres of olive, apricot, and fig trees; grapevines, chestnuts, and cypresses. ("The graveyard tree," Jackie explained. "You can tell where the old graveyard roads went, by looking for cypresses.") The fence was lined with red roses, and red poppies grew on the hillside, ivy on the yellow walls. From the back porch there was a view down the valley and out toward other Tuscan mountains, through spirals of smoke rising from the fires farmers had set to clear the brush around their grapevines. All the doors and windows were open, and we smelled the sweet scent of jasmine hanging from the back wall. Geraniums in planters. Lavender. Mimosa. Tall wisteria bent in the wind that Jackie hoped would bring the heavy rains now in southern France. In the garage was a sixty-liter cask of the local Chianti, in the cellar two thirty-liter casks of olive oil pressed last fall from their own olives, and in the vegetable garden lettuce and onions and juicy tomatoes harvested year-round.

"Everything grows here," Jackie declared.

It was true. Out their back door we could walk less than a mile, through stands of pine and birch, brambles and wild roses, and hike the Etruscan trail—"the closest thing to wilderness in Tuscany," Enrico said. On this ancient trade route we would look for wild boars and roebucks, hedgehogs and deer, hoping to catch sight of one of the wolves rumored to be in these hills. Everything seemed alive and, in the heat of the Italian summer, on fire. I have a friend in Santa Fe who has traveled all around the world, but until she went to Tuscany, she had always returned to New Mexico believing it was the most beautiful place on the earth. After a month here, however, she was no longer certain the Sangre de Cristo Mountains and Rio Grande would forever hold her interest. Now I understood exactly what she meant.

Jackie was happy to have moved here before the rest of Florence discovered the pleasures of country living. "Even Antella's becoming a little trendy," she admitted. The influx of newcomers, who had bought up most of the farmhouses and estates that once belonged to the nobility, had now directly changed their lives. Because their neighbor had tapped into their well, disrupting the flow of water, they had to install a set of cisterns to catch rainwater and build up a more reliable supply. A four-day construction project to place the concrete cisterns in the hillside was now well into its second week, though, and there was no end in sight, perhaps because Enrico had shown the laborers where the cask of Chianti was stored. Nothing, Jackie said, was ever accomplished after lunch, which each day started earlier and earlier.

"Stupid!" Enrico sighed, then blamed his inability to quit smoking on the construction delays. "You see," he explained, "I have no willpower." Jackie, smiling, emphatically nodded her head.

What worsened matters was the ongoing drought afflicting the region. It had not rained in months, though clouds kept building on the horizon. The spring ran dry every afternoon; there was only enough water for cooking, baths for Federico, and an occasional shower for the rest of us. Chickens and rabbits had once been stabled on the ground floor of the Spider House, and although the barnyard animals had now been replaced by antique furniture, paintings, and the accumulations of a growing family, a certain confusion still reigned. Neighbors wandered in and out, laborers jackhammered through twenty centimeters of cement in the cellar, a bull terrier named Zirca chased the soccer ball Ronnie had gotten in St. Gallen. An old Pekingese named Pimms, whose jaw Zirca had broken, dragged his tongue along the floor, collecting dust and dirt as he wandered in and out of the kitchen. "Despite what Italians think," Jackie said, "hygiene isn't happiness. They're the cleanest people anywhere, and it drives me crazy!"

All the same, Ronnie and I had two duffle bags full of dirty clothes, and so we brought them to the laundress in Antella. When we went to pick them up the next day, we found to our horror that we had been charged 103,000 lire—almost $85! Had she dry-cleaned everything, including our running shorts and socks? Was she taking advantage of naive Americans? We left without our laundry. Enrico later convinced the woman to lop 30,000 lire off our bill. But we were smarting from the realization that we, too, were innocents abroad, an idea reinforced in countless ways, none more glaring than the fact that we wandered halfway through the Duomo in Florence before we recognized that we were indeed in Brunelleschi's fabulous dome, the fourth largest cathedral in the world.

We were not alone in our innocence, as we discovered at the U.S. team's press conference the day before the Mondiale's opening ceremonies. In Florence's Centro Stampa, a state-of-the-art communications facility across the street from the train station, the coach of what one journalist called "the loneliest team in the world" fielded questions from members of the foreign press. "We'll try to cooperate with you," Bob Gansler began in a hoarse voice, like a beleaguered politician, "and hope you'll reciprocate." Whatever good will these writers might have shown him crumbled when the translator asked him to slow down and he snapped, "Obviously I'm in more of a hurry than you are!" Several people cackled. "Why are your training sessions closed to the press and public?" asked a reporter. "You think you have that much to hide?" More laughter. "Some like to shower with their windows open, some closed," Gansler said. What about the rumors that his job was in jeopardy? "If I believed every-thing I read in the American press," Gansler replied, "I'd be in trouble." "The truth hurts," said a journalist near me. Had he ever attended a World Cup match? "No," said the coach. "But I've seen all the [video] footage and read all the technical reports." "Good God," Ronnie whispered. Tittering spread around the room. It was as if we had sent the manager of a pool hall as the head of the American delegation to an international trade conference. "They're laughing at us," Ronnie muttered, nodding at the journalists. "They don't take us seriously."

Ours was nothing more than a sideshow to the rest of the Mondiale, proof to other countries that despite our economic and military power we were still beginners at the people's game, still isolationist in our approach to the world's favorite sport. We were here, I was told by more than one soccer aficionado, to learn how to be proper hosts of the 1994 World Cup—an education, many feared, we would be too arrogant to know we needed. Bob Gansler might believe, as he declared at the end of the press conference, that the experience of the World Cup was "data" he and his players needed to "collect." These journalists thought otherwise, judging from their disdain for the American coach. Success or failure in this tourna-ment was a function of national pride—occasionally, tragically, even a matter of life and death. We were long overdue for that lesson.

The organizers of the Mondiale, particularly Luca Cordero di Montezemolo, general manager of the organizing committee, under-stood their mandate quite clearly: to present the greatest show on earth, a month-long extravaganza during the course of which three million visitors and fifteen *billion* television viewers would watch a total of fifty-two matches. It would be a logistical nightmare, with twelve cities hosting twenty-four of the world's best national teams. Montezemolo, in the words of commentator Rob Hughes, had "spent four years pulling together strands of business, politics, security, media and culture to build an infrastructure out of chaos." A protégé of both the late Enzo Ferrari, whose sleek racing cars were the subject of a current museum exhibit in Florence, and Gianni Agnelli, the industrial baron who as head of the Fiat empire owned, among other companies, Ferrari as well as Juventus, one of Italy's best First Division clubs, Montezemolo thrived on challenges. He had been a rally driver at Monte Carlo and other sites. "I was very, very quick and daring," he told Hughes. "I finished one race in five. If I finished, I won. Other times . . . crash!" And he was not afraid to take chances in his preparations for the Mondiale. "It is our opportunity to show that Italy knows how to work," he said, "to show what it can offer in terms of technology, efficiency, and creativity."

Facing a dizzying array of problems, Montezemolo had no choice but to take chances in order to put the fourteenth World Cup together. "Italy, never forget, is the land of Machiavelli," Hughes writes. "Nothing is delivered until the last moment, and nothing is untouched by politics." Accordingly, the national government fell four times in the four years leading up to the Mondiale, leaving the elegant administrator in the awkward position of having to change tack again and again, renegotiating between opposing national parties. New stadiums were built in Bari and Turin; others were refurbished extensively—always, one can assume, with the kinds of problems Jackie and Enrico were experiencing with the construction of their cisterns. "What a country!" we heard from exasperated people everywhere, Italians and tourists alike. No doubt Montezemolo muttered these words constantly. Now the world would soon be watching what he had created, with the help of executives released from eight major Italian corporations, film directors Francesco Rosi and Franco Zeffirelli, the artist Alberto Burri, and thousands of workers and volunteers. All of Italy, it seemed, had a stake in the Mondiale's success.

"How can I not worry?" Montezemolo had said.

Aside from his country's honor, construction delays, political machinations, transportation and communications problems, and strike threats, there were also security concerns. In an interview with Reuters, Interior Ministry under secretary Giancarlo Ruffino, Italia 90's security chief, had said that while improving international conditions diminished the threat of terrorism, "We do not want to lower our guard, because the World Cup could represent a great stage for some crazed faction or offshoot of international terrorism." The massacre of eleven Israelis at the 1972 Olympics in Munich was still fresh in the memory of Gustavo Cappuccio, Italy's police commissioner. "Perhaps a unique moment for international publicity like the World Cup," he mused, "could lead someone to try to exploit the situation." There were reports of threats from the Abu Nidal Palestinian group; extra security measures would be needed for teams from potential target countries like the United States, England, and the United Arab Emirates. At the Olympic training center in Tirrenia, for example, where the American team was sequestered in what one writer labeled "monastic fashion" (the players were not allowed to spend the night with their wives or girlfriends until after the first match), there were one hundred and twenty-five security men on hand, twice as many as had guarded the squad at the Seoul Olympics.

Of more pressing concern than terrorists, however, were the hooligans from England, the Netherlands, and perhaps elsewhere. Three thousand police reinforcements were dispatched to Sardinia, where England would play its bitter rival from Holland; twenty-five hundred more were posted in Genoa, the port from which ten thousand English fans would travel to Cagliari; thirty thousand others, armed with automatic weapons, riot gear, and guard dogs, would patrol the rest of the Mondiale sites. Sophisticated intelligence units operated throughout the country, identifying hooligan leaders and their habits, consulting with public order experts from England, preparing for the inevitable fights and riots that would accompany any number of matches. As violence was certain to occur at this World Cup, at least among the hooligans, armored cars equipped with water cannons, helicopters circling stadiums, and thorough checks of every spectator would theoretically be part and parcel of every match. Yet no amount of security could stop all the hooligans.

Who were these angry men wrapped in Union Jacks, marked with tattoos—on their arms, backs, chests, and even lips—proclaiming their favorite clubs, the "wild ones" who went to soccer matches more interested in fighting than in the action on the field? In *The Soccer Tribe*, a brilliant study of the ritualistic nature of the people's game, anthropologist Desmond Morris suggests that the worst of the hooligans are the ones most afflicted by urban decay and poverty:

> [I]t is the young men from the more deprived areas of the city or town, living out their daily lives in crowded slums or boring, soulless housing estates, who are the typical offenders. Their outbursts of violence have little to do with the Soccer Tribe itself [the game, that is, with all its ceremonies, rules, and rites], which merely acts as a dramatic stage on which they can perform. Since society has given them little chance to express their manhood in a positive or creative manner, they take the only course left to them apart from dumb subservience, and strike out in a negative and destructive way. They know that at least they will not be ignored and that they will be able to make their mark on society, even if it is only a scar on someone else's body.

Perhaps the most devoted, excited, and/or angry fans always walk a fine line between creative tension and violence at a soccer match, whose appeal is as much tribal, religious, cultural, and cathartic as it is athletic. In a depressed economy like England's, for more and more fans that line may blur, sometimes with tragic results. In 1985 rowdies from Liverpool at a match in Brussels attacked supporters of Juventus, and in the ensuing riots thirty-nine people lost their lives, the majority of whom came from Turin. The so-called Heysel Stadium Riots had cost English clubs the chance to play in Europe for the last five years. Their fans' conduct at Italia 90 would determine if and when teams like Chelsea, Manchester United, and indeed Liverpool (ninety-five of whose supporters had died only a year earlier in a riot at another stadium) would be allowed to test themselves again against the top European clubs. Judging from the early returns, which came in the form of police blotters and newspaper accounts, the English fans were off to a bad start.

Three days before the opening ceremonies, and three weeks after his arrival in Italy, the self-styled king of the English hooligans,

Paul Stephen Cooper Scarrot, was arrested in Rome. He told a reporter from *La Gazzetta Dello Sport* that the London *Daily Star* had sponsored his trip; the English tabloid had published a photograph of him in front of the Colosseum. On the postcard he mailed to the *Daily Star* was his warning: "I am the greatest hooligan in the world. They'll never stop me. We're after the Dutch and we want to give them a right good kicking. We'll wait for them with tear gas bombs at Termini station." In fact, it was at the train station that he was caught, unsuccessfully "hiding himself," as a writer ironically noted in *La Repubblica,* in a Union Jack, "the red-white-and-blue of his country, armed not with tear gas but with a big, five-liter bottle of Frascati wine. He had gone to mix with the drunks in the station." There the police picked up the sometime house painter from London, a disheveled young man with a crew cut, covered with tattooed insignia of the Nottingham Forrest Football Club. Soon he would be deported, presumably to return to his favorite activity—"vagabonding" between pubs and soccer stadiums. However, there were other angry men waiting in the wings to take over the role of king of the English hooligans, and this was only one of the innumerable challenges Luca di Montezemolo and his staff would have to meet in the next month.

Nevertheless, despite a last-minute threat by technicians for the government television network RAI to delay the broadcast of the elaborate opening ceremonies, by game time it seemed that the organizing committee of the Mondiale had pulled everything together, as Montezemolo had predicted, if only at the last moment. Indeed, reflecting on the number of public works projects completed or started as a result of Italia 90, the administrator went so far as to say, "There should be a World Cup every year in Italy so we could get things done." In Milan, where defending champion Argentina would open the tournament against Cameroon, teams of gardeners were planting flowers until the eve of the match, "regreening Italy's mostcement-covered city with planter boxes," as one newspaper reported. "Until dawn workers repaved streets." I imagined the entire country holding its breath, praying for luck.

And luck was in the air Friday night. In Milan's overhauled

Stadio San Siro, a futuristic arena featuring an open roof in the shape of a grid, a series of spiral stairways that from a distance resembled giant shock absorbers, and seats for eighty thousand spectators, the World Cup's opening ceremonies revolved around a lavish display uniquely Italian in its particulars. Pop stars Gianna Nannini and Edoardo Bennato sang a duet, Riccardo Muti led the orchestra and chorus from La Scala in a performance of Verdi's "Va Pensiero," and twenty-four oversized soccer balls, representing the participating national teams, opened up into daisies, releasing hundreds of balloons. Beyond that, celebrating Milan's role as the world's fashion capital, dozens of models paraded around the field in designer theme-wear, costumes created by four of Italy's top designers: Valentino's red Statue of Liberty motif heralding the New World; Mila Schon's saris welcoming Asia; Missoni's tribal garb saluting Africa; and Ferre's half-opaque, half-see-through outfits representing Europe. A helium soccer ball six meters in diameter sailed toward the sky. The Mondiale was finally under way.

In a film about the 1988 European Championship, Craig Charles describes a match between the Soviet Union and Holland as "a collision of styles and cultures. The Russians: precise, honest, organized. The Dutch: colorful, worldly, spontaneous." The 1990 World Cup was "a collision of styles and cultures" writ large, and the first such encounter pitted Argentina—inventive, dramatic, controversial—against the West African nation of Cameroon—athletic, aggressive, individualistic. Argentina was a known quantity. Most of its players belonged to European clubs (which released them to play in the World Cup), as the country was eager to accept the enormous transfer fees its stars could command for their home clubs, hard currency to bolster a sagging economy. Its captain, Diego Maradona, arguably the greatest player in the game, was soccer's most visible presence. If he played well, pundits agreed, Argentina might become the first team to win back-to-back titles since Brazil in 1958 and 1962.

Cameroon, on the other hand, was a mystery. Even that nation's *marabous,* the clairvoyants from the capital city of Yaounde, though they had "seen" the World Cup, did not dare to make a prediction about this match, declaring instead that "the only thing to do" was to prepare a ritual bath for the Cameroon players. This the players refused to do, claiming to "have more faith in the power of their own legs than in the power of 'tree barks.' " In like manner, they turned down one sorcerer's offer to take several days off in order to make amulets or charms for the players—at $5,000 apiece! The Cameroonians preferred to play what they called a French style of soccer, "and one therefore doesn't understand why they have a Soviet coach [Valery Nepomniashi] who speaks only through an interpreter," Gianni Mura wrote in *La Repubblica.* "Then one realizes that the French interpreter 'translates' what he thinks should be done." In the Cameroonian Lions' only previous appearance in the World Cup at the 1982 event in Barcelona, they had set a record of sorts by tying all their matches (against Italy, Poland, and Peru) and *not* advancing into the second round. Thus theirs was the only undefeated team in World Cup history. With any luck, after tonight's match that record would be intact.

Cameroon, Ronnie said, was one of the teams of the future. The United States was fielding the youngest squad in the tournament, the average age of its players being twenty-three, but it was to Africa that many commentators looked for signs of soccer's next stage of evolution. The match between Argentina and Cameroon, then, was as much a contest between the present and the future as it was an encounter between the known and the unknown. The nation of Cameroon was perhaps most famous, in the public's mind, for having suffered through one of the more bizarre tragedies in modern times when in 1986 its Lake Nyos had released huge amounts of carbon dioxide, killing seventeen hundred people, herds of cattle, and countless other animals. The gas, volcanic in origin, continues to accumulate beneath the lake, raising the chances for another eruption. No doubt Cameroon's players hoped to change the prevailing view of their country. An upset of the reigning champions would insure their place in the history of soccer.

The match was from the outset a rough, fast-paced affair. As one of Cameroon's players would later say, they wanted "the world to know there is a country in Africa called the Cameroon!" Ordinarily, a World Cup veteran like Argentina might be tempted to hold something back in its three first-round matches, playing hard enough to get through to the next round but not so hard that the team uses all its energy and emotion. Against Cameroon, however, the defending champions had no choice but to play with abandon. Yet they seemed nervous, tentative, even sluggish. In their first and in certain respects best scoring opportunity, three minutes into the match, Abel Balbo had a clear shot on goal and tripped over the ball. The crowd was rooting for the Africans, partly because they were the underdogs and partly because they were not from Argentina, whose team was doubly cursed in the eyes of the Milanese: first, for the threat it posed to Italy's chances of winning the Mondiale, and second, for the fact that its captain, Maradona, was also the star of Napoli, one of AC Milan's chief rivals in Italy's First Division. That Napoli was the pride of southern Italy only added to their ire. All the money made in the north, I was told in Florence and Milan, in Turin and Bologna, disappeared in the south. To the northerners, Naples was the seat and symbol of the corruption endemic to the land south of Rome. Any harm to Napoli's star, famous for his theatrics as well as for his playing abilities, was in their view deserved. "In Naples they see him as the next-best thing to God," said one of Maradona's opponents; in Milan he was the Prince of Darkness.

Somewhere between lay a more accurate assessment of Maradona's worth. He has been called, along with Pelé and Johan Cruyff, one of the three greatest soccer players ever. Pelé and Cruyff had been brilliant team players, but Maradona was the genius of individuality, a man who could do anything with the ball. He had led Argentina's Youth Team to victory in the 1979 World Youth Cup, and garnered record-setting transfer fees in 1982 when he signed with Barcelona (where in two seasons injuries and a bout of hepatitis limited his playing time to only half the matches) and again in 1984 when he signed with Napoli; but it was not until the last World Cup that in the public imagination he assumed his place among soccer's elite.

"In 1986 all you could do was organize yourself and try to contain him," said Franz Beckenbauer, coach of the West German team that lost to Argentina in the finals. "He's a technically outstanding player who knows all the tricks," Beckenbauer told a film interviewer. "He's the perfect footballer. You must always count on him using the element of surprise. Any player who has to mark him has a thankless task." In Mexico City Beckenbauer chose midfielder Lothar Matthaeus to mark Maradona, because he was "the only one who had the mental speed to keep up with him"—that is, the sole player canny and perhaps creative enough to guess what Argentina's captain might do next. True, Matthaeus contained him to a certain extent, but Maradona's teammates took advantage of the extra attention paid to him to create their own scoring chances and thus defeat the West Germans.

"Other players make him a great player," Jackie Charlton once explained. The former star of England's 1966 World Cup championship team and Ireland's 1990 coach added, "I've seen him three times in these past two years, and he's done very little. Then all of a sudden he does something, and he's completely changed the game." Maradona was the most dangerous kind of player: like a leopard, he struck rarely, often when the other team least expected it, and effectively. "Eighty-five minutes of standing around," Ronnie liked to say, "then a spectacular goal."

His strengths? Resilience, balance, acceleration, change of pace on and off the ball, and the determination to keep going forward no matter how many defenders tried to trip him. His center of gravity was low to the ground, and because his legs were stronger than those of much bigger players, Maradona could run circles around almost anyone, especially in small spaces, screening the ball from one or more defenders, or displaying it for a moment to lure his opponent into an off-balanced position, or moving his feet like a tap dancer until he glimpsed an opening in the defense through which to push the ball, sprint after it, then shoot or pass. In these and a seemingly infinite variety of ways he tricked defenders, dribbling past them into the penalty area, where he could score from almost any angle, set up a teammate, or draw a foul—either a free kick which, with his uncanny ability to bend the ball around a wall of defenders, curving it past the four or five players lined up to cut down his angle on the goal, resulted in many tallies, or else a penalty kick: invariably a goal for him. He was an inventive dribbler and playmaker, a man who had the peripheral vision to know where everyone was on the field and the guile to exploit that knowledge: Magic Johnson with an attitude. And why not? He was the highest-paid player in the game, earning $2 million a year from Napoli (as well as a rent-free apartment) and $12 million more in endorsements, and he was the most physically abused: perfect ingredients for arrogance.

There are three ways a defender may take control of the ball— intercepting a pass; making a shoulder charge against a player who either has the ball or is going after it, knocking him off center, shoulder to shoulder, to get the ball; or tackling, that is, kicking at the ball, whether from the front, side, or by sliding at an attacker who has broken free of the defense. Tackling is the most violent, and Maradona, soccer's most visible target, suffered mightily at the feet of his would-be tacklers. Although like every player he wore shin pads (the game's only concession to protective covering, mandated more to diminish the chance of spreading AIDS through cleat and spike wounds than to protect a player's shins), still he took a beating. Kicked and tripped, hacked and upended, in every match Maradona spent an inordinate amount of time writhing on the ground, sometimes for theatrical reasons, sometimes in pain. No doubt he believed he earned his money.

The rule regarding tackling is simple: you may go in as hard as you like, but you must go for the ball, not the other player. Whether you block the ball with the side of your foot, kick at it with your instep or toe, or slide in from an angle to push it away, as long as your object is the ball it does not matter what happens to the other player. How the referee interprets a particularly hard tackle will determine if play continues, the tackle having been judged "clean," as it generally is, or foul. A superstar like Maradona, who came into the 1990 World Cup already suffering from a variety of injuries, real and perhaps imagined, including a bad right toenail, a sore ankle, and fitness problems, could expect many calls to go his way. He was not afraid to use the referee's benefit of the doubt for his own ends, sprawling on the ground whenever he lost the ball, clutching his shin, and pleading for a call.

Maradona did not have to act against Cameroon. The Africans' strategy was to knock him down as soon as he touched the ball. "I hate this," Ronnie kept saying. He, Enrico, and I had joined other journalists in Florence's Centro Stampa to watch the match on television. "Let him play," my friend urged.

"He's faking," said Enrico, throwing up his arms. "See how he's remade himself: short hair, a gold earring. Only he can get away with wearing jewelry"—a clear violation of the rules.

"Fucking Maradona," said a young man from Florence, a graduate student at Harvard's business school, who worked in the press center. "He's not a professional. He's like all the stars now. Not like Cruyff and Pelé. They never gave the people a reason to discuss them." Scandals hounded Maradona—a palimony suit, as well as rumors of drug use, visits to prostitutes, Mafia connections. The Mob, one story went, had lost millions betting on Napoli and now wanted him out of the picture. So did most of northern Italy, is what I was beginning to think.

"He falls down every time he touches the ball," Enrico said.

"He falls down thinking he *might* get kicked," said the graduate student.

But it was true that Cameroon had adopted a violent approach to the task of defending Argentina's captain. "Some of the tackling was almost gymnastic in its abandon," Paul Gardner wrote in *Soccer America.*

> Typical was an airborne entry from Aken N'Dip that left an ugly cleat mark on Maradona's left shoulder! . . . In every sense, Maradona was a marked man, for the crowd took great delight in whistling him every time he got the ball. The abuse climaxed in what sounded like a stadium-wide laugh when Maradona failed to control a simple throw in and allowed the ball to escape into touch.

Cameroon's tactics paid off. Although two of its players were ejected from the match, receiving red cards for flagrant fouls and thus automatically losing the chance to play in the next game, the Lions

intimidated the defending champions and dominated play, displaying brilliant dribbling and fearlessness when it came to shooting on
goal. In the sixty-sixth minute François Oman Biyik took advantage
of a mistake Argentina made in its penalty area, when Nestor
Lorenzo miskicked a ball he had meant to clear straight up into the
air. Leaping higher than anyone around him, arcing his back like the
spring of a trap, then snapping forward to head the ball on goal,
Biyik, Cameroon's top-scoring player in the World Cup qualifying
rounds, scored the most important goal of his life. Twenty-five minutes later, Biyik and his teammates, whose average annual pay
amounted to only $2,200 (FIFA would fine the ejected players $3,500
apiece), had defeated the defending champions, and the game's
wealthiest player. Theirs was the most stunning upset in World Cup
history. They left the field as heroes to millions of people in Africa
and elsewhere around the world.

"This is great for soccer!" Enrico exclaimed.

"Fucking Maradona!" The graduate student was smiling.

"I wonder how many Argentineans will commit suicide tonight," Ronnie said, and everyone near us nodded in agreement.

In a postgame interview Maradona said, "A generation has
failed," insisting that the younger players on his team lacked the
strength to sustain themselves in battles at this level. Argentina
would have to find that strength soon if it hoped to match the records
of Italy and Brazil, the only three-time World Cup champions. In its
remaining first-round games against the Soviet Union and Romania,
Argentina would need at least a win and a tie just to advance to the
next round. The second round of sixteen, which would proceed by
single elimination, would be comprised of the top two teams from
each of the six groups as well as the four best third-place finishers.
Even if Argentina qualified for the next round, Maradona believed
his team would not go much further in the tournament. "This is the
saddest Mondiale of my life," he said.

For Italians, though, and indeed soccer fans everywhere, an
upset was a terrific way to begin the World Cup. In Florence's
restaurants and bars that night, in newspapers and on television the
next morning, in Antella's shops and cafés in the early afternoon

and, later in the day, after the *riposo* or siesta, in a pickup soccer match at the house of one of Enrico's friends, Cameroon's victory was what everyone wanted to talk about. The 500–1 Lions' win (the odds against the United States had escalated to 5,000–1, according to an English newspaper) had given hope to underdogs around the world, including the makeshift team Enrico and I ended up on. We were the Cameroon of Poncho's place.

Poncho's was a small villa in the midst of renovation. The field was set on the edge of an olive orchard, between an aging crab apple tree and a dog run. The grass had been reduced to stubble by the dozen or so young Florentines who gathered here almost every weekend for day-long matches. While we played the gamekeeper arrived with his hounds, which barked at us whenever the ball rolled near them. We were not among superb athletes, yet some of these lawyers and judges and businessmen, who smoked and drank even as they ran around the field, possessed a level of skill many American college players might envy. Awkward as these men might be, untrained as they seemed, they nevertheless played as if they had been born with good touch. Dribbling a soccer ball was as natural to them as throwing a baseball is to most Americans. I chased a ball near our goal, and when it rolled over the imaginary goal line, the attacker following me asked, "Did that bounce off you?"

"Yes." I nodded.

"This is Italy: never tell the truth!" one of my teammates cried, running up to me. "You honest Americans!" he moaned, shaking his head. Ronnie, laughing, took the corner kick, which resulted in another goal for his team. The Lions we were not.

Our match ended before it grew dark. Into the surprisingly modern interior of the house we marched to wash up, open a round of beers, and settle down in front of the television to watch Italy play its opening-round match against Austria. Historic enemies, rivals on the soccer pitch since the 1930s, there was no love lost between these countries. During the introduction of Austria's team, the men in this smoke-filled room, professionals and aristocrats all, saluted the opposing players with raised right arms, chanting *"Heil Hitler!"*

"How will the match turn out?" I wondered aloud. Italy will

lose 1−0 or 2−0, was the consensus here. "But Italy's the favorite," I insisted.

"They'll choke," Enrico said. "There's too much pressure on them. Everyone expects them to win the Mondiale."

"But they beat Austria 5−0 in their last meeting," I reminded him.

Enrico shrugged. "It always happens," he said. "We even lost to *Malta!* What a country!"

But his and the others' fatalism vanished once the match in Rome's Stadio Olimpico began. Andrea Carnevale, a forward and Maradona's teammate on Napoli, hit the post in the opening minutes of play, bringing all of us to our feet—except the two, and only, women in the room, who would remain silent nearly throughout the match—shrieking as if in agony. Moments later, Austria's Andreas Herzog, a talented midfielder, kicked and spiked Roberto Donadoni in the upper thigh, sending him to the turf in pain, drawing a yellow card from the referee and from Enrico's friends cries of *bastardo!* Cupping their genitals, as if they themselves had been kicked by Herzog, they let loose a stream of invective Enrico could not translate. Italians, Jackie had said, were the most inventive cursers in the world, and now I could only imagine the extent to which that was true. In the coming minutes, as it became clear that Austria's strategy was to target Carnevale and Gianluca Vialli, "the Viper," as he was called, a forward celebrated for his lightning-quick strikes, in much the same way that Cameroon had attacked Maradona, the level of invective rose, according to Enrico, to new heights of absurdity. "They kick, those Austrians," Roy Hodgson had said in Switzerland. "They're vicious." No one in Poncho's living room would dispute that.

Yet Italy had the run of play in the first half, outshooting Austria 10−1, including at least five one-on-one chances within thirty yards of the goal. Klaus Lindenberger, Austria's thirty-three-year-old goalkeeper, gave a clinic in the art of saving goals, diving for hard shots and fisting balls away. Eighteen minutes in, when Vialli broke through the defense for another one-on-one opportunity, Lindenberger ran out to cut down the Italian's angle on goal, forcing him to shoot wide. In their six previous matches, the blue-shirted Italians—the *Azzurri*—had given up only one goal and scored only two. Classical defenders, they had trouble "finishing," as the saying went. Nowhere was that more apparent than in their match against the Austrians who, though known for their scoring prowess, could barely muster an attack. Each missed chance brought more anguished cries from this crowd. When the telephone rang and Enrico's brother, Lorenzo, learned that his wife was on the other end, he was too depressed to talk to her.

During the half-time intermission, while the match's only commercials flooded the television screen, under the lights outside we passed the soccer ball around. What Lorenzo and the others feared apparently was an Austrian counterattack coming on the heels of one-too-many missed chances. Discouraged in the first half by their failure to convert, say, Vialli's one-on-one with Lindenberger or Carnevale's half-volley from six yards out, an open shot he had somehow managed to kick over the goal, in the second half the *Azzurri* might let down and find themselves on the losing end of a 1–0 score. After investing $8 billion in the Mondiale, Italy might become the laughingstock of the world—of the international soccer community, that is, which for millions of people *is* the world. Upsets, as Cameroon had proved the night before and Romania earlier this same day, toppling the Soviet Union 2–0 in Bari, were part of the World Cup's fabric. Italy, which had once lost to "tiny Malta," as Enrico kept reminding me, and which could not put the ball in the net, seemed poised to add to that rich tapestry of loss, according to these young men. Their fatalism was endearing.

In the second half, the *Azzurri* picked up where they had left off, creating scoring chances. *"Olé, olé, olé,"* sang Enrico's friends, their despair immediately giving way to excitement. Ronnie turned to me and said, "It could be six–nil by now. I think the floodgates are about to open." Indeed, Vialli and Carnevale continued to pummel Lindenberger, to no avail. Donadoni was tripped in Austria's penalty area, and no call was made. "They're playing for a draw now," Ronnie said when Austria substituted Alfred Hoertnagl for Manfred Linzmaier, a defender for a defender. "They'd be happy to come away with a point from this match." But Italy, which in eleven previous opening-round matches had never lost, pressed forward, refusing to settle for a tie. In the seventy-fourth minute Azeglio Vicini, Italy's coach (the man who had forbidden his players to have sex during the Mondiale), replaced Carnevale with striker Salvatore Schillaci, a short, dark, feral scorer. The son of a Sicilian janitor, a grade-school dropout who had been named to the national team only nine weeks earlier, "Toto," as he was called, ran around the field like a wild dog. Four minutes after he entered the match, Toto slipped into Austria's penalty area, took Vialli's brilliant cross from the right goal line, and headed in what turned out to be the winning score. Schillaci's first touch on the ball electrified the nation.

In the smoky room all of us, including the women, jumped to our feet, screaming in delight. A television camera panned Stadio Olimpico, and we could see thousands of Italian flags waving, as if a military parade or the new Crusades were about to begin. Then a curious thing happened: the camera focused on Schillaci, the striker who until a year ago had been languishing with Messina, a club in Italy's Second Division, and instantly the cheering in Poncho's house turned to booing. Ronnie and I looked at each other, puzzled. Why were they giving the finger to Toto? Why call him names we could only imagine?

"He's from Palermo," said Enrico, "and he plays for Juventus."

"A team full of losers," Poncho explained, describing the club for which Schillaci had scored fifteen goals in thirty matches that season. Juventus was the arch rival of Fiorentina, Florence's First Division team.

Ronnie and I had witnessed an essential truth about Italy's history: although its unification had been one of the signal events of the nineteenth century, its cultural life at the end of the twentieth century continued to revolve around what could only be called tribal values. What had begun as a celebration of nationalistic pride had spontaneously shifted into an expression of tribal unity. For a moment we were back in the days of the city-state. The contradiction was fascinating. Italy would win this match, which was all to the good; that the victory would result from a goal scored by someone from the south who, worse yet, played for Juventus was more than these Florentines could bear, at least for a few minutes.

It was almost 11 P.M. when the match ended. Poncho filled a big pot of boiling water with pasta, Enrico stirred the sauce, bottles of Chianti emerged, and a hat was passed to pay for the meal; we were, after all, in the birthplace of the banking system. Television coverage of the *Azzurri*'s victory continued in the form of interviews with celebrities and political figures from around the country, analysis of the match with a panel of experts, and constant replays of the winning goal. "World Cup matches are often decided by individual bravery," Schillaci told a reporter. "Italia 90 represents for me a turning point, the crossroads of my career. I mustn't take a wrong turn." He was a national hero, and in Palermo people were literally dancing in the streets. Toto had temporarily redeemed the south.

"Italy has fifty million coaches," said Enrico, pointing his wine glass at the television screen, where yet another celebrity was discussing the match. "What a job Vicini has," he sighed, then steered me toward the table on which food was laid out, buffet style. "Everyone second-guesses him. Politicians. The press. Movie stars. Whatever he does is wrong. It's so stupid!"

Yet Enrico himself was the first to question Vicini, as he would readily admit. Although he professed to dislike the hoopla surrounding the game, still he could not take his eyes off the television, monitoring Italy's responses to this victory. At this crossroads, it appeared that Vicini, like Schillaci, had taken the right turn. Because he had given an obscure striker from Sicily a chance, the coach had been spared the ignominy of a draw, or worse. Instead, he had shown the world that the host country could field a formidable team. I looked at Enrico and thought: Everything is falling into place. Two upsets in the first two days, the favorite proving itself to be among the best, a new hero emerging from the pack of unknown players vying for World Cup fame—what more could soccer fans want? Eating pasta after midnight, steeped in Chianti, I could believe the opening weekend of the Mondiale might conclude with the United States stealing a win from Czechoslovakia, surprising the whole soccer community.

The next afternoon Ronnie and I made our way to Stadio Comu-
nale, the remodeled soccer stadium near the center of Florence. We
took our seats behind one of the goals, among two thousand fans
from the United States (many wearing American football T-shirts),
and settled in to watch our first Italia 90 match in person. It was
warm and overcast. During the pregame ceremonies, while
Smetana's music drifted over the public address system and two
squads of costumed marchers lined up at either end of the field,
thunderclaps blasted overhead. A group of Americans tried to sing
"The Battle Hymn of the Republic," but "glory, glory, hallelujah"
were the only words they knew. A young man walked past with a
sign that read Bad Czechs Bounce! Another shouted, "Do you take
Czechs?" "No!" the crowd replied.

"Exuberance is one thing," Ronnie said, "obnoxiousness
another."

The costumed marchers met at midfield in a pageant of yellow
and blue-and-red and red-and-white, waving flags at one another,
accompanied by cornets and drums. A marching band followed
them, and by the time the respective national anthems of Czechoslovakia and the United States had been played, thirty-three thousand
people had filled the stadium, including a fair number of Czechs who
must have been relishing their newly won freedom. Three minutes
into play, U.S. midfielder John Harkes broke clear for a solid shot on
goal. The fans around us streamed past the security forces and
pressed up against the fence to get a better look. "U.S.A.! U.S.A.!"
some chanted, but few joined in. We were not schooled in the fine
art of soccer calls. *Olé, olé, olé* sounded foreign on our tongues.

Like nearly all the Czechs and Slovaks in attendance and like
many Americans, I was at my first World Cup match. Excited as I and
my countrymen might be, I knew our feelings paled next to those of
the fans at the other end of the stadium. The night before Václav
Havel, activist and literary figure, had won the presidency in Czechoslovakia's first free elections. A playwright was now running an
entire country instead of the considerably smaller worlds of his
plays. "If a man gives up poetry for power," Mark Strand writes, "he
shall have lots of power." Perhaps Havel's writing would now be

confined to speeches, which would consolidate his power and raise the level of contemporary political discourse. He had risked trading his art for public service, and millions prayed that his sacrifice would pay off. His national team was playing its first "free" match. If it advanced into the second round, Havel himself might come to Italy to cheer it on.

This was, then, not only a meeting between the Old and New Worlds, between a historic soccer power (Czechoslovakia having been runner-up to Italy in the very first World Cup final in 1934) and a virtual newcomer to the game, but also between two countries shaped, at radically different points in their respective histories, by revolution. If ours was the younger squad, theirs was the most energetic. The Czechs did not intend to give an inch to "a team of college all-stars," as some journalists called the U.S. team, because this World Cup offered them a chance to display their talents to coaches and scouts from the West. These players, the majority of whom belonged to Sparta Prague, hoped in the coming months to sign lucrative contracts with Italian or West German clubs. Much as they might despise midfielder Lubos Kubik, who in 1988 had defected from Czechoslovakia and had been named to the national team only over their protests, they coveted his contract with Fiorentina. Kubik had said that since he played in Florence, he hoped the Tuscan fans would "adopt Czechoslovakia, and root for us, at least in our matches against the United States and Austria."

After fifteen minutes of play, it was apparent that the Czechs did not need any help from the stands. They outclassed the United States in every aspect of the game — skill, speed, strength, tactics, and creativity. Their style of play, as Jerry Trecker noted, was "a hybrid of recent Soviet and West German teams. From the Soviets they [had] borrowed a long-passing, counterattacking style of play that relies on keeping the middle relatively open to catch opposing defenders as they press forward into apparently safe space. They also [had] a 'Bundesliga' look about them, their players lean and polished, technically sound, given to quick, triangular passing movements." Like the country itself, which was divided between its Czech and Slovak peoples and languages, these players and their coaches looked to both the East and West for guidance.

The result? A nightmare for the Americans.

Ivo Knoflicek kept beating Desmond Armstrong—one of the faster Americans—down the flank; and when he centered the ball, there were usually more Czechoslovakian attackers in the penalty area than U.S. defenders. Worse, although Gansler had adopted a defensive approach to the game, his players made a number of mistakes in the back. One such lapse cost them a goal in the twenty-fifth minute. "The Czechs are always a step ahead of us," Ronnie said. "We try to hold the ball, take extra touches in the back, then do something with it. That doesn't work at this level. Great teams think ahead, *before* the ball arrives, then act. We get the ball, then react."

Czechoslovakia stopped every U.S. advance, shadowing Tab Ramos, Peter Vermes, and striker Bruce Murray so tightly that in the first half they rarely touched the ball. Tougher by far than the Americans, the Slavs battered their younger opponents, pushing them off the ball, winning most of the knockdowns—free balls—and intimidating them. "That's why I always have a prick on my team," Ronnie said, "someone who's not afraid to mix it up. Someone who can keep the other team honest." The ball sailed over our goal, landing in a flower bed at the edge of the grass. When the security force's pack of German shepherds strained their leashes, lunging at the ball, the Americans near us cried, "Be like the dogs!" urging on our players.

Nothing helped.

Seven minutes before the half, U.S. captain Mike Windischmann tripped midfielder Michal Bilek, and after the ensuing penalty kick, a rocket shot into the upper right-hand corner, the Czechs led 2−0. In their eight qualifying matches they had given up only three goals; it seemed unlikely that they would surrender their lead. "The ability to get out of pressure," Ronnie said, "that's the key against a team like Czechoslovakia." But the pressure only mounted in the second half. "See how they have two or three guys running off the ball with every pass," Ronnie said, "creating space and possibilities for through balls, one-twos, good shots? We wait till we get the ball before anything happens." Thus as soon as an American player touched the ball he was in trouble: the Czechs were waiting to strip it away.

One of the few bright spots for the Americans was the play of Tony Meola, the goalkeeper from Kearny, New Jersey. His World Cup debut was the proverbial baptism of fire. Often deserted by his defenders, he had to make several acrobatic saves and leave his line —come out from the goal mouth—again and again to punch balls away. In the fiftieth minute, he dived to tip away yet another shot, suffering a minor injury when he banged into the goal post. Back on his feet, rubbing his shoulder, he watched helplessly as the shortest player on the field, midfielder Ivan Hasek, eluded the U.S. defenders and headed in a corner kick. How the ball got through for the third goal of the match, with Americans guarding both goal posts—an unusual World Cup tactic—was a mystery.

Meola's frustration had already earned him a yellow card; in the wake of the referee's signal for the earlier penalty kick he had kicked the ball into the net. Now his mood spread to his teammates. Moments after Hasek's goal, U.S. forward Eric Wynalda was ejected from the match. Angling for position on a throw-in, Lubomir Moravicik had stepped backward on Wynalda's foot, and when the American shoved him from behind, Moravicik dove into the ground with a theatrical flourish. Wynalda had celebrated his twenty-first birthday the day before, and now he had fallen for one of the oldest tricks in the game; because he had retaliated, he received a red card and a hefty fine. It was, by all accounts, a harsh call, notwithstanding that in the first half the referee had cautioned Wynalda for elbowing Hasek in the face. From then on the United States would have to play a man down.

Surprisingly, shell-shocked as they were, the Americans did not completely fall apart, at least not in the short run. Indeed, in the sixty-first minute, defying the 1,500–1 odds against them scoring at all in the World Cup, Paul Caligiuri put the United States on the board, repeating his Port of Spain heroics by running half the length of the field, eluding a sliding tackle from the opposing sweeper and cutting around the goalkeeper "to slot home from a sharp angle," as one reporter put it. His was a brilliant goal, which brought the Americans back to life. Minutes later, Bruce Murray fell in Czechoslovakia's penalty area, and for a moment it appeared that a penalty kick might be awarded, which would almost certainly have closed the gap to 3 – 2. No call came, to our dismay. But soon Tab Ramos had us on our feet again, breaking free from his tight marking for back-to-back shots on goal, the first a half-volley from eight yards out that was deflected wide, the second a shot from the edge of the penalty area that went just high. With any luck the match might have been tied.

After that flurry, though, it was all downhill for the United States. The sun came out, and in the seventy-ninth minute Thomas Skuhravy, who had scored Czechoslovakia's first goal, scored again off a corner kick, a carbon copy of Hasek's goal. Two defensive lapses on set pieces—free kicks—were too much for the young team. "They look shattered," said a man near us. "It's going to take a while," Ronnie said. Another penalty kick was called on the Americans, and my friend threw up his hands. "We're so naive," he said. "We've lost our center, and we can't reorganize."

Nevertheless, against all odds, penalty kicks being successful 95 percent of the time, Meola saved Michal Bilek's second penalty, a chip shot designed to make a diving goalkeeper look bad, a kind of in-your-face move that backfired when Meola faked a dive and easily stopped the shot. It was another bright moment for the American keeper. Though he gave up another goal in injury time—the minutes tacked on after regulation time expires to compensate for the time lost to injuries, during which the clock never stops—and found himself on the losing end of a 5 – 1 result, Meola made the best impression of any American. Like Caligiuri, he wanted a contract with a club in his grandparents' homeland. Surely he had helped his cause, though it was Czechoslovakians like Hasek, Skuhravy, and Knoflicek who had cinched their chances in Europe.

On our bus ride back to Antella, Ronnie said of the Americans, "Don't count them out. They could surprise us. We'll see what they're made of now. They need to get sharper on defense, maybe slide another defender in there. We started things when we knocked balls on. Why didn't we do that earlier? Because it's not beautiful soccer? Fuck that. It's about winning over here."

It had rained in Antella while we were gone, and we returned to a cool farmhouse. The spring was full; there was enough water for us to take showers and wash our hair. Jackie had fixed a simple meal of *carpaccio* "cooked" in lemon oil, with cheeses, bread, and salad, and we sat out on the back porch, sipping Chianti. World Cupism had not killed us yet, though our illusions about the U.S. team had died. The next day we would plant grass seed in the patch of dirt between the porch and the fence lined with roses, watch the workers reel out of the garage after lunch, and go for a long run. Inspired by Roy Hodgson, Ronnie was reading Flaubert's *Madame Bovary,* and I had found a copy of Henry James's *Portrait of a Lady.* Now we would have time to catch up on our books, drive up the road to one of the local vineyards and share a bottle of wine, or wander back into Florence for more sightseeing. There were plenty of soccer matches left to watch.

6
. . . .
TIGER BURNING

O h, Rome! my country! City of the Soul!" Lord Byron declares in the fourth, and final, canto of *Childe Harold's Pilgrimage*, linking his fate to the ruins of the ancient city. Journeying through history, from descriptions of political intrigue to hymns of praise for Italy, from meditations on the nature of being to poetic homages and testaments, this most demonic of the Romantics discovered in "the Niobe of nations" limits to his suffering, a sense of scale, a sense of proportion:

> The orphans of the heart must turn to thee,
> Lone Mother of dead Empires! and control
> In their shut breasts their petty misery.
> What are our woes and sufferance? Come and see
> The cypress—hear the owl—and plod your way
> O'er steps of broken thrones and temples—Ye!
> Whose agonies are evils of a day—
> A world is at our feet as fragile as our clay.

Three days after the United States–Czechoslovakia debacle, Ronnie and I wandered through those same ruins, chastened by the Roman splendor. The Czechoslovakians had dedicated their victory to Václav Havel and his Civic Forum, the Americans were nursing their wounds in preparation for tomorrow night's match against Italy, and we were in the Colosseum, talking to a pair of refugees from Romania—two young men who were simultaneously delighted by their country's World Cup win over the Soviet Union, despairing at the continuing violence in the land they had fled, and starving. We gave them a handful of lire and walked on.

Here in the Flavian Amphitheater, an edifice of arches and columns and memory, I understood at last the significance of sports in our lives, the integral role they have played in the development of culture from the beginning of human society. Across the Tiber was Vatican City, the papal see and home of one of the world's major religions, and here was the main arena where Christian martyrs had been fed to lions, a favorite sport of the early Romans. Religion and sports, sports and religion: the lines between them often blur, since both reflect and respond to profound human needs. The current pope, a goalkeeper in his youth, had blessed the Mondiale before the opening ceremonies. Saves come in many forms.

"The roots of the Soccer Tribe lie deep in our primeval past," Desmond Morris writes, "when our early ancestors lived and died as hunters of wild beasts. Almost the whole of man's evolutionary history belongs to that hunting period, when the pursuit of prey was not a sport, but a matter of survival. It moulded us and made us, genetically, what we are today." He goes on to argue that, despite the advent first of agriculture, then of urbanization, "our ancient, hunting spirit . . . still needed the challenge of the chase, the exciting tactical moves, the risks, the dangers, and the great climax of the kill." Through the centuries our solution to that necessity has evolved, he asserts, from sport hunting to arena blood sports to arena ball sports, the most important modern example of which is soccer. Indeed, "soccer has outstripped all other forms of sport in global appeal," Morris believes, partly because "it manages to retain so many of the ancient hunting elements"—teamwork, free-flowing movement, fitness and strength, imagination and skill, tactics, concentration, vision, aim, danger, motivation, bravery, clear thinking. Hence "each soccer match is a symbolic event of some complexity."

There is no greater symbol of our relationship to sports than the

Colosseum. Here the Romans "brought the hunt to the people," Morris explains. "If the city-dweller could not rush out into the countryside to hunt, then the animals would be brought into the centre of the city and challenged there in an enclosed space, watched by thousands of frustrated hunters." What slaughter those frustrated hunters witnessed! Five thousand wild beasts imported from all over the known world were killed on the Colosseum's opening day, and over the next hundred days nine thousand more perished. In the following five hundred years countless gladiators, prisoners of war, martyrs, lions, elephants, and other wild beasts lost their lives in contests the spectators would cheer, boo, discuss, and rehash much as modern soccer fans do. When the taste for blood sports finally gave way, Morris reminds us, and the public tired of its descendants, bullfighting and lion taming and animal baiting, "the stage was set for a new era in the history of pseudohunting. A new form of sport was about to explode across the globe—the bloodless, animal-free arena sport: the ball-game."

Across the river from Catholicism's spiritual home, in a matrix of modern civilization, Ronnie and I walked around the Colosseum, exploring its nooks and crannies, archaeological excavations and cells. We were not so different from the plebeians who had gathered here to see mock naval battles, or gladiators killing elephants and each other. Our ideas about prayer had changed from those of the early Christian fathers; our favorite sport was for the most part blood-less. But we were linked, Ronnie and I and all the people we met in the soccer world, to those spectators who occasionally spared the life of a fallen gladiator who had fought well, signaling their pleasure with a thumbs up or wave of a handkerchief. Long ago we would have applauded the sight of a costumed Charon, ferryman of the underworld, finishing off the losers with a dagger, then turning the corpses over to an official dressed as Mercury, who would guide their souls to the underworld.

Since soccer is the arena sport of the modern age, to remember its distant origins reminds us of its enduring place in world culture. In the same way Czesław Miłosz, explaining "the good of reading the Gospels in Greek," reminds us "that it is proper that we move our finger / Along letters more enduring than those carved in stone, / And that, slowly pronouncing each syllable, / We discover the true dignity of speech," because "on every page a persistent reader / Sees twenty centuries as twenty days / In a world which one day will come to an end." Those twenty centuries collapsed around us in the Colosseum. It was hot, and we paid four dollars apiece for orange sodas, then slowly made our way to the Forum.

We had come to Rome to watch the United States–Italy match, making the trip by train down from Florence through olive orchards and potato fields, between hill towns and villas. We were staying with Claudio and Maressa De Vecchio in Acilia, a suburb near the sea, and in the morning we had been awakened by the call of a fruit seller. Claudio, a former semiprofessional soccer player who now worked with handicapped children, was a friend of a friend of ours from Middlebury, and he welcomed us into his house as if we were relatives. His wife was surely one of Rome's prettiest traffic cops, a voluptuous redhead who kept on her nightstand copies of Pablo Neruda's poems, Milan Kundera's *The Unbearable Lightness of Being,* and a new translation of the Kama Sutra. (No wonder, Ronnie and I agreed, Claudio's favorite English expression was "No problem!") Without a second thought, it seemed, Maressa drove us into the city each day—at speeds far exceeding the posted limits. This evening and the one following we would stay in Rome too late to catch a train back to Acilia. Claudio insisted that we call him to come and pick us up. But it might be as late as two or three in the morning, we protested. "No problem!" he said with a smile. Italian hospitality surpassed anything we had known.

Certainly the host country's patience was tested by the World Cup. Now that we were into the first week of action, it was possible to reflect on the course of the Mondiale. Although this extravaganza was expected to generate some $2 billion in revenue from the hundreds of thousands of supporters drawn to the twelve cities of the tournament, shopkeepers, hoteliers, bar owners, and the like reported that tourism, in fact, was down, owing to widespread fear of crowds and hooligans. Worse, the sale of alcohol was banned in the host cities on game days; this was a security measure particularly repugnant to Italians, since a main sponsor of the Mondiale was the Ministry of Agriculture and Forests, which wanted to promote Italian wines to the world. Restaurateurs complained that business was slower than usual, even if in many places, it was true, regular customers might be served a glass or two of wine on the sly. Still, the prospect of a dry dinner kept a fair number of Italians at home.

Curiously enough, it seemed that the petty criminals stayed home, too, at least when Italy was playing. During the match against Austria, for example, no incidents of petty crime were reported in crime-ridden Naples, and in Rome only one purse snatching was recorded, according to Reuters. The Mafia kept up a business-as-usual attitude, carrying out several execution-style killings in Sicily during matches between Austria and Italy, Czechoslovakia and the United States, and Egypt and the Netherlands; but hooliganism had yet to rear its ugly head in quite the way most observers had expected. Because England and the Netherlands, the countries with the worst offenders, had been relegated in their first-round matches to the island venues of Sicily and Sardinia, Italy's security forces had thus far managed to contain much of the violence there, arresting and deporting dozens of young men.

Even so, several British journalists asserted, England's sorry play in its opening match against Ireland, a rain-slopped 1–1 draw distinguished only by the relentlessness with which both sides pursued what Ronnie called "an ugly brand of soccer," trading long balls to no effect while displaying little in the way of technique and creativity, could be blamed on the hooligans. The five-year ban from European competition that UEFA, the governing body for European soccer, had imposed on English clubs in the wake of the Heysel Stadium tragedy had retarded the development of English soccer. Insular by nature, in the rapidly evolving world of modern soccer, England could ill afford to miss any chance to participate in matches on the Continent. The game was leaving England behind, according to many writers, in the same way that the European Community would soon call the economic shots in this part of the world, regardless of England's reluctance to join. The ancient Anglo-Saxon pride, manifesting itself in hooliganism, and a "rush and kick" style of soccer in an age of short passes and technical brilliance was hurting England. This Saturday in Cagliari, in the long-awaited match against Holland, England might pay dearly for its fans' behavior. Hooligans from both countries were bracing for battle.

Meanwhile, violence had broken out in an unexpected quarter. On Sunday in Milan, before and after West Germany's 4–1 thrashing of Yugoslavia, a thousand West German fans had gone on a rampage, breaking shop windows, damaging underground railway stations, fighting with Yugoslavs, Italians, and the police. The riot had begun in front of the six-hundred-year-old Gothic cathedral in the Piazza del Duomo, and millions of dollars worth of damage had resulted. Summary justice was the rule here: eight German fans were immediately sentenced to eight months in jail. "These people represent a culture of violence," said the judge, "and we cannot be sure that in the future they will be able to resist this kind of violence again."

What was obscured by the rampage was West Germany's magnificent victory over Yugoslavia. "The Germans prepare for football matches the way they prepare for war," Henry Kissinger wrote in the *Sunday Correspondent:* "their games are meticulously planned and anything achievable by human foresight, careful preparation and hard work is accounted for." The former diplomat took a historical view of West Germany's rise in the soccer community, reminding readers that its success in the last six World Cups—one championship, three times a runner-up, and one third-place finish—came on the heels of disaster: "West German football entered the postwar era with no particular tradition, professional leagues being as novel as the frontiers of the new state." (This was also an apt description of U.S. soccer in the post–Cold War era.) Now those frontiers and borders were changing. The formal reunification with East Germany was only days away, and West Germany's impressive showing against Yugoslavia made it difficult not to think that this year history might be on the side of Franz Beckenbauer's team.

Lothar Matthaeus, the famous central midfielder marking his seventy-fifth international appearance, began his third World Cup with two goals, the second "a scorching shot at the end of a searing solo charge," as one writer put it. Matthaeus had profited from his decision two years earlier to play for Inter Milan, maturing into the role of captain of his national squad. Now he was making his bid to be the premier player of his day. He and his teammates had made a fine start in overcoming some of the problems Kissinger had remarked upon:

> The West German national team suffer from the same disability as the famous Schlieffen Plan on which German strategy in World War II was based. There is a limit to human foresight; psychological stress on those charged with executing excessively complex manoeuvres cannot be calculated in advance.

Nevertheless, it was important to remember that, as Kissinger noted, "their game is shadowed by the underlying premonition that in the end even the most dedicated effort will go unrewarded." Perhaps that explained the behavior of the rampaging fans; notwithstanding West Germany's success on the soccer field, a certain level of frustration and anger was common, it seemed, "to a people who may not in their heart of hearts believe that joy is their ultimate national destiny." One way or another, the Germans would continue to command our attention.

The fifteen thousand Scottish fans in Genoa, on the other hand, were by all accounts positively gleeful, singing and dancing in the streets of the seaport, despite a humiliating 1−0 opening match loss to Costa Rica. This was abundant evidence of what Colin Malam labeled "the Scots' propensity for self-destruction." Ronnie and I, both of Scottish descent, certainly understood that inclination, and as we walked from the Forum toward the Tiber, discussing that match, my friend said, "The Scots just didn't recognize their opportunities." Twenty years before, the many chances the Scots had missed might have caused a riot, for it was the Scottish fans who had invented modern soccer hooliganism, a contribution to world culture comparable to their chefs' addition of haggis to international cuisine. "No wonder we self-destruct!" Ronnie chuckled. In Lisbon, Barcelona, and at Wembley Stadium in London, Scottish hooligans had invaded the playing fields, torn up the turf and goalposts, then run riot in the streets. Once it had been de rigueur for these hooligans, having drunk the pubs dry, to bite police dogs. But all that had changed with the tightening of drinking laws at matches in Scotland. Now the Genoese welcomed the revelers who took pains to distinguish themselves from the English. The Scots would have fun, but they would not turn violent, no matter what happened to their team. "The Scots habitually find the smallest nation they can to trip over," Rob Hughes wrote in the *International Herald Tribune.* Depressing as that habit might be, still the drama it provided was good for soccer. "I love upsets," Ronnie found himself saying almost daily.

Only a day earlier we had joined Claudio to watch the next best thing to an upset: Holland's 1–1 draw with Egypt. One of the most talented teams in the Mondiale, the 1988 European Champion Dutch side had played sixty minutes of scoreless soccer with the unheralded Egyptians before finally taking the lead on a goal by Wim Kieft, a lead they would relinquish eight minutes from the end on Magdi Abdelghani's penalty kick. "Egyptians catching Dutchmen on a hot humid night knew how to pace the contest," Rob Hughes observed, "particularly when one side had prepared for the match exclusively for four months and the other's superstars had dates with surgeons in between chasing Europe's rich club prizes." Ruud Gullit, Holland's captain who had been described as "a blend of imposing physique, athleticism, skill and the ability to mesh together players into a formidable unit," had spent the previous season recovering from his third knee operation. Against Egypt the tall, sleek Dutchman, dreadlocks flying about his head, had missed chance after chance. Gullit, two-time European Player of the Year Marco Van Basten, and defender Frank Rijkaard, teammates at AC Milan, needed to recover the championship spirit they had known on both the club and European levels if they hoped to win the World Cup, the one prize that had eluded them. A runner-up in 1974 and 1978, one of the best sides in the 1980s, the Netherlands had become a perennial bridesmaid in the World Cup. Their fans and hooligans were demanding a better showing.

Ronnie and I walked along the Tiber, stopping from time to time to gaze across the muddy water. We saw Isola Tiberina, the Island in the Tiber, which housed the Church of Saint Bartholomew, once the destination for pilgrimages of the sick and infirm. The considerably larger islands of Sicily and Sardinia were now thronging with pilgrims afflicted with a different sickness—violence. But here it was peaceful, and I was thinking of Ronnie's comments about the Holland–Egypt match: how good it was to see an ancient people finding a place in the modern soccer world, how sad to realize Gullit's best playing days were behind him, how small Egypt's goalkeeper had seemed after Kieft's goal; he had fallen to the ground, clutching his legs, pretending to suffer from cramps. "His excuse," my friend had said, "for looking so bad on that goal."

Walking back into town toward the Pantheon, I remembered that Rafael Alberti, a Spanish poet who had spent years of exile in Rome, had written a marvelous ode to a goalkeeper, a hymn of praise that might have shamed the Egyptian, who otherwise had played a fine match. Platko, the hero of Alberti's poem, was Barcelona's goalkeeper for a celebrated match in 1928, and the poet addresses him as if he were his familiar:

Nobody forgets, Platko,
no nobody, nobody, nobody,
you blond Hungarian bear.

Not the sea
that jumped in front of you without being able to save you.
Not the rain. Not the wind, not even the stiffest wind.

Not the sea, not the wind, Platko,
blond, bloody Platko,
goalkeeper in the dust,
lightning rod.

No, nobody, nobody, nobody.

Blue and white shirts, in the air,
royal shirts,
rival shirts, against you, flying and dragging you with them,
Platko, far-off Platko,

blond Platko beheaded,
tiger burning in the grass of another country. You, a key,
Platko, you, a broken key,
a golden key, fallen before the golden door!

No, nobody, nobody, nobody,
nobody forgets, Platko.

In these hypnotic opening lines Alberti memorializes a historical
figure; in the spirit of Homer and Virgil, the Spanish poet celebrates
the deeds of someone larger than life. Platko, in fact, resembles an
elemental force, and in this poem he is not unlike the heroes of the
Greek and Roman epics, whose actions depend on the will of the
gods, except that Platko's origins are common instead of royal. Nevertheless, he is godlike in front of the goal:

The sky turned its back.
Blue and scarlet shirts blazed
and died without wind.
The sea turned its eyes away,
collapsed and said nothing.
There was bleeding in the buttonholes,
bleeding for you, Platko,
for your Hungarian blood,
for without your blood, your moves, your great saves, your leaps,
the badges were frightened.

No, nobody, nobody, nobody,
nobody, nobody forgets.

Nobody forgets because one of the poet's roles is to be the memory
both for his people and his language. The striking images and insis-
tent repetition, exuberant metaphors and music—all turn a soccer
field into the landscape of dream. What Alberti uncovers with his
ode is the layer of myth that lies just below the surface of any event
in our daily lives, governing our actions and responses, whether we
choose to acknowledge this force or not. Platko leaps to save a shot
on goal—and he becomes a figure out of Ovid's *Metamorphoses:*

It was the sea's return.
There were
ten swift flags
wildly burning.
It was the wind's return.
It was hope's return to the heart.
It was your return.

The air commanded
the scarlet and heroic blue in the veins.
Wings, wings heavenly and white, broken wings,
embattled wings without feathers chalked the field.

And the air had legs
and trunk and arms and head.

And all for you, Platko,
blond, Hungarian Platko!

And in your honor, for your return,
because you brought lost energy back to the fight,
the wind opened a path to the enemy's goal.

Nobody, nobody forgets.

In short, Platko has restored to the game its primal mystery and magic, and his teammates respond in kind, discovering in themselves deeper reserves of energy. Platko is "in the zone," as contemporary athletes like to say of a player performing well above his or her ability, acting on an altogether different plane, where for a while everything seems to go exactly the right way. I suspect that those moments, occurring for artists as well as athletes, are vital to human evolution, history, and possibly survival. Alberti's gift to his readers is to have recognized such an instant, preserved it in a poem that itself represents an important human achievement, and thus insured that succeeding generations might know of Platko's gift to the fans in Santander. Like Achilles, Odysseus, Aeneas, and Dante on his way to Paradise, Platko can now enter our bones and blood, our language.

In so many of the circles I traveled in—intellectual, artistic, and social—it was inconceivable to believe a soccer player might become one of those "levers of the universe" that Apollinaire found on every street corner. A sports figure was an unsuitable subject for poetry and even for discussion, at least at the parties and gallery openings I attended back in Santa Fe. Not in Italy. At a newsstand in the Florence train station I had bought a copy of *Poesia,* an Italian literary journal featuring an entire section of poems as well as an essay on soccer; there was even a photograph of Pier Paolo Pasolini, the acclaimed poet, novelist, and filmmaker, dribbling a soccer ball. In bars, cafés, offices, kitchens, living rooms, and parks—millions of people, artists and writers, intellectuals and businessmen, laborers and pensioners—all were talking about soccer without the highbrow scorn I had found among my literary friends in the States.

We entered the Pantheon, the pagan temple converted into a Christian church, Saint Mary of the Martyrs. We stared at the opening in the center of the dome one hundred and forty-two feet above us; studied the various chapels and niches; lingered at the tomb of Raphael, whose epitaph reads: "Living, great Nature feared he might outlive her works; and dying, fears herself to die." I had come all the way to Italy to discover that for the last several years what I had pushed into the margins of my life was indeed central to my happiness—as it was to that of a good portion of the world's population. I, too, was sometimes guilty of a certain disdain for the very *idea* of sports, though I had devoted more of my life to that idea than to anything else, including literature. Frederick Turner suggests that the ancient Greeks idealized their athletes while we in America worship our sports stars. The difference? Idealized figures may become models for personal and collective behavior; objects of devotion change, at least in the modern age. Perhaps we have lost sight of the notion of sport as physical culture, as play. Yet what is writing if not another form of play? Somehow I had forgotten that.

Eventually we came to Villa Borghese, a large urban park once described as "a paradise of delight"; at the far end lay the U.S. ambassador's villa, where we were due for an evening reception honoring the organizers of the 1994 World Cup. After hours of walking around the busy city, it was a relief to wander through the park, where it was quiet and green and cool. Under the trees couples were kissing and caressing. Romans, I had heard, have a long history of courting in parks and parked cars, because they have nowhere else to go, living more often than not with their parents until they marry. "Of sexual particulars / In manuals vehicular," David St. John writes in a humorous poem, "By far the best we've got / Is the Kama Sutra by Fiat"—a text I imagined Claudio and Maressa knew by heart.

"What a country!" Ronnie said with a smile.

Approaching the ambassador's villa, an imposing edifice on a tree-lined street, I decided that the measure of immortality Alberti had bestowed on Platko was what most athletes wanted, including the U.S. soccer team that had taken such a beating on the field and in the local press. One headline read: "United, but small, States." Another journalist declared: "It's difficult to talk about soccer on the eve of Italia–USA. Giants in almost everything, on the soccer field the United States became dwarfs. Nice guys perhaps, and maybe even destined for a great future, but for now, dwarfs." And Giorgio Chinaglia, a former star in Italy as well as for the New York Cosmos, utterly dismissed the American efforts on and off the field. "Chinaglia—USA, a love that's over," was the headline to an interview with Chinaglia, one of the most recognizable soccer figures for American fans. "Soccer will never break through," he said, then described the demise of the NASL in dire terms: "One billion dollars thrown away, a clamorous breakdown. . . . The truth is that soccer will never take hold in the United States because Americans love sports that involve hands and eyes: football, baseball, basketball, boxing and tennis. Sports in which, among other things, it's possible to bet. Soccer remains on the fringes." The loss to Czechoslovakia had made it clear to him that, because of our presumption, soccer in the United States had regressed ten to fifteen years. "You can't invent soccer," he said. "There are coaches like [AC Milan's] Arrigo Sacchi who go around the world to learn, while the Americans think they know everything." Chinaglia predicted that Italy would win tomorrow night, 7–0.

He was not alone in his dismay, as Ronnie and I discovered in the receiving line at the ambassador's villa. We were standing next to Mick Luckhurst and Bob Neal, the Turner Network Television (TNT) commentators who had had the thankless task of calling the U.S.–Czechoslovakia match, and what they told us about American viewer responses was disturbing, if not entirely unexpected: less than 2 percent of the nation's audience had watched the game. Those who had tuned in had not been afraid to call the network and complain that the announcers had made excuses for the Americans' poor play.

"The switchboard lit up," said Neal. "Callers kept saying we were too *easy* on the U.S. team. I thought we provided a context: college all-stars at the World Cup. I hadn't counted on such a negative reaction."

"The toughest match I've ever called," Luckhurst added in a thick English accent. The color analyst, an international soccer player in his youth, had found his fortune place-kicking for the Atlanta Falcons in the NFL, and now he was reporting on his first sports love. "What could we say except point out what they were *trying* to do?" he said, then laughed an infectious laugh.

The guests moved slowly up the white pebble path leading to the villa. By the time we shook hands with Ambassador Peter Secchia and his wife, Ronnie and I knew we were underdressed for the occasion, our formal wear being a madras jacket dating back to high school for my friend and a wrinkled sport coat for me. The Ambassador's daughter, Stephanie, had wangled us our invitations to this event; when her father learned who we were and looked over our attire, I had the distinct impression that he did not like what he saw. We hurried into the garden, where a large crowd had gathered in the gloaming. Near a table covered with hors d'oeuvres we met Stephanie, a beautiful, reserved young woman with a deep tan and shoulder-length brown hair. She ordered drinks for us, then led us around the party.

I was hoping to see Henry Kissinger here. Chair of the World Cup USA 1994 Advisory Board, he was widely credited with persuading Dr. João Havelange, the president of FIFA, to take seriously the USSF's bid for the next World Cup. I wanted to ask him two questions: what was it like to go from secretary of state to informal ambassador of soccer? And was it true that the United States had "greased the wheel" to help the national team qualify for the Mondiale, as that cub reporter had suggested in Hershey? I had a sense of how he might answer my first question. "I have been an avid football fan ever since my youth in Fürth, a soccer-mad city in southern Germany," he wrote in the *Sunday Correspondent.* "My father despaired of a son who preferred to stand for two hours — there were very few seats — watching a football game rather than go to the opera or visit a museum." Perhaps his current position was the next natural step for him, combining as it did a lifelong passion with his love of public affairs. Skilled diplomat that he was, Kissinger was too smart to have answered my second question; I was certain of that. But I never got to ask him anything. If he had come to the reception, he was nowhere to be seen now.

There were other luminaries present. The most interesting, if seemingly out-of-place, was Tom Landry, the former head coach of the Dallas Cowboys. Had he traded football for soccer? No, though after his unceremonious sacking by the new owner of the Cowboys, it was possible that he had different feelings about the game he had done so much to promote. Now he was promoting a new cause, Dallas's bid to be one of the eight to twelve venues for the 1994 World Cup. Landry, like many of the well-dressed men and women in the garden, was lobbying interested soccer officials and others who might help in the selection process. Dallas had a leg up on the competition, because in the Cotton Bowl it had a sufficiently large stadium, seventy-two thousand capacity, to attract FIFA's attention, and because it had an established soccer tradition on which to draw. Its burgeoning youth leagues and the continuing success of the Sidekicks in the Major Indoor Soccer League (MISL) — "A bastardization of the game," Ronnie once said, "a sport closer to hockey than soccer; but it's all we have for players who want to go on" — insured a level of support and interest — organizational, commercial, participatory — vital to the success of the World Cup.

In the initial application to host the World Cup the USSF had executed preliminary agreements to reserve the use of facilities at seventeen sites, including Dallas, Kansas City, Philadelphia, Seattle,

Miami, Washington, D.C., and Pasadena. In the end twenty-six venues, including three sites in the New York–metropolitan area, would
mount bids to host World Cup matches. I assumed that each of the
bidding cities had sent representatives to Italia 90. The cities chosen
stood to reap considerable financial rewards. If the Super Bowl can
generate $150–200 million in a single weekend, imagine what a
month-long pageant might produce for hoteliers, restaurateurs, shop-
keepers, bar owners, and the like, especially given the anticipated
influx of foreign visitors. The World Cup, at the very least, will help
our trade balance, one reason why there were so many captains of
industry at the embassy reception.

Giorgio Chinaglia and others believed we had no business hosting the next World Cup. "The conditions necessary to organize a
Mondiale don't exist in the States," the former Cosmos star declared.
"The organizers are in desperate need of sponsors, but all the doors
are closed. I hope FIFA will make up for it. . . . If I were in Havelange's shoes," he added, "I'd cancel the United States and aim for
Africa or the Orient, where soccer is expanding." Certainly there
were obstacles to overcome: football stadiums would have to be
renovated to accommodate soccer's seating requirements, and artifi-
cial-turf playing surfaces would have to be replaced with grass, local
services reoriented, and the transportation industry persuaded to
make it easier, and inexpensive, to cross significant geographical
distances between venues, all in a climate of indifference (or worse)
to soccer.

Yet these business leaders seemed not only determined but
more than competent to make the 1994 World Cup a success. (There
were, as far as I could tell, no representatives here from any of the
Big Three auto manufacturers!) Dallas was prepared to invest $30
million in the renovation of the Cotton Bowl; American Airlines,
which has its corporate headquarters in the city, was "aggressively
entering the international soccer market," expecting to be named the
official World Cup '94 carrier; and Tom Landry was a terrific salesman for Dallas. Within the year he would say, "I think soccer is
probably the best sport available in America for youngsters. . . .
Soccer lets children develop coordination and physical attributes

without taking a pounding." He believed the audience for soccer in the United States was bigger than most people had thought. "And when Americans are exposed to World Cup soccer," he said, "it will be an enlightening experience."

The reception ended promptly at nine o'clock, perhaps because many guests wanted to watch Argentina try to resurrect its honor against the Soviet Union. Ambassador Secchia decided on the spur of the moment to take his family out on the town—"to some of the places that have been kind to us," he said—and he invited us along. Like the U.S. soccer team, the ambassador had not been treated kindly by the local press, which according to Jackie considered him another obnoxious American. But Ronnie and I found him warm and engaging, a generous man who liked to say, "My family is what I care most about." He and his wife, Joan, an elegant woman who might have passed as Stephanie's older sister, had been surprised at the amount of work their jobs entailed, and they would not have another free night until the middle of July. They had made a pact between them to stop working at midnight, a pact they had difficulty honoring. But tonight was different. Stephanie's younger sister, Sandy, was here with a friend, Joe (who as it happened had played last year for the Fort Wayne club in the American Indoor Soccer League), and Charlie, the youngest Secchia, also had a friend over from the States; there was no telling when the whole family might be together again. It took forty-five minutes to round up a pair of Italian security men, drivers, and enough cars to ferry us all to a small restaurant near the Pantheon. When at last the motorcade was ready to leave, I found myself in the front seat of the ambassador's limousine.

"What do you do for a living anyway?" he asked me.

"I'm a writer," I said.

"Oh, no," he sighed, turning to his wife with a smile. "Out of the frying pan and into the fire!"

The security men cut a path through the traffic, one leaning out the window of the lead car, waving a small signal flag at oncoming motorists. Once we had parked, the guards followed us at a discreet distance, armed and listening to the Argentina–Soviet Union match on transistor radios. I asked one the score; he was not allowed to answer, it seemed. Instead, he blended back into the crowd milling in front of the Pantheon, watching us closely. The ambassador said he could not leave the villa without them; he even had to take his exercise within the high walls of the compound, because it was too much trouble to organize security for a daily run through the streets of Rome. The Mondiale only heightened fears of a terrorist attack, but Mr. Secchia delighted in the spectacle. "We'll have to postpone our fourth of July party at the embassy," he grinned. "It's the night of the semifinals!" We walked up a side street, where a restaurateur greeted the ambassador like an old friend, then cleared a large table for us. Soon we were drinking wine and eating pastries and watermelon under the stars. Mrs. Secchia asked me to recite poetry, and I was only too happy to oblige her.

"Oh, Rome! my country! City of the Soul!" I began, hoping—in vain—to remember the next lines.

From the restaurant we wandered on to Piazza Navona for *gelato*—ice cream—and when the ambassador and his wife decided to turn in, the rest of us walked on into the Roman night in search of a discotheque. Along the way we met a social worker from Edinburgh, who told us in a thick accent that it had been impossible to tell from the Scottish fans dancing in Genoa's streets the other night that their team had just lost to Costa Rica, one of the long shots.

"It was like we won the whole World Cup," he laughed.

We could not find a discotheque we liked, and we were not drunk enough to dance in the streets. So we walked and walked, stopping from time to time for a drink or more *gelato*. It was after midnight before we called Claudio, yet he happily agreed to pick us up at the Vittoriano, the symbol of Italian independence. When six of us tried to pile into his Cinquecento—a two-seater—little Fiat commonly known as a "baby shoe," a dozen traffic cops descended on us to tell Claudio that he was breaking the law.

"But my wife's one of you," said Claudio. "A traffic cop."

They were not impressed. "Don't try to use influence on us," said one.

Claudio cursed them, pulling us into the car. They cursed back. When we were all crammed in, sweating and aching and laughing, he gave the finger to the cops, then drove the wrong way straight into oncoming traffic. The police let us go. The other cars swerved to avoid us, honking their horns. Claudio gave the finger to all of them.

Toward us Claudio was kindness incarnate. The next day he came home early to prepare a lavish four-course meal. We offered to help, but he waved us away. "You need energy for tonight's match," he said, steering us toward the television. "Rest up!" Thus while he cooked, we watched an Italian interviewer ask several American fans to predict the outcome of the United States–Italy match. Without exception the Americans believed Italy had no chance against us. Finally, an old man hedged, suggesting the score might be a 0–0 draw. "Do you believe in God?" the interviewer asked. The old man shrugged.

Over dinner Claudio described the matches he had seen the night before, Spain's scoreless draw with Uruguay ("A sleeper," Ronnie said of the Latin American team that had not won a World Cup match in twenty years, though in 1930 it had been the very first champion of this event) and Argentina's 2–0 victory over the Soviet Union. Despite the score, Claudio believed the defending champions had done nothing to resurrect their honor. Maradona had again used his infamous "hand of God," this time to deflect a sure goal off a Soviet header. Once again no call was made. Playing before thousands of his fans in Naples, Maradona had, in the words of a British journalist, "contrived to make a mockery of a World Cup dedicated to the spirit of fair play." No doubt his fans, many of whom had arrived at the match wearing Maradona masks and clutching photographs of him like icons, excused his behavior. But Claudio and countless others considered him a cheater.

Was the tide of sentiment turning against Maradona? It was too soon to tell, but I wondered if all the parents in Naples and Argentina who had named their sons after him would one day regret that decision? In the Mondiale there were at least four players who had adopted his name—Egypt's Taher Abu Zeid was known as the Maradona of the Nile; the Balkans and Carpathians had their own Maradonas; and Cameroon's François Oman Biyik, the Maradona of Africa, had scored the winning goal against the real Maradona. Would that magical emblem eventually turn into a badge of dishonor?

"Drink up," said Claudio, opening another bottle of table wine. He himself professed not to drink — "I am in training," he had said the previous day — though he consumed as much wine as anyone we met in Italy. "Drink up," he repeated, filling our glasses. "You'll need the energy."

After dinner Claudio drove Ronnie and me to a transit station, directed us to the Stadio Olimpico bus, and wished us good luck. As the bus lurched through the late afternoon traffic, we saw vendors packing up their carts, Italian flags hanging from hundreds of windows and balconies, and thousands of people walking toward the Tiber. The pope had rescheduled the annual Corpus Domini procession, starting it an hour earlier so that the faithful could watch Italy play the United States; and when we joined the crowd thronging from the Tiber into the stadium, I felt as if I were on my way to a holy shrine. Security outside the gates was extremely tight. We were frisked several times, and at each stop policemen armed with clubs and automatic weapons searched everything we had, even flipping through my notebook, examining my scribbled entries. A pair of helicopters circled the stadium. Inside, there were policemen and German shepherds everywhere. I had never heard such a deafening sound as the roar of the crowd, and the wave of noise mounted minute by minute. It seemed that all of the eighty thousand fans were on their feet, waving flags and cheering the Italians warming up on the pitch, hissing and booing the American players. The scoreboard read: Italia 0–USA 0.

"A good result," Ronnie joked.

The noise grew during the introduction of the teams, drowning out both national anthems. Ronnie had to yell just to make himself heard. "Bad news," he shouted in my ear, pointing at the Mexican referee. "He won't respect us, won't call anything our way. This could be a repeat of the other night," he groaned. Indeed, the referee from the United States–Czechoslovakia match had been taken to task for ejecting Eric Wynalda; even FIFA's General Secretary Sepp Blatter had said the call was "too harsh," though nothing had been done to reverse Wynalda's suspension for this match. Given Mexico's feelings about watching the World Cup from the sidelines, it was difficult to believe this referee would not pull a similar stunt with another American player. At the very least, it was too much to expect him to act at every moment in an impartial fashion: Italy, after all, was playing in its capital. In the 1934 final, which had pitted Czechoslovakia against Italy here in Stadio Olimpico ("The house that Mussolini built," according to Enrico), the referee had been seen in Il Duce's box before the match. Italy won in extra time, 2–1. This referee might have as little interest in seeing the home team lose.

Not that he had to worry in the early going. Although Bob Gansler had juggled his lineup, inserting Marcelo Balboa, Jimmy Banks, and John Doyle to give his team a defensive advantage, the Italians consistently beat the Americans to the ball and dominated play. In the ninth minute Gianluca Vialli ran by Desmond Armstrong for a hard, though unsuccessful, header on goal. A minute later, the Viper fooled three American defenders at the edge of the penalty area, letting a pass go through his legs to Giuseppe Giannini, the only player from the local club Roma, who blasted a left-footed shot by Meola for a goal. The *Azzurri* had no reason to let up once they took the lead. Suffering from a dearth of goals, a good lambasting of the United States would give them confidence for the rest of the tournament. Minutes later Paolo Maldini delivered a fine cross to Roberto Donadoni, who headed another strong shot on goal. Tony Meola made a fine save, but his efforts seemed stopgap measures.

"Italy's knocking at our door," Ronnie shouted.

Scores flashed on the scoreboard: Yugoslavia, "the Brazil of Europe," according to England's coach, had defeated Colombia 1–0; and Cameroon, on the strength of two goals by thirty-eight-year-old Roger Milla, had beaten Romania 2–1 and thus become the first team to advance into the second round. The United States had hoped to be Italy's Cameroon, but when Paul Caligiuri committed a professional foul with twelve minutes left in the half, tripping Giannini in the penalty area to stop what might have been a one-on-one with Meola, it looked as if Italy was on the verge of a rout. Caligiuri could have been ejected for his foul; the referee chose instead to give him a warning and Italy a penalty kick. Vialli stepped up to the penalty mark, and I remembered that in 1934 the United States had lost to Italy 7–1, also in Rome. I was afraid the same might happen tonight, but Vialli was too loose, too certain he would score. His shot hit the post, and Italy's momentum faded.

John Doyle, inserted into the match to add muscle and aggressiveness to the American defense, took control in back. Tab Ramos continued the strong play he had shown at moments against Czechoslovakia, and Bruce Murray won several knockdowns. The United States was still disorganized, still ball watching, waiting for the play to begin instead of acting, yet the team had survived Italy's initial onslaught and now found its own reserves of confidence. The Italian fans were quick to notice, booing the *Azzurri* once it became clear that the Yanks could hold their own. In injury time Peter Vermes beat a defender with a clever move and crossed the ball into Italy's penalty area. Walter Zenga made a fine save. The referee blew his whistle to signal the end of play. The noise died down. The United States was still very much in the match.

"A fine half for the lads," Ronnie said in a normal voice.

On the screen by the scoreboard a video of Luciano Pavarotti singing began. On the field a boy with knee pads was juggling a soccer ball hundreds of times without losing control. Trapping it in the hollow between his hunched shoulders and head, he dropped to his knees, then lay face down in the grass for a full minute before rising to his feet to juggle again, all without letting the ball touch the ground. At intermission during matches in Rome, Milan, Florence, and Bologna, I would see the same spectacle: Pavarotti and a boy juggling a soccer ball. The high and the low. It was as if the Mondiale were conspiring at every turn to remind me of both the source and solace of my art—its origins in the commonplace, its search for the sublime.

"It's a good thing Italy isn't pressuring us," my friend said.

"It looks like they're playing half-speed," I said.

"The secret to the first round is to get through without using up all your energy," he said. "But that could backfire for Italy. In 1966 they lost one-nil to Korea. They just don't play well against weak teams. They're better on defense, without the ball. Italians like to win it back," he added. "It's like the workers back at Jackie's: they have to be prodded into action. But once they react, watch out!"

"And what do we have to do?" I asked.

"The unpredictable," he said. "Runs from the back don't always have to be down the flanks. Send someone up the middle. And get the ball to Ramos. Let him create some scoring opportunities."

In the second half the Americans responded. John Harkes had a superb header five minutes into play. A minute later Salvatore Schillaci, national hero now and proud new father, came in only to be contained by Desmond Armstrong. And fifteen minutes after that, Paul Caligiuri served two beautiful crosses from the right. Italy had its chances, but now the team was flustered, reacting poorly to the mounting U.S. pressure, missing easy passes and traps. The crowd jeered.

"Now we're knocking at the door," Ronnie said, surprised.

In the sixty-ninth minute the door opened for an instant. Tony Meola cleared the ball with a long dropkick, which Bruce Murray won in the knockdown before being fouled. On the ensuing set piece, a free kick from just outside Italy's penalty area, Murray struck a hard, swerving shot around the wall of defenders. Zenga pushed it away, but Vermes was there for the rebound, driving a low shot from six yards out, which slithered under the goalkeeper's legs and, for a tantalizing moment, looked as if it would roll into the net. Defender Riccardo Ferri cleared it out of the goal mouth. Had Vermes "roofed" it—shot high—he would have scored.

"Fifty million Italian hearts just stopped," Ronnie said. "One more foot, and this match would be tied."

The Americans kept up the pressure, and the crowd harped on the *Azzurri*. Harkes had another solid chance, Murray won more knockdowns, and in this half the United States outshot their opponents. Inexplicably, eight minutes from the end, Gansler replaced Murray, and with him went the Americans' momentum. "Never break up a good thing," I wrote in my notebook. All the same, the United States managed one last chance, Marcelo Balboa almost scoring on a half-volley from thirty yards away. By the slimmest of margins, as Roy Hodgson had predicted, Italy escaped disaster. Its disgruntled fans filed out of the stadium before the final whistle, while the Americans in attendance gave the U.S. team a standing ovation. The *Azzurri* were through to the next round, and the Yanks had redeemed themselves. It had been the kind of match after which soccer players perform an interesting ritual, trading shirts with their opponents. "These are not swapped, sweaty shirts to be sold on," Craig Charles explains, "but kept at home and laundered proudly in memory of an opponent's honest day's chivalry." Indeed.

On our way out of the stadium we fell in with Father Ed Leahy, a Benedictine monk and headmaster of Saint Benedict's Academy in Newark, New Jersey, and Rick Jacobson, a salesman who moonlights as St. Benedict's soccer coach. They were here to support their star alumnus, Tab Ramos, who they said had picked the perfect time to play well: a good club from Holland was interested in him. Surely the scouts liked what they had seen tonight. We walked along the Tiber at a brisk pace, excited by the outcome of the match, describing over and over Murray's set piece, Vermes' rebound, the ball rolling toward the Italian goal.

"What a difference another foot would have made," said Rick, a burly, animated man. Then, studying the quiet Italian fans around us, he added, "It was pandemonium here after Italy beat Austria. Cars honking. Kids blasting those air horns. Everyone shouting. But tonight it's like they lost."

"In a way they did," said Ronnie.

In Naples the night before, Father Leahy and Rick had seen pandemonium of another sort surrounding the match between Argentina and the Soviet Union. "The hotel manager begged me for my Maradona T-shirt," Rick explained. "I think he would have given me *anything* for it! I had to give it to him," he said with a laugh. "Then we met a local man who told us he'd saved up three weeks' pay to buy a ticket to the match. 'It'll put me back,' he said, 'but it's worth it. It's the little I can do for Maradona. He's given so much to me and my family.' "

"What about the 'hand of God?" I wondered.

"He got away with it," Rick said. "Just like the guy who pickpocketed Father Ed the other day." He nodded at the priest. "I'm glad it was you, not me," he added playfully. "Imagine stealing from a holy man!"

Father Leahy, a wiry man with cropped gray hair, grinned. "Imagine," he said.

"Have you been to see the pope?" I asked him.

He shook his head, laughing. "I've been here six days, and I haven't been to the Vatican yet. If I don't go soon, I might be out of a job!"

Theirs had been a hectic schedule of travel from one soccer match to the next. From the Mondiale Father Leahy would continue on to Hamburg to visit another Saint Benedict's alumnus, then to Spain for a Spanish course, which would help him communicate with Tab's parents. Soccer and religion were inextricably intertwined for him. His work was St. Benedict's, and the previous season it had ranked first in the United States among high school soccer teams. For the last several seasons the best players from all over New Jersey had ended up at that small prep school; Tab's success in the World Cup was perhaps only the beginning for Father Leahy and his coach. We accompanied them to Stazione Termini, making plans to meet for dinner before the U.S.–Austria match in Florence. Leaving the station to walk to Piazza della Repubblica, where Claudio would pick us up, I asked Ronnie if Saint Benedict's was a boarding school. He shook his head. "Then how do they get so many good soccer players?" I wondered. "Where do they stay?"

"They manage," said my friend, winking.

It had begun to drizzle, and it was pleasant in the cooling air to sit on the low stone wall surrounding the Fountain of the Naiads, watching the streetwalkers across the way. Cars circled us, horns honking, young men and women leaning out of the windows, waving Italian flags. A truck painted red, white, and green kept reappearing, its driver jumping up and down in his seat, shouting. A convertible passed with its top down, all its passengers on their feet, its windshield wipers jutting out over the hood, swiveling back and forth, wiping the air. The noise had picked up since our walk along the Tiber, but there was something false about it, as if these celebrants were working at their revels, forcing themselves to be happy about a dismal result.

Midnight. The local journalists were already filing their stories, trying to account for Italy's inability to rout the United States. The morning headlines would read: *"Azzurri* on a Diet" and "We Have Discovered America." Meanwhile, the Italian players were at last permitted to spend the night with their wives and girlfriends. Would they play more freely in future matches, score more goals? The U.S. players must also have been celebrating, after a fashion. Their Mondiale was for all intents and purposes over, but they had recovered from the Czech debacle; with any luck they might have drawn with Italy, and the match against Austria would have been for a place in the second round. They had proven to themselves, and to much of the soccer world, that they could come back.

The rain let up. The traffic and noise increased. Across the road was the seedier side of Roman night life. Prostitutes (who dressed down to distinguish themselves from the Brazilian transvestite hookers in elegant attire) and their pimps, drug dealers, refugees from Eastern Europe, homeless families from Africa, a vendor hawking Mondiale souvenirs. We wondered what was taking Claudio so long. Was the postgame traffic that heavy? Had we misunderstood his directions? We were exhausted, hungry. We had needed all the energy we could muster to attend that soccer match, and now we were wrung out. An unmarked police car pulled over in front of the crowd across the way. Three men in uniforms got out . . . and bought an Italian flag from the vendor. They returned to their car and circled the fountain half a dozen times, their siren blaring, the flag waving out of their window. Then they drove away, honking at the whores. Everyone was forgiven tonight.

7

. . . .

AFTERBURN

Montisoni, an abandoned monastery near Jackie's house, was a good place for a pair of runners to take a breather. Sprinting up the last steep curve in the road below the monastery, Ronnie and I would think of our destination as a refuge, where we could rest, check our pulse rates, and decide whether to run further or return to the Spider House. Late one morning, before the heat grew oppressive, we started out from the end of Jackie's driveway (by the plaque commemorating her neighbor's heroic activities in the Resistance, a marble tablet damaged by villagers still angry over his "betrayal" of Mussolini) and jogged down the road toward a nunnery that had been converted into a house. Here we turned right, steering clear of two plucked geese draped over a fence to dry, and ran into a field, picking our way along wagon-wheel ruts, surrounded by olive trees and shocks of damp hay.

We were in good spirits. Two days earlier, the United States had redeemed itself with its narrow loss to Italy, and this afternoon we would drive to Genoa to watch Scotland play Sweden. We kept our eyes fixed on the uneven ground, praying not to twist an ankle nor see a viper. The summer before, in this very field, a farmer reaching into a clump of hay had been struck and killed by such a snake. The expiration date on the antivenom vaccine Jackie kept on hand had passed. If one of us were bitten, she had reminded us before we left, we would never make it to the hospital in time. We ran with our heads down until we entered the woods at the far end of the field.

Here we could follow a wider, muddier path to the cobblestone road leading up to Montisoni. So we relaxed our guard, stretching as we ran, skipping and kicking up our heels and turning sideways to do jumping jacks. Midway through the woods, leaping over a puddle, I landed on a viper stretched out along the side of the path, a thick rope of a snake asleep or digesting a meal. I jumped straight up into the air, twisting away from the surprised viper slithering slowly into the underbrush; flailing my arms, I knocked my friend off-balance, and he momentarily threw out his back. We must have looked like the Keystone Kops. We walked the rest of the way to the road, then sprinted up along the crumbling stone wall. We took a longer break than usual at the monastery.

Montisoni, built in the thirteenth century and occupied through World War II, had fallen into disrepair during the 1960s, due to a national shortage of priests, monks, and nuns. From here we could see an abandoned oratory on the next mountaintop. There were simply not enough religious to go around. Italy's industrialization and rising level of prosperity—the fruits of Mussolini's ambitious modernizing efforts, according to many people in this area, including Enrico's parents, who had adored Il Duce—had coincided with a decline in the number of young men and women choosing spiritual vocations. The country was flush, and that new wealth was also what had fueled the spectacular rise of Italian clubs like AC Milan, Juventus, and Napoli on the international soccer scene. Like the muse, who seems to settle in different parts of the literary world at different times, now inspiring poets and writers in Latin America, now those in Eastern Europe and South Africa, soccer's angel wanders from country to country, club to club. In the last thirty years that fickle angel had drifted from Brazil's Santos to Holland's Ajax to Bayern Munich in West Germany to England's Liverpool and now to Italy. Where to next? Africa? America? Asia? Unlike the muse, who blesses alike writers from rich and poor countries, perhaps preferring in our time those who labor in difficult political conditions, soccer's angel seems to like money.

An infusion of cash was what Montisoni needed. Although it had once housed holy men and, during the war, members of the Resistance, now its windows were barred and barricaded, except near the steeple on the second floor, where drug addicts had ripped down the wire netting covering the window to a small room and moved in. The squatters had no interest in upkeep. Stucco peeled from the walls, revealing a layer of stone and brick. Waist-high grass grew in the courtyard, surrounding an unpruned apricot grove. Heaps of trash were piled on either side of the building. In what might have been the basement we found an open room, a crypt of sorts, lined with graffiti. Charcoal and ashes spilled out of a make-shift fireplace near the door. Here were wadded newspapers and the covers to two issues of *Zip,* a pornographic comic book. There was blood on the floor, near a broken syringe. The village of Antella had acquired the monastery and a large tract of land encircling it, hoping to create a park. They had a long way to go.

Invigorated by our brush with the viper, reluctant to run back through the woods just yet, we changed our workout, adding interval training to what had been a routine "LSD run"—"Long Slow Distance running," not hallucinogenic. Thus on the hills and flats behind the monastery we ran a series of timed sprints, raising our pulse rates to their maximum levels, then jogging or walking until we recovered enough to sprint again, working ourselves into "oxygen debt," a kind of physical afterburn in which an athlete can improve his or her endurance and overall fitness. The object is to recover as fast as possible.

This is the principle around which modern soccer coaches organize practice sessions. Short and long sprints, on and off the ball: a variety of running situations resembling game conditions. In a match a midfielder may make 150 to 250 sprints ranging from 5 to 95 yards each. "Practices should reflect that," Ronnie said, catching his breath. On a wall next to the monastery was an altar into which the Stations of the Cross had been chiseled, and that was where we stopped to check our pulses for the last time. Twelve years older than I, Ronnie recovered much faster than I did. Tired and wary, we ran slowly through the woods and field, stretching on the road up to Jackie's.

After lunch we borrowed Enrico's Fiat and headed for the coast. I came into my own driving among the Italians, first in a downpour, then under clearing skies, passing nurseries and factories and mountains, entering tunnels at speeds I was afraid to convert from kilometers to miles per hour, imagining—in one flight of short-lived madness—that I had missed my calling and should have been a race car driver. It was a two-and-a-half-hour test of my nerves, and our wallets. No wonder Italians take the train, we realized, after filling up the gas tank and paying the tolls.

"There are ways to encourage mass transit," said my friend, reaching for his wallet again.

Once we came in sight of the Ligurian Sea, nearing Italy's oldest port and the birthplace of Christopher Columbus, our conversation turned to Cameroon's thirty-eight-year-old Roger Milla, who the other night had become the oldest player in World Cup history to score a goal, and who had then scored again to insure his team's 2–1 victory over Romania. The son of a railroad man, until quite recently Milla had been content to play out his career with Jeunesse St. Pierroise, a semiprofessional club on the Indian Ocean island of La Réunion, near Madagascar. He had left the national team a few years before the World Cup finals, angered by the Cameroon Soccer Federation's refusal to take care of his dying mother while he and his teammates were in Saudi Arabia for a friendly match. It was only after his country had lost in the African Nations Cup that Milla was persuaded by Paul Biya, his friend and president of the Republic, to rejoin the team for the Mondiale. Everyone in Cameroon, it seemed, celebrated his decision to forgive the federation and "put his experience and legs in the service" of his country. Now he was a national hero and an object of international fascination. How could this five-foot-nine-inch, 150-pound player continue to perform so well at his age?

An Italian newspaper hired a sprint coach to analyze Milla's physical gifts:

> The finding? Milla has the ability to shift gears quickly; calf muscles that contract more rapidly because

they are shorter than normal; longer-than-normal Achilles
tendons, and feet that are quick and flexible, which allow
him to control the ball and *"beat his opponents to the
punch."*

There were sorcerers in Cameroon who wanted to take credit for
Milla's success, but Ronnie had a simpler explanation: "Fitness," he
said. "And he's managed to avoid serious injuries." Then he smiled.
"What he's lost in speed," he suggested, tapping his head, "he more
than makes up for in brains. See how he's always in on the important
plays? He knows how to conserve his energy, when to give it everything and when to rest."

Although no one in Cameroon kept reliable statistics, it was
believed that Milla had scored about a thousand goals in his career,
none more important than the winning tally against Romania, which
raised his currency in the international soccer community such that
semiretirement no longer seemed like a good idea. Already there was
talk of him playing in Italy or Spain, and offers were on the way from
clubs in England, Austria, and Mexico. Curiously enough, he was
even thinking of playing in the United States, though the MISL and
APSL lacked the money to be viable options for him. In short, he had
the chance—even this late in his career—to cash in on his scoring
abilities.

Nor was he alone in hoping that he might end his playing days
in America—"the land where everything is possible," said Stefano
Tacconi, Italy's backup goalkeeper. While Tony Meola dreamed of
playing for an Italian club, of sharpening his goalkeeping skills in his
parents' homeland, his *Azzurri* counterpart, Walter Zenga, was saying *"Mama mia,* give me 100 lire. I want to go to America!" Even
Gianluca Vialli, the soccer viper, was interested in finishing his
career in the New World, according to Giorgio Chinaglia, who in an
interview went on to declare that "so many players ask me about
American teams. I tell all of them that today a soccer player can earn
no more than $2,000 a month in America." That wealthy soccer stars
might consider playing minor-league ball in the New World, I
thought as I slowed down for the exit to Genoa, was a testimony to

the *idea* of America, perhaps the most important legacy of Columbus's journey across the Atlantic. We paid one last toll, drove down to the sea, then up along a dry river bed toward the box-shaped stadium that resembled a factory.

"What would it mean if all those players came to America?" I asked aloud as I parked the car.

"It would certainly up the ante, wouldn't it?" Ronnie said. "We'd have to get serious."

"And if that happened," I said, "what kind of soccer would we play? What would be an *American* style?"

He thought for a moment. "A style that could assimilate a number of styles and adjust to anything. Structured, but allowing for individual creative play. Who we are as a people," he said, "that's how we should play."

We walked up the road and soon found ourselves in the middle of a street party. Thousands of Scots in kilts and Swedes waving flags were toasting one another. Despite the ban on the sale of alcohol, scores of drunken fans weaved in and out of restaurants and stores. A shirtless Swede came up to me and said, "Good luck, Scotland!" He asked my name and where I lived. When I told him, he looked puzzled. Then, in a drunken slur, he said enigmatically, "You won the war! You won the war!" A Scotsman borrowed my pen to write on the back of a Swede's hand his name and the address of the hotel where he was staying. When he returned it, he made a point of distinguishing himself and his countrymen from the English hooligans. "We only sing when we're losing," he said cheerfully. "Just wait till you hear the Tartan Army!"

The luck of the draw clearly favored the citizens of Genoa. The Mondiale was for them a lucrative and festal occasion, a counterweight to the experience of the Sicilians and Sardinians, many of whom said openly that the World Cup was a fiasco. Numbers of people in Cagliari now used only one word to describe anything English: *Brutto.* Ugly. Earlier in the week, two hundred English hooligans had attacked Irish fans outside the stadium in Cagliari; the next day dozens more squared off with a local Italian youth gang at a railway station; and this day police and carabinieri, a paramilitary force, had to contend with a full-blown riot. Marching two thousand English supporters to the stadium for the England–Holland match, separating them from the Dutch fans (who included in their ranks some of the world's most infamous rowdies), the security forces fell victim to what one journalist called "a series of vicious and un- provoked attacks" when hundreds of hooligans broke from the pack and started hurling rocks at them. Running battles, tear gas, pistol- whippings and beatings with clubs, hooligans sneaking down side streets to attack police from behind, helicopters hovering overhead, vanloads of carabinieri racing from street to street, and skinheads saluting one another Nazi style: *Brutto*. What made matters worse was a British Intelligence report that the top leaders of the English and Dutch hooligans had met a month earlier to plan this uprising: the violence was orchestrated. Five hundred Englishmen were ar- rested, and British Sports Minister Colin Moynihan said the riot was "a sickening reflection that a mindless minority of thugs can bring English football into international disrepute." His countrymen's dream of England returning to European club play seemed dimmer than ever, and the worst was perhaps yet to come. "It's great to be frightened and to conquer your fear and make a bit of trouble," one hooligan told an Italian journalist. If England advanced into the second round, hooligan leaders warned, more violence would fol- low, because on the mainland it would be more difficult for security forces to monitor the comings and goings of all the rowdies. *Brutto* might become the Mondiale's most common slur.

In Genoa it was an altogether different story. Security was rea- sonably loose in Stadio Luigi Ferraris, and when we took our seats near the Scottish end of the stands, we were overwhelmed by the sound of the Tartan Army singing "When the Saints Come Marching In." On one side of the stadium were hundreds of Scottish flags, signs like SWEDES ARE NEEPS and banners proclaiming the names of seemingly every clan in Scotland. On the other side were Swedes in short pants, flags draped over their shoulders, their faces painted in blue and yellow stripes, with waves of *olé, olé, olé* surging from them. A frantic usher ran up and down the steps in the aisle next to us, a wild-eyed look about him as he checked people's tickets and directed them toward their seats. No one escaped his scrutiny. A Scotsman near us, nodding at this overly officious usher who seemed on the verge of a nervous breakdown, said, "The only Italian working in Italy!"

Both teams took the field, and their fans traded rounds of cheering, each side trying to outshout the other. "This is how we warm up," Ronnie said, pointing at the Swedish players. "A little running, a little striking. No more structured warm-ups. I want my guys to get loose on their own. They know what they need to do before a match." The Scots, on the other hand, were more organized about their pregame activities: some players served long balls in from the wings, others did one- and two-touch passing exercises, and still others made short runs on and off the ball. Perhaps they had more to prove this night. Sweden, it was true, was in the same position as Scotland, fighting for a place in the second round. But its opening-match loss to Brazil was not unexpected, and since the team had not been to the World Cup since 1978, Sweden's players may have felt less pressure than the Scots, who in each of the previous four World Cups had failed to make it beyond the first round. Scotland's loss to Costa Rica, which had cost some of its players several nights' sleep, frightened the whole team.

The country, too. "A rueful doom ruffles the Scottish spirit," Alastair Reid writes, exemplified in their fans' determination to sing in defeat. Talented as the Scots might be, the feeling I had in Genoa was that they would find a way to disappoint their followers. I remembered Leslie Norris's description of the Scottish soccer tradition. "The most skillful players in the world," he told me. "Because the kids grow up playing on those narrow city streets, they have to rely on their touch. Good passing and clever dribbling are what they've given to soccer. And," he added with a smile, "they're the greatest self-destructors in the history of the game. Once they had to send three of their players home the day of a World Cup match because they stayed up the whole night drinking!"

No doubt many of the Scottish fans had spent the entire previous night drinking, too. Yet there was no sign of fatigue among them. When their team came out fighting against Sweden, drawing three penalties for rough tackling in the opening minutes, the faithful made a deafening noise. Ten minutes into the match, they were rewarded for their patience when Stuart McCall scored off a corner kick, beating two defenders to slot the ball inside the far post and put the Scots up 1–0.

When play resumed, Ronnie said, "First touches on good teams are always good. That first touch has to be away from pressure," he explained, "away from your feet when a defender's on you. See how they're always moving off the ball? We don't do that."

"Why not?" I said.

"Maybe we're overcoached," he offered. "Maybe Roy's right. We play too much by coaching, not by talent. Even in tight situations, these guys"—the Scots and the Swedes—"know where to play the ball. They don't receive it, then decide. They know their options before the ball arrives."

Such instinctual knowledge made for an exciting match. The players worked the ball around the field, each team testing the other's mettle. Midfielders sprinted upfield, forwards dropped back on defense, and defenders took to the attack. On either side there was constant interchange of positions. At the start of the first half there had been a row of empty seats behind us; before long they were occupied by more than a dozen policemen who had abandoned their posts. Our usher threw up his hands. "Now he *knows* he's the only Italian working in Italy!" the Scotsman near us roared. The noise mounted behind the Scottish goal, and when the half ended with Scotland still in the lead, our neighbor disappeared, perhaps to join his countrymen.

In the second half the Swedes stepped up the pressure, adding to their short-passing conservative mode of play an occasional long through ball. But they were unable to exploit their height advantage over the scrappier, long-ball playing Scots, who in the eighty-third minute scored again on Mo Johnston's penalty kick. Two minutes later, Sweden struck back when Glenn Stroemberg, a star in the 1980s but lately relegated to the bench, volleyed in a hard right-footed shot off a long pass from midfield. Had Scotland let down, or had Sweden simply woken up? Perhaps both were true. In the last minutes of the match the Swedes produced what Reuters called "a furious finish, but it was too late."

"They play like socialists," Ronnie joked on our way out of the stadium. "There's no pressure on them to succeed."

An orderly crowd filed into the streets, Swedes and Scots hugging one another, exchanging hats and souvenirs. "Good luck, Scotland," a young Swede said to us. "Thanks," Ronnie said. "We'll need it, because we're from America!" The Swede slapped him on the back, then wandered off into the night. It turned out that I had parked the car directly in the crowd's path, and so we spent more than an hour watching the Tartan Army march past, thousands of Scotsmen singing on their way down to the sea, where they would party with the Swedes until early in the morning. Scotland had reclaimed its honor. Assuming Sweden went on to defeat Costa Rica, the Scots would only have to draw with Brazil to advance in the tournament. I wondered aloud if Brazil, having already made it into the next round with a victory over Costa Rica that night, might be tempted to use its reserves against Scotland and play for a draw, saving its starters for later matches?

"Not likely," said my friend. "Sweden's rich. It has investments in Brazil. Brazil won't jeopardize that for Scotland."

Our speculations would prove moot four days hence when Scotland fell 1−0 to Brazil, and Costa Rica, one of the Mondiale's Cinderella teams, took Sweden 2−1. Scotland would fail for the fifth straight time to advance into the second round of the World Cup, and Sweden would be humiliated. No pressure? A Stockholm newspaper would call the Swedes "traitors," declaring that the national team was filled with "inflated fools dressed up as soccer players. Thirteen [the number of players who had seen action in the three losses] scared rabbits who let their nation down when they were obligated to win. Thirteen tourists [to Italy] who created the biggest fiasco in Swedish soccer history."

Nevertheless ("a favorite Scottish qualification," Alastair Reid notes), the Swedes had played well against the Scots. In a match interview, Andy Roxburgh, Scotland's manager, said: "It was like a cup final, and it's very sad there had to be a loser. It was only a snap of the fingers between winning and losing." The fans on both sides realized they had witnessed a classic confrontation, a hard-fought, well-played match. They walked past us in a spirit of revelry and camaraderie. When at last the street was clear, Ronnie and I got in the car and drove off, utterly spent, but I entered the stream of traffic on the highway back to Florence wide awake and terrified.

"My pulse is forty-eight," Ronnie informed me on our way into a tunnel, cars and trucks racing past us. A minute later, he said, "Now it's forty-two."

"I'm sure mine's over a hundred," I said, "I must be in oxygen debt. These drivers are putting me into afterburn!" I made a silent vow not to drive again in Italy.

It was an easy vow to keep, for a day.

The next morning my wife, Lisa, arriving from a visit with her older sister in London, emerged from the Florence train station with her own stories about the Italian stretch of an otherwise uneventful trip: a missing passport; a drunken ticket collector whose advances she had had to ward off; an elderly "gentleman" who had offered to protect her, only to try to seduce her himself. She had not slept at all, and she had almost nothing good to say about the "charms" of Italy. Henry James's portrait of Isabel Archer's innocence was a little too close for comfort now, she thought, examining the novel I was still reading. I put the book away.

A long nap restored her spirits. Later in the afternoon, we joined Ronnie on the back porch, and Lisa was dazzled by the splendor of the Tuscan countryside. It reminded her of Vermont, where we had spent our first six months together: the rounded hills, the heat and haze, the slower pace of life. That summer we had house-sat for Ronnie and his wife, taking care of their friendly golden retriever, harvesting from their large garden quarts of strawberries for glacé pies and daiquiris. Lisa practiced her violin upstairs, and I wrote in the barn. We lived as if under a spell. In the fall I coached Middlebury's B soccer team, Lisa played with the Vermont Symphony, and we made plans to marry. Now we felt as if we had come full circle.

That Lisa had not seen Ronnie since our stint in Vermont only added to our pleasure. We sipped Chianti, sampling a spread of local cheeses. We had so much to talk about.

We kept our voices low. Blessed as we felt, we knew all was not well with our hosts. The work on the cisterns dragged on and on. Every day, it seemed, one of the laborers left the spigot running on the cask of Chianti; now the garage smelled like a winery, the cask would have to be replaced soon, and no one could say when the construction might be completed. What is more, ants had dragged off the grass seed Ronnie and I had methodically planted in front of the fence; we had already replanted that plot of dirt once, and although we had sprayed insecticide over the area several times, it looked as if we would have to do the whole thing over again. These problems were nothing next to the real concern of the moment. Even as Ronnie, Lisa, and I traded stories, Jackie was upstairs packing for a stay in the hospital. The next day she would have surgery to help her carry her child to term, all other remedies—bed rest, medication, daily injections of hormones—having failed. Her doctor was not optimistic about her chances of successfully delivering this baby; the operation would be a last-ditch effort to save her pregnancy.

In her absence we would take care of Federico and Enrico. When Enrico left to drive her to the hospital in Florence, we went inside to cook tuna pasta, a local specialty Jackie had served us during our stay, then turned our attention to entertaining Federico, assuming our most difficult task would be to comfort the little boy. But he welcomed having another woman in the house, especially one who doted on him and blithely ignored his bedtime. Enrico was a different story. Upon his return from the hospital, he told us he had lost his appetite. Our pasta, it was clear, was missing something. To complicate matters, he had mysteriously developed some of Jackie's symptoms, the most prominent of which was high blood pressure. "I can't calm down," he said, filling his wine glass. "That is my defect." He gave up all hope of quitting smoking. Lighting one cigarette after another, refilling his glass again and again, he stayed up late with Federico, watching World Cup coverage on television.

Enrico was even more unsettled in the morning. Jackie had

taken his only bottle of aftershave, and he was in despair. Ronnie dug out a vial of cheap cologne he had picked up somewhere on his travels and never used. "Try this," he said. Enrico grabbed the vial, and within minutes he had used up all the cologne. "He smells like a French whore," Ronnie whispered to me as we followed our friend down to the cellar to check on the water pump. "Stupid!" Enrico said to the valve on the pump. "What a stupid country!" Then he drove to the hospital.

This was Ronnie's last day here. After the United States– Austria match, he would accompany Father Leahy and Rick Jacobson to Rome, and the next day he would fly back to the States. It was in every respect a sad morning until Jackie called to tell us her surgery had gone well; she was even planning to leave the hospital a day early. "My doctor's going to meet a battle-axe," she said in a feisty tone, "if he thinks I'm staying here any longer than *I* want to!" It was time for Ronnie and me to set out for the match. Jackie's fighting spirit had enlivened us considerably.

While Lisa stayed home to entertain Federico, we caught up with Father Leahy and Rick at a restaurant adjacent to the Hotel Corona. They had more tales to tell. A sportswriter from the London *Times,* stuck in a traffic jam in Naples, had been robbed when a thief had reached into his car, grabbed his wallet and camera, then run off in plain sight of a policeman in the car directly behind his. A group of Juventus fans, plotting revenge for the Heysel Stadium tragedy, had vowed to cause problems for England and its band of supporters if the team advanced as far as the semifinals, which in that half of the draw would be held in Turin. And the Franciscan monks in Italy had been granted a special dispensation allowing them to stay up past their bedtime to watch World Cup matches on TV.

"What a country!" we all agreed.

On the train to the stadium we saw members of the Orange Football Club, a team from Los Angeles that, according to its promotional literature, "enjoys sharing its love of soccer with others, as well as seeing individuals establish a personal relationship with God." The club had visited more than thirty countries; at every

World Cup match I had noticed these orange-shirted men waving signs, like flags, imprinted with a simple message: John 3:16. Now I realized they were referring to a Biblical verse, not a soccer player.

Father Leahy seemed not to notice them. "Maybe soccer's the sport of monolithic societies," he was saying. "Maybe our pluralistic society isn't right for the game. We have too many distractions, too many places to go." Our conversation turned to Thomas Merton, the Trappist monk who had written so many important books in his short life. "They say he never wrote outside work hours," said the priest, shaking his head in admiration. "A model to us all." I wondered, had Merton needed that discipline, though he had chafed against the strictures set down by his father superior? "We all need it in the order," said Father Leahy. On our way into the stadium, he told me how much he missed the orderliness of the monastery. "Travel's vital," he said, "but it throws me off." I thought of Merton's ill-fated journey to Bangkok, a pilgrimage undertaken at a critical moment in his life. In Asia he had hoped to discover his future course of action—whether to become a hermit, give up writing altogether, or leave the order and pursue his interest in Buddhism—but his voyage had ended in his accidental death. Did his fate weigh on Father Leahy's mind? I did not ask; he had grown quiet. I could but dimly understand how difficult it was for him to leave his monastery, even if only for a matter of weeks.

Once in his seat, however, the priest appeared to be back in his element. He scanned the stadium for Mr. and Mrs. Ramos, who were sitting with the other U.S. players' families, then he turned his attention to their son, who was finishing his warm-up. "Why are Tab's socks down?" he asked Rick. "Is he hurt? I've never seen him do that."

Rick shook his head, bewildered. "Maybe he's too hot," he offered.

The sun was setting, and still it was muggy. Both teams left the field, prompting a contingent of American fans to start chanting *"Olé, olé, olé."*

"Ten days ago we were a crowd that didn't know how to react," Rick said. "We scored a goal and cheered for ten seconds. Everyone

else scores, and the cheering goes on for fifteen minutes." Father
Leahy stood up to wave to the Ramoses. "Obviously a goal means
more to others than to us," said the coach.

"We're learning," said the priest. "We're still learning."

Goals were especially "precious items," as Bob Gansler had
called them, to the Austrians, who had yet to score in the Mondiale.
Technically, each team had an outside chance of qualifying for the
second round. The winner of this match would have to score enough
goals to surmount the goal differential of another third-place finisher,
providing that it also finished the first round with two points—that
is, one victory or two draws. Because the United States had lost by
four goals to Czechoslovakia in its last Florence appearance and thus
would have to win this game by something like 7−0 to have any
hope of advancing, the team was actually playing only for pride,
trying to build on its success against Italy. The Austrians, on the
other hand, while not a strong side, had in Anton Polster one of
Europe's top goal scorers, and a host of reasons for wanting to take
out their aggression on their younger opponents. This was the first
time these countries had ever played against each other, and Austria
came out applying pressure.

"We're in trouble," Ronnie said after only one minute of play.

Minutes later, though, several things caused him to change his
mind. First, on a set piece from John Harkes, which John Doyle
headed down in the penalty area, Peter Vermes kicked a hard half-
volley over the goal, a point-blank shot that would have scored if he
had kept it down. Then Austria's pressure let up, and Ramos worked
a fine combination with Vermes and Bruce Murray, who was winning knockdowns off Tony Meola's long dropkicks and punts, some
of which landed on the edge of Austria's penalty area. "There's a lot
more movement up front than we've had," Ronnie said. "We could
win this match."

Almost immediately he realized that he had spoken too soon.
Austria broke through the American defenses twice within a matter
of minutes for one-on-one shots on Meola, which he saved in brilliant fashion. "Their forwards are hungry for goals," Ronnie said,
"and they're faster than we are."

"Explosive," Rick added. "We could have 80 percent of the play and still lose two–nil. They're tough, the Austrians."

Rough, too. Defender Anton Pfeffer caught Murray on the chin with a pair of right hooks, the first of which left him writhing on the ground, dazed and upset. The second, delivered soon after he got back on his feet, angered the American striker so much that for the duration of the first half he seemed more interested in retaliating than in playing.

"Take him aside, Tab!" Rick called.

"Calm him down!" cried Father Leahy.

"Get him out of there before he gets the boot," Ronnie muttered.

Murray was in danger of falling for the same trick Czechoslovakia had pulled on Eric Wynalda, earning him a red card, a one-game suspension, and a $7,000 fine. The match had turned ugly—*brutto*. Nine yellow cards would be issued before the end of the night. In the thirty-third minute the referee handed out a red card—not to Murray, though his behavior warranted such a call, but to Austria's Peter Artner. Roy Hodgson had said the Austrians were vicious tacklers, and Artner's over-the-ball foul on Vermes, a tackle that could have broken the American's leg, was one of many examples proving his point. The Austrians would have to play a man down for almost an hour. For the first time in the Mondiale the United States had an advantage.

But the team did nothing in the remaining minutes of the half to exploit that edge. Indeed, Murray continued to lose his temper. "Somebody should be babysitting him," Ronnie said. "They'll bait him till he swings." Then Murray pulled an Austrian down, and although the linesman wanted him to be ejected, the referee only handed him a yellow card. "Just watch," Ronnie said, "if he gets the ball, in the air or on the ground, they'll clock him." Still he was not finished: he kept going after other players, and when the half ended in a scoreless tie, Murray walked off the field to the sound of Austrian supporters hissing at him. He had acted in a childish manner, and he had gotten away with it. It was another bleak moment in American soccer history, and these Austrian fans would not let him forget it.

Others in the crowd, though, were in good spirits, especially the Italians monitoring—on transistor radios they had smuggled through security—the progress of the Italy–Czechoslovakia match in Rome. In the first half a cheer had gone up when Toto Schillaci, whose followers in his home town of Palermo wanted him to be the new mayor, had scored his second World Cup goal. During the next half an even louder burst of applause rocked the stadium when Roberto Baggio, Fiorentina's star forward, scored what Pelé called the greatest goal yet in the tournament, a daring run from midfield in which he "survived two tackles," Claire Lovell wrote, "dribbled into the penalty area and sent the goalkeeper the wrong way with his shot." Then the cheering abruptly turned into an angry chant, a chorus of untranslatable curses hurled at Fiorentina's owner. At the end of the season he had transferred Baggio to Juventus for a record $13 million, precipitating a minor riot in May at the club headquarters in Florence, a clash between protesters and police. Baggio had not wanted to leave Florence, not even to team up with Schillaci, who would be his frontline partner. "Stupid!" was how Enrico had characterized Fiorentina's owner. "He runs his team for a profit, like a *business!*" he spat, accenting the last word in such a way that it resembled an obscenity. "It's an art!" And Baggio's goal was by all accounts a work of art. By the end of the U.S.–Austria match many Italian fans here must have wished they had stayed home to watch their banished hero in action.

Perhaps the American players also wished they were elsewhere. The second half was a disaster for them. They came out trying to control the ball—to no avail.

"You mean to tell me they're going to play possession when they're up a man?" Rick said of the Americans dribbling sideways across the pitch and making short passes among themselves. "I don't believe it. It doesn't take a genius to know you can't get four touches without getting cracked by these guys!"

Polster, who had been shut down in the first half by Doyle, was replaced by Andreas Reisinger, a speedy midfielder who was cautioned almost as soon as he entered the match. Whatever hope the Americans might have had in Polster's absence vanished four minutes into play when Andreas Ogris scored on the counterattack following a Ramos corner kick, outrunning the whole U.S. defense for another one-on-one with Meola that this time was successful.

"If we lose this game down a man," said Rick, "we go back to where we were ten days ago. I can't believe he just ran past four guys —and Windischmann, our *captain,* let him go without taking a swipe at him! I don't care if he misses. At least he should disrupt him enough to give Tony a chance."

Minutes later, on another breakaway, Windischmann committed a foul of that sort, earning himself a yellow card (which should have been red, according to FIFA policy, since this was a professional foul) but preventing another goal.

"Finally!" Rick said. "You gotta' whack him. Hey, that's the game!"

But Windischmann's gesture came too late to reverse the course of the match. In the sixty-third minute Gerhard Rodax scored a second goal for Austria, taking a cross from Michael Streiter right through the U.S. defense for another successful one-on-one with Meola. "After the Czech game, I didn't think it was possible to be more embarrassed," said Rick, "but I was wrong."

"What should the United States do?" I asked.

"Play to Tab's and Peter's [Vermes'] beat," he said, "but they can't even get them the ball. Austria's smart. They'll bring in two fresh guys down a man and keep running hard. They have us so disorganized we can't sort out a thing. We've just taken ten steps back."

Yet with ten minutes to play the United States mounted a partial comeback, discovering that Ramos-Vermes beat long enough for Murray and Vermes to get several good, low shots. Then Ramos fed Murray for a shot that slithered through the Austrian keeper's legs for a goal. "It took us sixty minutes to figure out how to play a man up, but I'll take it!" Rick beamed. The United States played well right up to the end, mustering a final breakaway when Eric Wynalda, back from his suspension, sprang loose. But there was to be no draw tonight, no points garnered in this World Cup.

"I've got a pit in my stomach," Ronnie said as we left the

stadium. Rick was close to tears, and Mr. Ramos, Father Leahy assured us, would cry all night long. Outside the locker room, John Harkes's father, a fiercely proud, white-haired Scotsman, was also on the verge of tears. "By God, I can't believe it," he said in a quavering voice, his whole body shaking in the glare of the street lights filtering through the trees. "Why?" he kept asking no one in particular. "Why?"

I imagined him speaking for all of Kearny, New Jersey. That community, that mix of ethnic loyalties, had placed such hopes on the elder Harkes's son, Tony Meola, and Tab Ramos, the talented threesome who had played with and against one another since childhood. He was speaking, too, for a part of our country that had delighted in the prospect of a band of "college all-stars" taking on the world at its own game. In the end it was important to remember that our team was the youngest in the tournament, though such a reminder did not diminish our pain. Ours is a relatively young culture, raw, unarticulated, powerful; the callowness of our soccer team, viewed in a certain light, was perhaps inevitable. John Harkes and his teammates had worked hard to become one of the World Cup's surprises: a Cameroon, a Costa Rica, an Ireland—all advanced into the second round. That the United States had not turned into a Cinderella team was no surprise to most soccer observers, but still that knowledge rankled. We like to think we can do anything. In sports, as in the international arena, we are used to getting our own way. It hurts to discover that we are not invincible. Perhaps our failure in Italia 90 was only a step in what will eventually appear to be an inevitable march toward change in our relations to the rest of the world. Our players would grow from this experience; the same might be true of the nation. "By God, I can't believe it," Mr. Harkes repeated, and we nodded. There was more to say, but it was time for me to bid farewell to Ronnie, Rick, and Father Leahy. The last part of my journey I would take alone.

8
. . . .
THE INVISIBLE FOOT

*T*he Feast of Saint John the Baptist, the patron saint of Florence, is celebrated every year with a game of *calcio storico*—football in costume or livery, a rough-and-tumble source of modern soccer. On June 24 thousands of people assemble in Piazza Santa Croce to watch four city teams resurrect the style and substance of a famous sixteenth-century match between the Whites of the Santo Spirito district of town and the Greens of San Giovanni. It was during the Siege of Florence that a one-day truce was negotiated with the invading Imperial Army of Charles V, solely for the sake of *calcio.* The White-Green ur-soccer match played that winter afternoon in 1530 gave the weary Florentines a rest from battle, uniting them for the next stage of their defense of the city.

Calcio remained popular until the eighteenth century. Although authorities like Desmond Morris do not believe it can be called a true forerunner of modern soccer (because once the game was no longer played, it lay dormant until after soccer's rules had been drawn up), still *calcio* is a spiritual ancestor of the people's game. Eager to see this spectacle, I wandered through the low-lying district of town that once was the center of the dye trade, toward the square in which Girolamo Savonarola had burned books and heretics. Security was tight, a helicopter briefly hovered overhead, and it took me several minutes to make my way to a seat in the temporary stands opposite

Santa Croce, the church in which Michelangelo and Galileo are buried. It was late in the afternoon, yet the sun beat down on my back as I waited for the formal procession to begin. Soon I was sweating heavily. I wished that the policemen at the gate had not forced me to empty my water bottle, fearing that I would use it as a missile.

Tons of dirt had been trucked in to create the field enclosed on all sides by these makeshift stands. Teams of workers then raked out a playing surface as smooth and even as a baseball diamond. *Calcio* had been revived in 1930 to commemorate the fourth centenary of the death of Francesco Ferrucci, the legendary commander of the Republic who, Mary McCarthy wrote, was "taken prisoner and killed at Gavinana, in the fateful Pistoiese hills, during a last brilliant action against immensely superior forces—'You are killing a dead man,' he murmured as he fell, already covered with battle wounds, to the enemy commander's treacherous dagger." Until the late 1980s, *gioco del calcio storico* was a fixture in Piazza della Signora; while the government argued over what to do with the Roman foundations discovered and dug up under the piazza, *calcio* had found a provisional home at Santa Croce.

Seeing a statue of Dante on the corner, I remembered that since the 1966 flood, which forced the local craftsmen and their families to leave their workshops and apartments, this quarter had become the center of the city's leather business: two facts that in their odd conjunction seemed germane to my explorations. A simple theme was at the heart of this enterprise: the juxtaposition of high and low. Dante, a cultivated man expected to write his poetry in the literary Latin of his day, had chosen instead to use vernacular Italian for his *Divine Comedy,* one of our civilization's artistic touchstones. And what is more elegant than a leather vest, handbag, or jacket made in Florence, though animal skins furnish the material for these marvelous trappings? In an irreligious time, in the absence of a sense either of community or of history, I mourned the passing of what Allan Bloom calls "a common experience inviting high and low into a single body of belief" even as I welcomed the chance to live in "interesting times." I was nostalgic for Dante's all-encompassing world view, and at the same time I coveted the leather vest the man seated next to me was wearing. A poetics might be fashioned out of those contradictory impulses.

My travels had turned into a search for sources—of soccer, of poetry, of myself. As a player I had on occasion been accused of holding something back to spare myself injury, relying at crucial moments on the skill I had acquired over the years instead of a certain recklessness necessary for success. Soccer, like life, demanded more, demanded the kinds of headlong efforts one might first experience on the field. In sports and writing, in love and life itself, too often I had held back, afraid to take chances, afraid of being hurt. "No, it was not because it was too far / you failed to visit me that day or night," Czesław Miłosz cautions at the end of "Elegy for N.N.," a poem in which he chides his lover for not accompanying him into a new life. "From year to year it grows in us until it takes hold, / I understood it as you did: indifference." I realized that I was prone to indifference, to spiritual inertia, in my affairs and in my relation to the world. That I had suffered many injuries on the soccer field was, I now believed, one of life's little ironies. Whatever failure and confusion I had endured in adulthood were nothing compared to what I might have experienced, in joy *and* pain, had I only risked more.

I thought of a story James Wright had told about his teacher, Theodore Roethke: how one night he called the older man in a fit of despair, needing to talk about poetry. "I'll be right over," Roethke said. Yet when the older poet arrived, drunk and excited, he was in no mood to talk about literature. He suggested instead that Wright accompany him to the fights. The younger poet tagged along, claiming later that he learned more about poetry from Roethke's passion at the fights, the way he would scream "Get him! Get him!" and jump up and down in his seat, than from anything he had said in the classroom. Roethke, in short, demanded from life a healthy dose of gusto, without which poetry and love and life itself wither. In *calcio* I hoped to find that gusto.

From a distance came the sound of drums and bugles. Billed as a tourist event, *calcio storico* nevertheless seemed to attract a local crowd. Italian was the only language I heard in the square, and I saw more families than I had expected. Even so there were many empty seats, perhaps because the second round of the World Cup was under way. Argentina was playing Brazil in Turin, a match certain to generate a considerable amount of excitement and discussion. Acceleration was the new theme of the Mondiale. In the first round eight teams had been eliminated over the course of twelve days; now it would take a third as long to get rid of eight more. Gone was the leisurely pace of teams playing for a draw, saving their energy for later matches. Single elimination was now the rule. The day before, in overtime, Cameroon had continued its winning ways, defeating Colombia on a pair of goals by Roger Milla, while Costa Rica came to the end of its magical run, losing 4–1 to Czechoslovakia. Two more teams would be gone in a matter of hours, and by the next weekend the quarterfinals would be over. Everything was moving faster now, except the historical procession entering Piazza Santa Croce.

What surprised me was the stately manner in which some five hundred costumed figures paraded around the *calcio* field. Seven drummers in red-and-white striped outfits set a martial beat for the first of the famous standard bearers, a group of flag throwers representing the sixteen magistratures of Renaissance Florence. They took positions in the middle of the field, waved the long red-and-white and blue-and-white flags in a synchronized display, then tossed them back and forth, furling and unfurling great bolts of color. They formed a tight circle in and out of which they wove the flags, then put on a tumbling exhibition, running and leaping over one another. They made the air shimmer. And when they left the field, trumpeters entered escorting the standards that would be placed in front of either goal, like toll booths. Next came men-at-arms, knights in full armor, magistrates, members of the artisans' guilds, more drummers and horn players, a man on horseback, soldiers armed with antique guns shaped like large boomerangs, and finally the players from Santo Spirito and Santa Croce, young men calling out to their friends in the stands, throwing flowers into the crowd, oblivious to the pomp and circumstance surrounding them: chaos in the midst of order, a kind of wild heart at the center of ceremony—sanctioned by every-one in the square, who delighted in the juxtaposition of regal and riotous, proper and primitive.

"Pontello! *Bordello! Vaffanculo!*" the crowd started chanting, yet again cursing Fiorentina's owner whose double misfortune it was to have sold his club a day earlier and this afternoon to be obligated to play the role of *calcio* dignitary. The spectators around me shook their fists at an apartment balcony overlooking the field. In the world of sports perhaps only George Steinbrenner, the owner of the New York Yankees, has been more reviled than Pontello.

Two more teams entered the arena, flowerless, presumably be-cause they would play the second match of the day; they were followed by eight horses and the white calf that would be presented to the winning side. The field was almost full when the players from Santo Spirito and Santa Croce removed their capes and began warm-ing up, running up and down the lines of costumed figures standing at attention, hugging one another like wrestlers, faking tackles, lim-bering up in the middle of a grand tableau vivant that now included a party of religious officials. Bells rang in the church. Drums beat. A man sang in Latin over the loudspeaker, ushering in the games with the reading of the "Magnifico Messere."

A gun fired. Everyone, except the players, ran off the field, scattering in every direction: a curious sight after such a stately entrance. The players stripped down to their shorts and shoes. The gun was fired again, the ball was thrown up into the air, and a game combining elements of soccer, rugby, and mob football was under way. Players threw the ball to one another, and those who held it too long were soon tackled. Others were tackled for no apparent reason; at any moment in the match there might be as many as half a dozen grappling sessions going on. Twenty-seven players to a side made for a crowded field. Only the two captains, who stood in front of their standards, escaped the violence. Santo Spirito scored first, throwing the ball over the end line into the wire mesh running along the line, which turned out to be the goal. The gun was fired, and while a flock of startled pigeons circled the piazza, the players changed sides, their captains slowly trudging to the other end of the field—a ritual repeated after each of the match's fourteen goals. The nobility of the historical procession vanished in the wake of *calcio*'s violence, which only now and then was interrupted by flashes of athletic grace and skill: a behind-the-back pass, some deft footwork and fancy dribbling, an improvised pick-and-run. It was like team handball— except that no one seemed to know how to throw or catch—gone barbarous, a savage form of sandlot football, a brawl. The crowd loved it. I was dumbstruck.

Dust hung in the air, and my attention drifted to the facade of the church. I was living through a privileged moment in our recent history, a respite of sorts between the Cold War and the "New World Order" politicians were touting. On one side of the Mondiale was the end of communism, marked by the fall of the Berlin Wall; one by one the countries of the Warsaw Pact were striking out on their own; and there were signs of the Soviet Union's impending collapse. On the other? Historical forces were gathering speed in the Middle East, and soon the world would focus its attention, hatred, and hope on a man named Saddam Hussein. This was, indeed, a special time: ethnic tension in places like Yugoslavia, Czechoslovakia, and the Soviet republics was simmering, and the world economy was not in a free fall. The Cold War would close with a whimper, not a bang; the European Community was about to take its place on history's stage; and widespread Islamic fundamentalism, unleashed by the Gulf War, belonged to the future. The world would never be the same. What remained constant, the Mondiale revealed, were certain human needs. In 1530 the Whites and the Greens had played *calcio* in Florence to give the defenders of the city a break. Four and a half centuries later, Italia 90 offered another intermission to a world on the threshold of radical change.

The first game concluded in a ragged fashion, Santa Croce winning handily. A band of costumed figures returned and formed a circle in which to play drums, fifes, and bugles for the bruised and bloodied players running around the field, soliciting applause from the crowd. Grounds keepers watered down the dirt before the next match began; within minutes the new players were kicking up more dust. I gave myself over completely to the heat and spectacle, and when at last a small cannon was fired to signal the end of play, I was as startled as the pigeons circling the piazza. Dazed, I saw the captain of the Greens of San Giovanni accept the white calf. Had they won? I could not say. The field filled again with the entire historical procession, which paraded out of the arena. A solemn drumbeat set the tempo, as if this were a funeral march. The helicopter reappeared, drowning out the buglers. The cannon was the last to leave. Fireworks erupted over the city. I headed out into the crowded streets.

I was parched, sunburned, famished. I walked to the river, where I found a vendor selling slices of watermelon and liters of mineral water. I drained one bottle, poured another over my burning scalp, and packed a third for the bus ride back to Antella. I slurped down several slices of watermelon and climbed onto the bus, sticky fingered, soaked, and sweating. When I got off in Antella, where villagers had gathered outside the café to watch the Holland–West Germany match on TV, I decided to walk the three steep miles up to Jackie's house. I knew that Lisa, Enrico, and Jackie, who for the first time in her pregnancy was saying that she would carry her child to term, would be watching the match. It pleased me to think I was out walking in the still evening air while so much of Italy was preoccupied with a soccer match involving their new European Community partners. Passing a farmhouse, I heard an eruption of cheers, and I tried — in vain — to imagine which side these peasants might support. Nor could I guess who had scored, if in fact the cheering had been for a goal. I walked faster up the hill.

It was full dark when I arrived at Jackie's. No one there could tell me what might have occasioned the applause I had heard, because neither side had scored yet. Enrico fixed me a dish of *carpaccio,* cheese, and bread dipped in olive oil, then ushered me into the den to watch the rest of the match. The big news from the first half was that West German striker Rudi Voeller and Dutch defender Frank Rijkaard, rivals from Italy's First Division, had been sent off for fighting. Rijkaard, a star for AC Milan, had spat three times at Roma's great scorer — a grave insult, Enrico thought, believing that Voeller had been unfairly ejected. The referee had no business breaking up a feud borne of a match between Roma and AC Milan.

"This is like watching Italian soccer," he said at the start of the second half. "Five of the Germans and three of the Dutch play for clubs here."

Indeed, for West Germany's Andreas Brehme, Juergen Klinsmann, and Lothar Matthaeus, all of whom played for Inter Milan, and the Dutch/AC Milan trio of Marco Van Basten, captain Ruud Gullit, and Rijkaard, this match in Milan was another version of crosstown rivalry. Six minutes into play, Klinsmann scored on a cross from Guido Buchwald, and in the eighty-fifth minute it was Brehme who looped the ball around the Dutch goalkeeper for what would be the winning West German goal. Holland's only score, Ronald Koeman's penalty kick before the final whistle, came as the result of Van Basten's clever acting when he made a push look like a full-blown trip. The most exciting play throughout the second half centered around Gullit and Van Basten, Klinsmann and Matthaeus: Italy's finest.

West Germany's 2−1 victory over the Netherlands, then, was a perfect example of a phenomenon a columnist for the *Economist* would describe on the eve of the championship match, explaining that each national team was nothing more than "a temporary rearrangement of individuals who play most of their football in a world market." The *Economist* commentator was less than sanguine about the changes wrought by the internationalization of the soccer market, charging that because the labor force is mobile, the technology simple, and money abundant, "the players increasingly play against each other in the colours of the richest clubs, all of them in Europe." Thus, "a sameness has come over the game," the columnist asserted.

> Players who play in a dozen of the top clubs learn each others' methods. They train to the same standards of fitness, eat more or less the same food, fake injury in the same melodramatic way. They are coached by like-minded officials, several of whom used to play for the same clubs. If

one experiments with a different playing formation, the others immediately hear about it; if it is any good, they quickly copy it. No wonder this year's World Cup has seen fewer goals per game than any of its 13 predecessors.

The homogenizing effects of the global soccer market, the Europeanization of the game, the sacrifice of native instincts and playing traits to what might be called an international style—these were the culprits, critics believed, behind the demise of Brazil, which earlier this day had suffered an ignominious defeat to Argentina. The three-time champions were already out of the World Cup, and no one was less surprised than the great Pelé, who from the beginning of the tournament had criticized coach Sebastiao Lazaroni's tactics. He charged that Lazaroni's new defensive approach to the game, use of a European-style *libero* or sweeper (a defender who plays behind everyone except the goalkeeper) and devotion to a counterattacking style would never suit Brazilians. Nor was Pelé alone in his condemnation of Lazaroni's "It's better to play badly and win than to play well and lose" approach to soccer. Rob Hughes of the *International Herald Tribune* concluded an open letter to the Brazilian players, in which he reminded them that it was their duty "to elevate the contest to art form," with this warning:

> We are, in short, afraid that Brazil is coming too close to uniformity. We fear that, just like the concrete jungles that demolish architectural national identities, watching Brazil win will become no more, no less of a routine than watching everyone else is.
>
> The fantasy will be smothered, and the joy in your Brazilian expression might, like the rain forests, become an endangered natural resource.

Careca, Brazil's leading scorer in the qualifying matches for the Mondiale, defended his team's evolution from the samba style of soccer that Pelé and others had perfected twenty years earlier to a different beat for the 1990s. "We play the way the *lambada* is danced," he explained. "You start very, very close, almost crushing your partner, then at the right moment, you strike." Unfortunately, it was Maradona who had struck today, waiting until the eightieth minute to show the world, perhaps for the final time, why he had been the best player of the last several years. Taking the ball at midfield, he dribbled down the center—at a full sprint—between two defenders, passed to his left between two more Brazilians, then watched Claudio Caniggia finish with an easy shot. "The only chance Argentina had, they did it," Lazaroni said after the match. "We had the action, but we did not have the goal." Brazil had come close, hitting the post twice, missing open shots, dominating play. But the *jogo bonito,* the beautiful game of another era, was gone.

"Brazil did not deserve to lose," Maradona admitted. But he was quick to add that, contrary to the impression his team had made thus far in the tournament, "Argentina is not dead. When we're alive, we're dangerous. This victory has charged us up."

"I think it will be West Germany–Italy in the finals," Enrico said before we turned in for the night. "I hope it won't be Maradona."

The solution to sameness, according to the *Economist,* was to bring variety into the soccer market. The next day Lisa and I discovered a modicum of that variety in the match between Ireland and Romania. We had to drive to Genoa because of a threatened train strike. ("They think striking is a function of democracy," Jackie had said at breakfast. "They've been good because of the Mondiale. But there's no way that could last.") Leaving early to spend time on the beach, we were disappointed with the overcrowded seaside resort. Couples lay next to one another on the sand like match sticks; the water looked polluted. It was hot, close, irritable weather. In a dirty restaurant along the boardwalk we ordered fruit drinks and pork sandwiches, which were much better than we had expected. By then it was time to walk to the stadium, where I had arranged to meet Francisco Elizalde and his sons, including Paxti, who had played for Ronnie at the University of Vermont. Thanks to Francisco, I would have superb seats through the finals. Here and in Bologna, Milan, Florence, Turin, and Rome, the Elizaldes and I would meet, watch a match together, then go our separate ways. It was as if we were members of a church with a traveling congregation: we only met at soccer matches.

Francisco—or Frank, as he liked to be called—was a short, stocky man with dark hair and a lively wit. Born and raised in Barcelona, where in his words he had been "a mediocre soccer player" until a knee injury ended his career, he now had the misfortune of following his passion, Spanish football, from his home in Manila. "Almost as much of a soccer wasteland as the U.S.!" he said, grinning. He would know: a former president of the Philippines Football Federation and friend of Dr. Havelange, FIFA's head, Frank was privy to the inner workings of the game's hierarchy. Whatever else he might be—an extremely successful businessman, his country's delegate to the International Olympic Committee, and a self-styled "sports nut" whose wife, he said, believed his "mania" was what kept him out of trouble—Frank was a soccer man at heart.

"Some guys too long in sports administration start to look at it in terms of power," he said. "Not me. I don't want to pull strings to sit anywhere but among the real fans."

And that was where we sat, albeit in expensive seats.

Frank had just returned from a brief tour of Manchester, England, where he had inspected possible sites for the 1996 Summer Olympics. The best part of the trip? That his hosts had flown him to Cagliari to see the England–Holland match. "How was that?" I asked.

"Brutto!" he replied with a laugh. "Those hooligans are impossible. Nothing like these happy-go-lucky Irishmen!" He nodded at the thousands of green-shirted Irish fans singing at the tops of their lungs, drowning out their national anthem. "Sounds like a Gaelic war chant," he cried.

"Jesus Christ!" screamed an Irishman behind us, attracting the attention of a middle-aged man twenty rows away, who waved a Mexican flag in our direction. He was wearing a sombrero and a serape with "Mexico" stitched across it, and he was dancing toward the aisle.

"He's an honorary Irishman," Frank explained.

The Romanian national anthem started up, and a hush settled

over the stadium. More than 150 Romanians here for the World Cup had applied for political asylum, citing as their reason for wanting to remain in Italy the recent violence in their homeland—the bloody suppression of dissident protests; the wave of attacks on the part of miners loyal to the National Salvation Front president, Ion Iliescu; threats from the secret police and "closet communists." Fearing retribution in the government's crackdown, these fans had more cause, perhaps, than any others in the Mondiale to welcome their team's advance into the second round. Romania's success on the soccer field prolonged their stay abroad, and maybe even their lives; for many believe they had been allowed to leave their country only because the government did not want them interfering with the crackdown—not, as they had been told, as a reward for their part in the December 1989 overthrow of dictator Nicolae Ceauçescu.

"I have been shot once and I don't want to go back and be shot again," a young man from Bucharest told Reuters, unbuttoning his shirt to display scars from bullet wounds he had sustained in the revolution, a common sight among the asylum seekers.

This contest was a modern example of the 1530 *calcio* match played to halt a battle. During the Ireland–Romania match there would be no fighting in Bucharest or Belfast, and the Romanian fans in Genoa, noticeably silent through the playing of their national anthem, would be safe.

Once the match was under way, the noise picked up on the Irish side, the Romanians numbering only a thousand or so. "What a blow it will be for Italian tourism if Ireland loses," said Frank. "All the Irish fans will go home, and three Romanians will be left—without money and seeking political asylum." A Romanian defender played a long ball back to his goalkeeper, slowing down the action. The Irish fans booed and hissed. "They'll wear you down, these Irishmen," Frank said, "especially in this heat. [Coach] Jackie Charlton's done a good job with this team. They're basically just scrappy players. Not a lot of skill. But he's got them playing more like the English than the English."

Romanian midfielder Gheorghe Hagi, the Maradona of the Carpathians, finished a splendid run with a hard right-footed shot that went just wide. Frank shook his head in admiration. "Such skill," he said reverently. This was a classic confrontation between an old-style, long-ball-playing Celtic side and a modern, skilled, creative Central European team. Frank was betting on the Irish, who in twelve previous World Cup entries had never made it past the qualifying rounds. Having come this far, they were already calling themselves "The Cameroonians of the British Isles." "They can win because they have more heart, more spirit than the Romanians," Frank declared.

I was not so sure. The Irish, it was true, had temporarily put aside their religious and sectarian differences to root for a national team comprised of players from both Northern Ireland and the Republic of Ireland, an aging squad that in the last three years had become one of the better sides in European soccer. Most of the players belonged to the top clubs in England's First Division or Scotland's Premier Division, and this was in all likelihood their last hurrah. Nevertheless, the Romanians had something to play for above and beyond whatever joy and short-lived peace they might offer their countrymen. In the coming months twelve members of this team would enter the global soccer market, earning more than $14 million in transfer fees for the Romanian Football Federation. For the first time in their lives, they had the chance to cash in on their skills. If it was disappointing to play in front of only a handful of their fans, it must also have been exhilarating to know the stands were filled with talent scouts. Hagi, for instance, would cost Real Madrid $4 million to play there next year; his paycheck from the Spanish club would be considerably larger than the one he had received at Steaua Bucharest, the late Ceaușescu's favorite club. Indeed, he was playing this match, in the early going as well as in flashes throughout the night, as if his entire future was on the line.

On one level the Irish were playing for national pride, the Romanians for a way into the new economic order. The political scientist Benjamin Barber argues that the two strongest forces operating in the world today are the globalizing impulses of the free market system versus the reassertion of primal values, which may take the form of nationalism, religious fundamentalism, or tribalism. Italia 90 was a field where these forces met and mingled. No player was immune to nationalistic feelings, nor exempt from the lure of the global market. The writer for the *Economist* believed that variety could offset homogenization, but the problem was deeper than that. How could any indigenous playing style survive the circular action of the market that "knows all about prices but nothing about values," as the Mexican poet and essayist Octavio Paz reminds us? Brazil's samba style of soccer was a value foreign to the international soccer market. Likewise, isolated from European soccer, the Irish (and the English) had managed to hold on to certain tribal values, and perhaps that was what gave them more heart. Yet I could not imagine them defeating a far superior team on spirit alone. The Romanians were too skilled, too stylish, and too poor to let themselves lose, or so I believed.

Frank was the better judge of character, however. Ultimately the match was a lackluster affair, as the heat and humidity took their toll on both sides. The Romanians were unable to use their better skills to counter the tough play of the Irish, who seemed to run down every ball. Irish coach Jackie Charlton was known to some as Saint Jack, as several green and orange banners proclaimed. (There was even a variation on the ubiquitous signs of the religious club from Los Angeles that read Jack 3:16.) Charlton, according to Rob Hughes, had "a simple approach: Stop the other team from playing." And the Gospel of Saint Jack worked. At the end of regulation time there was no score, and thirty minutes of extra time yielded no goals. "Ah, for fuck's sake!" cried the Irishman behind us. The Mexican dancing in the aisle threw his sombrero onto the field.

"Penalties," Frank said.

Now we would see a shoot-out, what Hughes called "that Russian roulette apology for soccer": players from both teams trading penalty shots until one missed and the other scored. The exhausted players lay in a circle at midfield, drinking from water bottles, stretching their cramping legs, summoning the courage to approach the penalty mark. Jackie Charlton walked among his men, shaking their hands or rubbing their heads, letting them decide their shooting order. "If they are confident enough to do it," he said after the match, "they'll select themselves."

The tension mounted. Photographers jockeyed for position behind the goal at the Irish end of the field. The goalkeepers paced
around the penalty area. "I can't watch," Lisa said when the first
Romanian took the ball, carefully set it on the mark, shot—and
scored. She was not alone in her anxiety. In Dublin, Prime Minister
Charles Haughey, conducting an afternoon news conference on the
heels of a European Community summit meeting, abruptly stopped
answering questions to join other heads of state crowded around a
television outside the conference room. Even Saint Jack looked
away, though afterward he claimed he had been monitoring the
action on the video screen above.

One by one, eight players approached the line, and eight scored.
Then Romania's Daniel Timofte, a twenty-three-year-old substitute,
shuffled up to the mark, head down, visibly shaking. "This guy's
green," Frank said. Lisa shut her eyes. The Irish goalkeeper saved
Timofte's weak right-footed shot. When Dubliner David O'Leary, also
a substitute, almost a decade older than his Romanian counterpart
and Ireland's last hope, fired home his shot, the Irish fans started
singing.

"The Romanian was ordered to miss," a Peruvian gentleman
said to Frank, who was reminded of an even more heartbreaking loss
four years ago in the European Cup championship match in Seville.
In that shoot-out Frank's beloved Barcelona had fallen to Steaua
Bucharest, thanks to the goalkeeping heroics of Helmut Ducadam,
who had seemed to know in advance which way the Barcelona
penalty kickers would shoot.

"Why wasn't Ducadam in the goal tonight?" I asked.

"He ran into the Securitate," Frank said. "The torturers. They
ripped his arm out of its socket. That was the end of his career."

O'Leary danced a jig, and the singing went on and on. In Dublin
the prime minister hugged a television reporter, danced his own jig,
and cried, "I am absolutely over the moon!" Charlton told a reporter
he relished this victory even more than the 1966 World Cup championship he had won with England. "I'm delighted for the Irish
people," he said, knowing full well that most of the factories and

offices in Ireland had closed early today so that everyone could watch the match. "There will be a party in this town like you've never seen before," he promised, "and there won't be a moment's trouble." As for Saturday's quarterfinal match in Rome? "We'll start worrying about the Italians," he said, "when we sober up."

Lisa and I left before the party was in full swing, driving down the coast to Chiavari, a village on the Gulf of Genoa. After the heat, crowded beaches, and excitement of the shoot-out, it was fine to stroll along the stone-inlaid walkway next to the sea. It had cooled off, and the emerald water was calm. We found a little restaurant overlooking the sea, took our waiter's advice to order the house special—*frutti di mare* served over the most delicate pasta we had ever tasted—and drank a bottle of wine. We lingered over our cappuccino, imagining what it would be like to live here for the rest of our lives. When our waiter brought us the bill, I asked him about Chiavari, and he stifled a laugh. I looked at Lisa, puzzled. She shrugged. Accenting the wrong syllable of the town's name, the waiter finally explained in broken English, changed the word into slang for "fuck." I felt my face turning red. Although service was included in the bill, I gave him an extra tip. And when we headed back to the car, flushed with good food and wine and high spirits, we had all but forgotten soccer, until we came upon a large crowd spilling out of a bar and over the walkway.

"What is *that?*" said Lisa, pointing at the sea.

Beamed over the jetty, onto the water, was a televised projection of the Italy-Uruguay match; it looked as if the soccer field in Stadio Olimpico was propped on the Ligurian Sea. What a marvelous world! No wonder these fans had such beatific expressions on their faces: Baggio and Schillaci, De Agostini and Beresi, Zenga and Bergomi—all were walking and running on water, at least in Chiavari. This impression was only reinforced by Toto's miraculous goal in the sixty-fifth minute, an astonishing shot at the end of a short run that made Paul Gardner think of "those trick ones that Harlem Globetrotters use, the ones that seem to turn corners and do little dances in mid-air." Aldo Serena added a goal in the eighty-third minute to seal

Italy's 2−0 victory and perhaps secure a place for himself in the sanctifying rites of the Chiavarians. By then Lisa and I were on our way back to Antella. It was a beautiful night to drive.

The next night was another matter.

Enrico, Lisa, and I drove through heavy traffic to Bologna to watch England play Belgium for a spot in the quarterfinals. The peace and pleasure my wife and I had known in Chiavari did not hold for the sleepless residents of Rimini, a coastal resort along the Adriatic Sea, which had become the campsite for four thousand English fans. Early that morning several hundred hooligans had made good on their promise to wreak havoc on the mainland, attacking a group of Italians rejoicing in their country's success. They had rioted in the streets, smashed store windows and cars, fought running battles with the police. By late afternoon some 250 Englishmen had been deported on a chartered plane; extra security forces were called in for the evening's match. The rising tension we felt upon arriving in Bologna was a far cry from the excitement we had known on Italy's opposite coast. Outside the stadium, a brisk walk away from the cathedral whose splendor had supposedly driven Martin Luther to reform the German Church, were hundreds of police in riot gear, clutching automatic weapons. We saw armored cars mounted with machine guns, piles of debris, throngs of loutish English supporters.

"It looks like Berlin just before the war," said Enrico.

We were frisked and searched repeatedly on the way in. Taking our seats among a group of Belgians at midfield, we saw that the English fans were sequestered at one end of the stadium, guarded on both sides by two long lines of policemen, four deep to an aisle: a pair of blue bands bordering a crowd of angry men and women waving Union Jacks. Frank and his sons slumped into their seats beside us. They were upset, not by the Englishmen, though the tension in the air did nothing to lighten their spirits, but by the course of the Mondiale. Already saddened by Brazil's early exit from the tournament, now they were in despair: Spain had just outplayed Yugoslavia in Verona only to lose 2−1 in overtime. They had come straight from their hotel in Bologna where they had watched midfielder Dragan Stojkovic, the Maradona of the Balkans, act like his namesake, complaining and pretending and suddenly striking— twice—for the goals fated to send Spain home. The Elizaldes had never expected their team to lose so soon.

A helicopter flew over the stadium, filming the crowd. "If you've got a police record anywhere in the world," Frank said, "they know where you're sitting. That film goes right into an Interpol computer in a truck outside." The helicopter passed again and again, no more than a hundred feet above the playing ground. Around the columns leading up to Santa Luca, the church on the hill behind the stadium, the lights went on like a golden banner in the distance. In the night sky a sliver of the moon appeared. "First rule of riot control," Frank said, "at the first sign of trouble, use your club!" He wanted to be in Verona, commiserating with his countrymen. He let out a heavy sigh.

The "Wave" began, thousands of spectators raising their arms in sequential fashion, a good-natured, collective motion undulating around the stadium until it reached the English section of the stands, where not a single arm was raised. "In Cagliari," Frank said, nodding at the Englishmen, "they gave the Nazi salute during their national anthem, then drowned out the other one. *Brutto!* My theory is these are the old warriors who used to fight England's colonial wars in Africa and America. Now there aren't any wars for them, so they fight at soccer matches."

Once the game was under way, though, it became clear that he respected the English, brutishness and all. "The Brits are the better side," he declared early on. "So what if seven of them are plumbers and only four have any skills. And if [Steve] Bull comes on, watch out!" he said of the young forward who, according to columnist Stuart Jones, was "useful only as a rampaging substitute sent on belatedly to cause distress among defenders who may be tiring." Frank pointed at the fans draped in Union Jacks. "Bull's just their kind of slob."

Again this was a clash between old and new styles. England was a long-ball, physical team that had modernized its tactics only enough to occasionally employ a sweeper, as if to tip a hat toward the European soccer community. Belgium, on the other hand, was a skilled and clever side that played possession ball, controlling the action at either end of the field; all the Belgians lacked was a world-class goalkeeper to be considered a favorite in the Mondiale. Certainly Enrico, Ronnie, and I had admired the talents of midfielder Enzo Scifo, Belgium's star. In the last few years he had been criticized for selfish play, but he regained his form in time for the World Cup. Rooting for him, I found myself rooting for the Belgians, who dominated play. Forward Jan Ceulemans, making his last international appearance, hit the post in the fourteenth minute, and Scifo hit it in the fiftieth—to no avail.

Five minutes before the end of the first half, England's Gary Lineker, the leading scorer in the 1986 World Cup, centered a ball to John Barnes, a forward with Liverpool, who put it into the net, only to have the goal called back for an offside infraction no one in England saw. A group of Belgian supporters off to our right, relieved by the call, taunted Barnes, who was black, hooting like gorillas, a slur they would use throughout the match.

"Nothing new for Barnes," said Frank. "I'm sure he's heard enough racist trash in England." He looked at the Belgians. "They were the worst colonizers in the world."

"Animals," Enrico agreed. "Stupid!"

Curiously enough, this was the first World Cup match Enrico had ever attended. Everything about it, including the hooligans, Belgian racists, and a flurry of fake falls ("These guys take second only to professional wrestlers for acting skills," Frank said), thrilled him. "I always support the losing team," Enrico said midway through the second half, "so I can see extra time."

Steve Bull came on in the seventy-fifth minute, and play turned rough. When the referee whistled the end of regulation time, granting Enrico his wish for more soccer, a group of English fans started throwing sharpened coins over the heads of the carabinieri guarding them, into the Belgian section of the stands. A small riot broke out. More police arrived, some waving clubs, others leading German shepherds, forming an even wider wall between the English and Belgians, where they stayed until the match was over. Bull had his chance in extra time, but it seemed that England was simply waiting for a shoot-out. Suddenly, with less than a minute to go, England's David Platt, a substitute midfielder, volleyed home a free kick from Paul Gascoigne, thus defeating Belgium. The security forces remained in place. Not until the rest of the stadium was cleared were the English fans herded out to a caravan of orange buses, each escorted to the train station or a campground by a squad car and a van filled with police. Another skilled club was out of Italia 90, and the quarterfinals were set. Delighted to have seen so much soccer, Enrico could not keep his mind on the road. His driving back to Antella was terrifyingly erratic. Lisa and I were grateful to make it home alive.

But even Enrico would grow tired of extra time. Fully half of the matches from the second round to the final were decided in extra time or in a shoot-out. Passionate fans now believed that too many defensive teams afraid to lose were paralyzing the game. The *Economist*'s diagnosis of soccer's ills seemed altogether correct: a sameness of approach in training, coaching, and playing styles led to low-scoring matches that were often frustrating to watch. Perhaps only in Beirut, where during each Mondiale broadcast Lebanon's fifteen-year-old war stopped for a few hours, was extra time universally welcomed. "The World Cup's a godsend," a Christian in East Beirut told one reporter. "We really needed a diversion, even if it's only for a month." For those living among the rival factions, the dearth of goals was probably a blessing, since the quiet only lasted until someone scored—then the militia emptied their automatic weapons at the sky. For others, Italians in particular, the low goal count was becoming a problem as serious as the game-day ban on alcohol sales. The chorus of complaints reached a crescendo on the last day of June when Argentina defeated Yugoslavia in another shoot-out.

The five o'clock Saturday match took place in the heat and haze of Florence. While Lisa was being treated to a four-course meal Enrico's mother had cooked and brought over to Jackie's house, I took my seat next to the Elizaldes, who had just come from their hotel pool. "The Brazilians were packed in the water," Frank said, "still discussing their loss." As the match began he added, "The Brazilian press has demanded an apology from the coach. And they had to whisk the team away from the airport in Brazil because they'd forgotten to line up security. They might have been killed!" He shook his head. "This could have been Spain–Brazil," he sighed, watching Yugoslavia build its attack.

Maradona was nursing a bad ankle, and whenever he touched the ball he had to withstand the close marking of Refik Sabanadzovic, who had once spent three days in a coma after colliding with an opponent, as well as the taunting of the crowd, which had devised a variation on the curse I had heard directed at Fiorentina's ex-owner: "Diego! *Bordello*! *Vaffanculo*!" One of the glories of a rhyme-rich language like Italian, I reflected, was the instant music available to poets and cursers. "That screws up the atmosphere," Frank said, scowling at the screaming fans.

In the thirteenth minute Yugoslav defender Davor Jozic volleyed a cross from Safet Susic over Argentina's net. "He should have just tapped it," Frank muttered. "He was almost close enough to *walk* it in." In soccer circles Yugoslavia had a reputation of being at once cosmopolitan and unpredictable: its players had been among the first from the Eastern Bloc to seek, en masse, their fortunes in the West. Skilled as they were, "Europeanized," too, they did not often cohere into a team, settle their tactics, focus on the match at hand. Yet Pelé believed them capable of upsetting anyone; their victory over Spain was proof of their considerable talents. At the same time, on any given day they could lose to a much weaker team. An astute political observer might have discerned in their inability to draw together signs of their country's impending dissolution, but those changes were a year away. Despite their problems, the Yugoslavs were getting the better of Argentina.

"That's your best offensive weapon," Frank said at the sight of Maradona writhing on the ground near Yugoslavia's penalty area: "Taking the ball and falling in front of the goal!" Acting or not, Maradona was awarded a free kick, and his shadow, Sabanadzovic, was soon booked for delaying the game, lingering by the ball to give his teammates time to set up a wall of defenders. Maradona did not bend his shot hard enough to score around the wall, but moments later he set up two good chances in front of the goal, drawing sighs of admiration from Frank. "That little guy can see in the back of his head," he murmured. "The son of a bitch!"

Sabanadzovic must have been thinking the same thing. Before the match he had said, "Maradona may not be playing the wonderful football he is capable of for 90 minutes at this World Cup. But he can decide a match in one minute, just like he did against Brazil. . . . I will not be able to relax for a second, because that's when he gets you." Now he had let down his guard, and twice Argentina's captain had shown flashes of his former greatness. Sabanadzovic stepped up his pressure only to find, after fouling Maradona in the thirtieth minute, that he had gone too far. His second yellow card became a red card, and when he was sent off the field, Argentina played up a man for the fourth time in the Mondiale. But it could not exploit its advantage, stymied by what Frank called "Yugoslavia's packed defense." No one could get through.

Not that the Argentineans were trying especially hard to score. They were content, even with their numerical edge, to wait for counterattacking opportunities, which the defensive-minded Yugoslavs were not prepared to offer. "A boring game's about to get even more boring," said Frank. "It's a good thing they wouldn't serve us any booze at lunch, or I'd be down for a siesta!" Then: "Argentina's problem is that only a couple of its players are based in Argentina. They should send a video around: this is how your teammates play!" A Yugoslav fan with a bullhorn led the crowd in another round of the *Diego*! *Bordello*! chant, and Maradona smiled.

"I don't know why he's playing so far forward, unless he's hurt or a decoy," said Frank. "But he's not the commander anymore. Flashes, yes. But that's it. And if he's not commanding Argentina, no one will. Yugoslavia could steal a victory." Indeed, just before the first half ended, the Yugoslavs had several chances in front of Argentina's net, two coming off corner kicks, a third from a solid header on goal—the most exciting action yet, besides the spectacle of the police dragging off the youth with the bullhorn. At half time Luciano Pavarotti appeared on the video screen, and Frank remarked, "Best thing so far."

The second half was no better.

"There's only one thing wrong with this game," Frank said. "One of these teams is going to win."

His mood did not improve even when Maradona played a free kick to a teammate, who headed the ball off the post. "Even Argentina's fans are quiet," he said. "I support the eliminator. Save us the trouble of watching this!" And so it went until the referee signaled the end of regulation time. "I started out rooting for Argentina," Frank said, "but now I don't care. The Yugoslavs probably deserve it more. They've played harder." In the opening minutes of extra time Dragan Stojkovic, the Maradona of the Balkans who had wanted to show Argentina's captain that there was room for another star at midfield, created three wonderful scoring chances—a chip just over the post, a half-volley high, and a diving header. "My admiration goes out to these Yugoslavs," said Frank. "They're not supposed to have any balls, but that's not the case today."

In the second fifteen minutes of extra time, however, it was Argentina's turn to attack, though it waited until the last minutes to begin. Maradona received a ball right in front of the net, kicked a weak shot directly at Tomislav Ivkovic, Yugoslavia's goalkeeper, then fell to the pitch, clutching his shin. The crowd hissed at him. His theatrics no longer impressed anyone, not even the referee. Argentine midfielder Jorge Burruchaga chest-trapped a deflected shot and, unlike his Yugoslav counterpart in the first half, literally walked the ball into the net, only to have the referee whistle the goal back. Burruchaga had used his arm to control the ball, or so went the call. It was as if the spell of Maradona's "hand of God" was broken. Argentina's captain ran up to the Yugoslav bench, fist clenched, and both teams emptied onto the field. Spectators screamed at one another, throwing cups and shirts at the players. When order was restored, Maradona took three dangerous corner kicks in a row, each nearly resulting in a goal, just before the final whistle blew.

"Maradona played a lousy game," said Frank, "but he's still so goddamned brilliant! There's only one player of his caliber in the world."

But in the shoot-out, he missed his penalty kick, a chip shot any goalkeeper could have saved. Yet Argentina prevailed. Maradona, leading his teammates on a victory lap around the field, leaped the fence behind Yugoslavia's goal, slipped on a bench he was trying to climb, got back on his feet (without limping), and jogged past the stands, booed every step of the way. He was utterly shameless.

"Those Argentineans are the luckiest people in the world," Frank sighed, "at least in soccer."

The same could not be said of the Irish, legendary guardians of luck. It was true that Jackie Charlton's team had advanced into the quarterfinals without having won a single match. What is more, the pope had blessed Saint Jack's players at the Vatican, and in Stadio Olimpico there were thousands of noisy Irish fans to cheer their countrymen on. Against Italy, though, the luck of the Irish ran out. The Italians moved the ball gracefully around the field, testing their opponents' stalwart defense. Toto Schillaci scored once again, Walter Zenga closed in on English goalkeeper Peter Shilton's World Cup record of 499 consecutive scoreless minutes, and their teammates displayed enough skill and artistry to thoroughly dominate the hardworking Irish. This splendid match helped me forget the heat and boredom of the Argentina–Yugoslavia debacle. Ireland added little in the way of style or brilliance to the game, but soccer fans everywhere were grateful to Saint Jack for having taken his team so far, seemingly on heart alone. That appreciation extended into the political arena. The Irish parliament, it was rumored, planned to grant Charlton a permit to fish any river in Ireland, at any season, for the rest of his life. By the time I boarded a train the next day to travel to Milan for the West Germany–Czechoslovakia match, I had regained hope for the people's game.

Later in the afternoon, on a bus ride from the train station in Milan to the stadium, I overheard a conversation in English between an elderly Italian gentleman and a German youth. "Who will win the World Cup?" said the Italian. "Germany, of course!" said the youth. "The difference between Germany and Italy," said the older man, "is that we hope to win, but you Germans *expect* to win." The young man nodded vigorously. I remembered Jackie's joke about the new order arising out of the European Community: that the artistic Italians would create the laws, the rhetorical French would elaborate on them, and the dutiful Germans would follow them.

"Germany!" the youth repeated.

And why not? That same day the border restrictions between East and West Germany were lifted, and the nation's currency was unified. Germany was, for all intents and purposes, one country again. More than fifty thousand Germans filed into Stadio San Siro, chanting *"Deutschland, Deutschland."* When I caught up with Frank Elizalde and his sons, he said, "We might as well be in Hamburg or Frankfurt." Had we seen the last of the violence that had erupted here on the opening weekend of Italia 90? I wondered. Or had that impulse gone underground? Perhaps for the time being the Germans had other things to think about.

Our seats were in the sun, the heat wave had not abated, and I could understand how the sod on the pitch had dried out and died the week before the Mondiale. The grass had been replanted, but it had yet to establish deep roots. From the first touch of the match clumps of the new turf were pulled up, and soon the field was pocked with divots. Czechoslovakia was booked twice in the opening fifteen minutes, struggling to contain the attacking Germans. Ten minutes later, Juergen Klinsmann beat two Czechs on the left wing, sprinted between two more in the penalty area, and drew a penalty kick, which Lothar Matthaeus slammed home for his fourth goal of the tournament. Although it was the only score of the day, no one complained about overly defensive soccer, for the Germans took seventeen shots, three cleared by Czech defenders standing on their goal line.

"The problem was a misunderstanding between our forwards and their defenders," West German coach Franz Beckenbauer would joke after the match. "Their defenders weren't standing where our forwards had told them to."

If not for those last-gasp saves, Czechoslovakia might have been humiliated in much the same way that it had humbled the United States, and for the same pressurizing reasons. Not until Czech midfielder Lubomir Moravcik was ejected in the sixty-ninth minute did the team from Europe's newest democracy find its form. Czechoslovakia dominated the last twenty minutes of the match, overcoming its numerical disadvantage to create a pair of scoring chances, and still this was not enough to halt what was beginning to look like West Germany's inevitable march to a third World Cup title.

"We haven't seen too many goals," said Frank, who was in a much better mood than yesterday. "The Germans are going to know they've been in a game," he added as we left the stadium. "Those Czechs are tough."

I took a bus to the center of town where I wandered around Piazza del Duomo, in the shadow of the monumental cathedral built over the course of six centuries. I was in the fashion capital of the world; everywhere I looked I saw beautiful women. Less than a month earlier, West German youths had rioted here, rampaging through the streets before and after the match with Yugoslavia, breaking windows, fighting with police, and chanting *"Sieg Heil! Sieg Heil!"* Now all was calm. The hooligans had been jailed or deported, repairs had been made, and tonight the city was at peace. In honor of German reunification I ate bratwurst at an open-air cafe and drank a pint of nonalcoholic beer—all I could get with the game-day ban.

The shadows deepened in the piazza, reminding me of the haunting paintings of Giorgio de Chirico who had lived and exhibited here at various times in his life. "In the involuntary role of incendiary," Félix Labisse once declared, "he was the agent who touched off the explosive charge of Surrealism." I could feel the same energy in the air. In this lull between the death of the old order and the birth of the new, we might witness spectacular changes in the arts and literature, social thought and political discourse—all of which, creative and destructive, would shape our future. I walked back through the piazza, making a silent petition to "the great Solitary of modern painting." Courage and creative fire were what I wanted.

A crowd was gathering outside the train station, a thousand people or more, mainly Africans, waiting for technicians from a local communications firm to finish setting up a hundred-foot square video screen on which a truck equipped with a generator was about to project the Cameroon–England match. On this screen I watched the most exciting game of the Mondiale, another classic confrontation, an old-fashioned Anglo-Saxon team taking on an African version of soccer's future. Only a week before, FIFA's Havelange had decided, on the strength of Cameroon's performance in Italia 90, to add a third African spot to the 1994 World Cup—at Europe's expense, since half of the teams eliminated in the first round were from the Continent. (Of the twenty-four spots available in the draw, by far the majority are reserved for teams from Europe, home to the traditional soccer powers.) The *Economist*'s commentator believed that the game's future lay most probably in a rich country like the United States (which, he admitted, had yet to develop its "own style: elaborate moves with code words, plenty of team huddles and psyching-up, seven-foot players who lurk near the front to head in the goals"). But the crowd outside the train station clearly felt otherwise. These were fierce partisans of Cameroon, and I was in their company.

I loved the Indomitable Lions' skill and athleticism, passion and toughness. I loved the fact that half of Cameroon's team was amateur; defender Bertin Ebwelle, for example, who worked in a bank, had to extend his leave in order to play in this match. No doubt the *Economist* was right in asserting that Cameroon's "best young players will quickly be lured to rich Europe, where they will be moulded into Italian or German ways." That was how "the Invisible Foot," soccer's analogue to the free market's "Invisible Hand," worked. But for now the soccer world could only welcome what these outsiders offered: excitement. Theirs was a style of play that underscored the primary nature of the English kick-and-run. In a contest between the creative and the brutal I would always choose the former.

I had more than aesthetic—and, indeed, sentimental—reasons for cheering on Cameroon. The winner would play West Germany in the semifinals three days hence in Turin, whose residents had not forgotten the Heysel Stadium tragedy, the thirty-six Juventus fans killed in the Liverpool supporters' stampede. "We remember Heysel," read the graffiti in that industrial city. "We are waiting for you hooligans. Juventus comrades, we will avenge you." Turin's mayor, Maria Magnani Noya, was terrified by the prospect of England advancing any further in the tournament. "The events involving hooligans in recent days show the danger linked to the presence of these characters in Turin," she said, urging FIFA to swap the semifinals in Turin for Naples. "The memory of the tragedy of Heysel . . . could aggravate the danger of the hooligans and unleash a mass reaction." But FIFA would not honor such a demand. As Luca di Montezemolo, general manager of Italia 90, explained: "A swap of the semifinals is a non-starter, both because we have unlimited faith in the police and because it would be a sign of senseless surrender." The mayor had less faith than Montezemolo in Italy's security forces, yet she was left with little recourse but to root against England. "Up with Cameroon!" she declared on the eve of the match, a sentiment echoed everywhere.

But Cameroon entered the game at a disadvantage. Four of its players had been suspended for rough play—a handicap, one team official complained, akin "to playing with only one leg." Few soccer observers outside Cameroon disputed the suspensions. In the London *Times* David Miller called the West Africans "both one of the cleverest and the most unscrupulous teams, in terms of unfair tackles." Who could defend their overzealous shoulder charges? This night, however, as Miller later noted, "it was their skill, unfortunately for England, that was the more prominent" of their characteristics on display. England struck first, midway through the half, when David Platt, last-second hero of the victory over Belgium, scored from six yards out on a cross from defender Stuart Pearce. But Cameroon had the run of play. In the opening minutes François Oman Biyick, the Maradona of Africa, broke through England's defense for an unobstructed attempt on Peter Shilton. At forty-two the renowned goalkeeper was the oldest player in the World Cup, and he saved Biyick's hard shot with the agility of a man years younger. Just before the end of the first half Biyick had another chance, breaking into the clear only to lose control of the ball moments after his teammate Thomas Libih had headed a shot barely over the goal. No one at intermission believed England's 1–0 lead would stand.

A taxicab parked under the temporary video screen was suddenly moving toward us. Few had noticed the driver approaching his car, opening the door, revving the engine. Like others, I had turned my attention from the half-time entertainment to the Africans danc-ing around the communications truck, scores of robed men and women swaying in the warm evening air: a swirl of bright colors—red, green, and violet—in the light and glare of the train station, a flowing version of the tableau vivant the costumed figures had cre-ated in *calcio storico.* The cabbie honked his horn, and the crowd slowly parted for him, laughing and slapping the car as it passed. The dancers cheered, pointing at the video screen. For the second half, Cameroon was bringing on Roger Milla, its aging hero who had already scored four goals in Italia 90. The crowd surged forward into the space left by the cab.

Milla immediately put his stamp on the match, dribbling around defender Mark Wright to set up a marvelous scoring chance for Stephen Tataw, which England broke up at the last moment. Seven minutes into the half, Milla received a pass from Biyick in the penalty area—and a clumsy foul from Paul Gascoigne, England's best player. Emmanuel Kunde converted the penalty, and the match was tied, though not for long. Four minutes later, Milla delivered a perfect pass to Eugene Ekeke, who chipped the ball over Shilton's head for Cameroon's second goal. Now almost everyone was dancing under the video screen. A woman in a magenta robe twirled around me. I could not believe my luck.

The Lions truly appeared indomitable, swarming all over the field, sweeping forward for more chances on goal, refusing to play it safe. Milla created another splendid opportunity in the seventy-ninth minute, feeding Biyick in the penalty area, who back-heeled a shot Shilton was fortunate to deflect. The crowd jumped up and down. A drunken Italian tried to pick a fight with an Englishman. The woman in magenta danced between them until the Italian wan-dered away.

Then disaster struck. Cameroon's Benjamin Massing tripped Gary Lineker in the penalty area, a vicious foul that earned Lineker a penalty kick—and the tying goal. For all their attacking, Cameroon had left holes in their defenses. Had they stayed back, protecting their goal, at the end of regulation time they might have been heading for the semifinals.

There was no dancing during extra time, though Cameroon dominated the early going, "putting the English defense under relentless pressure," Paul Gardner wrote, "with smooth, flowing soccer in which forwards, midfielders and defenders were all involved." The crowd around me was tense, silent — with good reason. In the 105th minute, Lineker, dribbling into Cameroon's penalty area, drew a flagrant foul from goalkeeper Thomas N'Kono, who dragged him to the pitch. Lineker's second penalty shot of the night put England ahead to stay, 3 – 2. "England's victory," Gardner declared, "was another example of a World Cup game won by the 'wrong' team, a game lost by the team that had produced by far the better soccer."

Stunned, I trudged into the station, where I gradually realized that I had missed my train. I had been so absorbed in the match that I had lost track of the time. The train to Florence had left nearly an hour before. Now I had to find another way home, which involved sneaking onto a local train in the middle of the night, haggling with a conductor, then alternately standing and squatting in the aisle for the entire trip back to Florence. A small price to pay for soccer at its very best, or so I thought until the loss of sleep caught up with me later in the day.

What depressed me was that the better teams, my favorite teams, kept losing. Scotland, Romania, Brazil, Spain, Yugoslavia, and now Cameroon — all were out of the Mondiale; and England, *brutto* outcast England, which had not reached the semifinals since winning the title in 1966, was in the final four. On the Fourth of July, when I boarded a train for Turin, I was not only sad about the outcome of the World Cup but also frightened. Lisa had left in the morning for England, where she would catch a flight back to the States, and I would not be able to talk to her again until she had completed her travels. Her parting words to me had been: "Do you really think you have to go to this match?" I wondered. The train was filled with drunken Englishmen, skinheads and hooligans swearing and saluting one another Nazi style, trying to pick fights with anyone. I kept my head down, attempting to read the tough-minded poems of Yannis Ritsos. "Verses no longer know what to do in the dry mouth," he had written in a Greek concentration camp in 1953. The words blurred on the page. No one took my ticket. The noise did not let up.

When the train pulled into the station in Turin, riot police were waiting for us, wearing long blue mitts with which to ward off the hooligans' flags and sticks. Helmeted, armed with shotguns, they escorted the Englishmen to special buses that took them directly to the stadium. I walked out into the sunlight and saw thousands of fans milling in the park across the street and almost as many carabinieri. An Italian had just stabbed a German, mistaking him for an Englishman. Tempers flared. Two gangs squared off, taunting one another, their fists and flags raised and shaking. Police rushed in. More carabinieri arrived. An ambulance was on its way. I boarded a tram bound for the stadium.

"They treat us like fucking rubbish!" cried a middle-aged Englishman near the back. He was drunk, wrapped in a soiled Union Jack, and weaving between a pair of young Germans in short pants, who looked like body builders. "Like caged rabbits," he continued. "What a fucking country!"

The tram pulled away from the curb. No Alla Violenza read a sign stretched between two apartment buildings. But it was too late for that. Ten years after the so-called Battle of Turin, a riot in which English fans angered by their country's 1–1 draw with Belgium had wrecked dozens of bars here, and five years after the Heysel Stadium tragedy, Italian *teppisti*—hooligans—were waiting for the English. Last night, wearing scarves in the black and white colors of Juventus to honor those who had died in Brussels, they attacked Englishmen camping in the city, after a futile search of the train station. The night before, a truck driver from York in northern England had been stabbed in the thigh when fifteen Italians had attacked him and two friends for speaking English, according to *La Stampa*. Back in England, in more than a dozen towns from Brighton to Hull, gangs of hooligans celebrating the victory over Cameroon had rampaged through the streets, smashing store windows and cars. *Brutto*.

Halfway to the stadium, stalled for a moment in traffic, the angry Englishman leaned out the window and called to an elderly Italian woman walking down the sidewalk. Catching her attention, he spat in her face. "What fucking rubbish," he muttered. He forced the door open on the other side of the tram and stumbled out into the traffic. No one on the tram said a word.

The new stadium in Turin can hold eighty thousand spectators. Although authorities expected forty thousand Germans and eighteen thousand English supporters to help fill the stands, there were many empty seats because of all the threats. The English and Germans were separated at the gate, and during the playing of their national anthems each side tried to drown out the other. A shame—and a loss, or so Luciano Pavarotti might have said. Asked to judge the anthems of the eight quarterfinalists, he had decided in favor of England and West Germany. "For me, all the anthems are beautiful," he explained. "They still move me emotionally because of the patriotic and lyrical elements, which I still feel when I see the players singing. But musically, the English and German anthems have something extra. Perhaps it's because of their noble origins, or the way they are covered in the dust of ages, but certainly they have a fascination that no other anthem among these eight can boast." I heard none of the music—only the roar.

"They let these guys out of jail just for the game," said Frank Elizalde as he and his sons took their seats, "then put them back until the next one."

The noise from the English section of the stands mounted furiously in the opening minute of the match, when Paul Gascoigne took a corner kick from Chris Waddle and fired a shot from the edge of the penalty area, which German goalkeeper Bobo Illgner dived to deflect. Two more English corners followed. Soon Gascoigne was dribbling circles around German defenders.

"He plays like a bloody Brazilian!" Frank exclaimed.

Indeed, the English players, as Mike Woitalla wrote, "were finally beginning to take to their new game—the modern game with a sweeper in the back, two outside backs to work the wings and three midfielders who rely on short-passing and pace instead of aimless balls in the air." Gascoigne was the centerpiece of England's attempt to ape its European neighbors' style of play. Skilled as he was, however, Gascoigne was only one of eleven English players. His teammates continued to play kick-and-run, and if some of their passes were less "aimless" now, still they were long. Europeanized as English soccer might become, it would nevertheless retain its tribal roots.

The Germans soon found their bearings. Thomas Haessler and Olaf Thon took several long shots, Lothar Matthaeus marked Gascoigne tightly, and the German fans overwhelmed the English partisans with their applause. Juergen Klinsmann fell to his feet near the penalty area, and the referee ignored his plea for a call.

"I think the ref's trying to show him that artistic talent and falling don't go together," Frank said with a laugh. "What I like about these teams is that they play hard, but clean. Unlike the Argentineans. They're the dirtiest players in the world."

Yet for all the fair play, in the thirty-sixth minute West German striker Rudi Voeller, who had been suspended from Sunday's quarterfinal match with Czechoslovakia because of his fight with Holland's Frank Rijkaard, went down with a severe injury to his calf. A standard soccer ritual in this situation is for the team with the ball to play it out of bounds so that the referee can stop the match; after the injured player has been treated, the team awarded the throw-in will play it directly to the other team. In this case a variation was worked on that rite: because Voeller was hurt too badly to return to action and yet did not want to rule out the possibility of playing on, he lay on the sideline where the trainer attended to him, while his teammates played a man down. The crowd chanted, "Rudi! Rudi!" but he was finished for the day. Karlheinz Riedle replaced the speedy striker limping back to the bench, supported by his trainer, and immediately went down with a leg injury of his own, though he recovered enough to keep playing.

"England's defense is too strong," Frank said just before the half. "Germany can't get it in."

The match was still scoreless when the half-time entertainment began. Teenager Alfred Ryngol, the world-record holder for ball juggling (he had once kept a soccer ball in the air for more than two hundred hours straight), walked up and down the field in a casual manner, juggling the ball from foot to foot, removing one article of clothing after another: a juggling striptease that ended with Ryngol in his underwear, taking a feeble shot on goal. I thought of the concluding lines of my poem "A Boy Juggling a Soccer Ball." The boy juggles the ball in a variety of ways, then loses control of it:

> He wheels around, he marches
> over the ball, as if it were a rock
>   he'd stumbled into, and pressing
> his left foot against it, he pushes it
>   against the inside of his right
> until it pops into the air, is heeled
>   over his head—the rainbow!—
> and settles on his extended thigh before
>   rolling over his knee and down
> his shin, so he can juggle it again
>   from his left foot to his right foot
> —and right foot to left foot to thigh—
>   as he wanders, on the last day
> of summer, around the empty field.

The boy in my poem is a figure for the budding writer who, like Alfred Ryngol, will one day perform stripteases, though his will take place on the page. What an artist reveals, in his casual yet studied removal of all the masks he creates and wears, is nothing less than his vision of what it means to live at a particular moment in history. He hopes to be at once entertaining and profound, bringing his anxiety, dreams, and pleasure to light in such a way that his readers will discover their darkest questions articulated in an original and engaging fashion. Ryngol dribbled the ball clumsily out of the net, demonstrating that he could not actually play the game. He was an artist, not an athlete: all touch and little soccer experience. He flicked the ball back into the air and juggled his way upfield, collecting his clothes. When he was dressed again, he wandered off into the night, heading the ball "from side to side, softer and softer, / like the fading refrain / on an old 45." I felt as if I knew him in my bones.

"The problem with soccer today," Frank was saying, "is that defense has passed offense. The defensive players are too big, too strong, too fast. It's almost physically impossible to score."

But five minutes into the second half, West Germany was on the scoreboard. Defender Andreas Brehme took a free kick from twenty-two yards, which deflected off an onrushing English player, wobbled over Peter Shilton's head, and slowly bounced into the goal.

"That's the only way anybody's going to score tonight," Frank cried above the din of the crowd. "Poor Peter Shilton. What a freak goal!"

Shilton paced in front of his net, shouting at himself and at his teammates. Making his next-to-last international appearance, the legendary goalkeeper looked as if he might punch a goal post or do a hundred push-ups. His anger was a tonic. England had the run of play in the second half. Ten minutes from the end of regulation time, Gary Lineker took advantage of a mistake in the West German defense, converting a simple cross from Paul Parker into a goal from eleven yards out, which tied the match and sent it into extra time. Outnumbered by more than six to one, the five thousand or so English fans made as much noise as their German brethren had after Brehme's goal.

In London's Wembley Stadium, where the Rolling Stones were playing their first concert in eight years on their home turf, Mick Jagger was thrown off his stride in the middle of the group's current hit, "Almost Hear You Sigh," when the crowd suddenly cheered Lineker's goal, waving their transistor radios at the musicians. Presumably the rest of the country was celebrating, too, including the Labour MPs, whose "patriotic duty," according to deputy leader Roy Hattersley, was to "be in front of TV sets shouting their heads off." Even Queen Elizabeth was watching the match, and Princess Di, attending a classical concert, was kept informed of the score. Lineker's goal was a national event.

The thirty extra minutes of soccer were among the most exciting in the Mondiale. First, a Klinsmann header off a cross from Brehme drew from Shilton a miraculous save. Then Klinsmann shot point-blank—wide. Chris Waddle hit the German post. Guido Buchwald countered with a shot off the English post. And so it went. "It doesn't get any better than this," Frank said. "Historic. Up and down. Lots of opportunities. A great game." Its most stirring moment came when Gascoigne, who had emerged as the best young player in the tournament, was booked for rough play. His second yellow card of the tournament, which meant that he would be suspended for the next match, whether it was the championship or consolation game, left him in tears. He was crying again when time ran out.

"Both teams deserve to win this match," Frank said.

But in the shoot-out West Germany was the better side, knocking home all four of its penalties; though Shilton correctly guessed the direction of each kick, he could not stop them. England's Stuart Pearce and Chris Waddle missed their penalties, making the fifth round unnecessary. The new Germany advanced into the World Cup final.

Bobby Robson, England's coach, had nothing good to say about deciding the match in a shoot-out. "Play on," he told reporters, urging sudden-death overtime in place of penalties. "Eventually someone will crack. Football is a game of endurance and fighting spirit." He had a point. England might well have won this match had it been fought to the end. Many soccer observers contend that sudden-death offers the best solution to overly defensive matches, since it is in the interest of both teams to score rather than play on and on. No doubt tonight the English fans would have welcomed a change from the shoot-out format. Not permitted to leave the stadium until the other spectators were gone, they sang for their team, cheering Pearce and Waddle, Shilton and Gascoigne, Parker and Steve Bull, and all the others who had helped redeem English soccer.

I hurried out of the stadium, boarded the wrong bus, and promptly found myself wandering around Turin. I fell in with a young Canadian in the same predicament, who was equally nervous about being mistaken for an Englishman. We walked through the streets of the industrial city, Fiat's home, afraid to ask directions, afraid to stumble blindly on. We heard firecrackers—or was that gunfire? Even as we tried one side street after another, joking to keep our spirits up, mobs were forming all over England, spilling out of pubs to smash windows and cars, especially those of German make. More than six hundred people were arrested, millions of dollars of damage done, and at least three people killed. In Brighton, outside a nightclub, fifty teenagers from Italy and Scandinavia were pelted with bricks and police cones. Missiles smashed through two windows of a German bus carrying a girls' choir in Hemel Hempstead. There were riots everywhere. It was as if the entire country turned on itself. I walked through Turin's dark streets, hoping that I would not run into Italian hooligans determined to take out the same kinds of resentment and revenge on someone who looked and talked like an Englishman.

"How much Italian do you know?" asked the Canadian.

"Not enough to fool anyone," I answered. "You?"

He shook his head and let out a nervous laugh.

In the end we mustered the courage to ask a group of Italian youths how to get to the train station. There we heard more firecrackers, more cursing from English fans, more threats. I boarded the right train, which was filled with skinheads, hooligans bearing Chelsea FC tattoos on their arms and lips, drunken young men chanting Nazi slogans. I headed for the dining car, where at this hour I could get only a sandwich and a soda. Here two hooligans harassed a young man dressed in the black and white colors of West Germany. "I'm Austrian," protested the young man, backing out of the car. "Not German!" One of the hooligans followed him out, and I was left with the other, waiting for an attendant to arrive. He seemed as uncomfortable as I was, shifting his weight from foot to foot, coughing nervously. "Well, we're out of the Cup," he said suddenly, "but we'll fucking well win it next time." I did not say anything. He grew more nervous, fidgeting and cracking his knuckles. "We'll fucking well win it next time," he repeated, then abruptly stalked out of the car, muttering, "What a country. What a *fucking* country." Without his friends, his gang, he was terrified, and I could almost feel sorry for him. The train sped toward Genoa. The attendant was nowhere in sight, but I was willing to wait. I was that hungry.

9

. . . .

CONSOLATION PRIZES

*J*ackie's neighbors were hosting a wedding reception for their son and daughter-in-law, and we were invited. Late Saturday afternoon, Enrico, Jackie, Federico, and I wandered over to the neighbor's house, where a small crowd was gathering in the backyard. It was hot, and the drought had turned the grass brown, though in the shade where the tables were set up there was a cooling breeze. As bottles of Chianti and mineral water appeared, and dishes of food were laid out on the tables, the men in formal attire removed their coats and rolled up their sleeves. Three older women praised the view of the valley and olive trees, and children darted in and out of the house. Most of the guests, Jackie told me, were from Florence. Shunned for his work in the Resistance, the neighbor, an architect, had few friends in Antella, and the newlyweds seemed to have little connection to the village, nor had they invited many of their own friends. We might have been at a simple family get-together.

The bride and groom were in their early thirties. She had once been pretty, Jackie assured me, but it was already clear that she would not age gracefully; bags were forming under her eyes, and her pleasantly plump figure was on the brink of giving way to obesity. He was nondescript, memorable only insofar as he appeared grateful to be marrying at all. There was something desperate about this pairing, as if the guests drifting toward the tables considered the bride and groom fortunate at this late date to have found each other, the first several choices on either side having long ago married others. We sat down to eat bread, cheese, cold cuts *in gelatina* (in aspic), and cold salads—pasta, shrimp, and potato. The men kept checking the time. Wine flowed. This reception was as much a pragmatic statement as a celebration of union. The marriage would not last.

There was another reason for the somber mood. The architect, it was true, had had to learn to live among his enemies (I never did find out what had become of his wife), and his son's nuptials were probably less than ideal. But what was of most pressing concern, even at this reception, was the fact that in the following night's World Cup championship match Italy would not be represented. The moment of Italian soccer was passing. Later this evening the *Azzurri* would play England in the consolation match in Bari. A victory, and thus a third-place finish in Italia 90, would not salve the pain. Italy's loss to Argentina in the semifinal was a national disgrace. Italians everywhere were in mourning.

It was as if a spell had broken. A general strike was planned for the middle of the week (the day I was supposed to fly home), the government was expected to fall ("That won't even make the headlines," Jackie said), and now people went about their daily tasks without the sense of possibility that for the last month had reigned over the nation. The dream of Italy at the height of its soccer glory meeting West Germany in the midst of reunification, of the old Axis alignment rehabilitated and restored to the international community, had dissolved in the face of Argentina's surprising win in Naples, a match that had at the same time divided Italians along ancient ethnic lines and united them in grief.

"Fucking Maradona!" Enrico muttered, and everyone at our table nodded.

That had become his favorite expression, replacing "Stupid!" as his catchall phrase for the world's ills. He had finally quit smoking, and now he focused his pent-up agitation on Argentina's captain. Nor was he alone in his feelings. In the last week Maradona had managed to alienate even staunch supporters. His mistake? He had tried to pit Neapolitans against northern Italians, tried to exploit for his own ends

Italy's bitter north–south rivalry by urging Napoli's fans to root for him and Argentina instead of for their countrymen who, he insisted (and not without justification), looked down on them.

"After so much racism, only now they scurry to remember that Naples is part of Italy," he said in an interview. "Now that they have slapped the Neapolitans in every possible way, someone tells them they are Italians, that only Italy counts. It is incredible, absurd, offensive."

His comments infuriated millions of Italians. The mayor of Naples, Pietro Lezzi, welcoming the semifinal match awarded to his city, said, "Maradona is a famous and great soccer champion but this time he has gone too far with opportunist statements, showing that he does not understand the difficulties of our country." Toto Schillaci, who had endured his share of insults in the north and whose four goals in Italia 90 had brought his countrymen together in a celebration of his new heroic status, was even more emphatic: "It is not true that Maradona's city is discriminated against by the rest of Italy," he said. "The fans have no need to support him." What is more, he went on to declare, "The insults have ended. I have dragged to my side the people who have opposed me the most. . . . Italy is finally reunited."

Reunited, perhaps, in its antipathy toward Maradona, whose brilliance on the soccer field would no longer excuse his behavior. In addition to the rumors of his drug use, visits to prostitutes, and Mafia connections, now there were stories of late-night sprees during the Mondiale in Rome and elsewhere. The recent scuffle he and his relatives had started with security police over his younger brother's driving without a license only fueled the public's anger. Now his injuries, real and imagined, like his long periods of lethargic play, irritated more spectators than not. That he had spearheaded Argentina's victory over Italy worsened matters, in the same way that he touched a sensitive Italian nerve with his pleas for Neapolitan support.

"It is horrible to discover that there is so much racism in Italy against the Neapolitans," he argued, "racism that my own national team has suffered when it played in the north."

He was right, of course, which only deepened Italy's shame. No one wanted to hear that from the player most responsible for the country's exit from the World Cup. Schillaci's dream of Italian reunification would, on closer inspection, prove as illusionary as Germany's: legal terms and political decrees are no substitute for shared spiritual, cultural, aesthetic, and tribal values. Maradona had blundered onto a truth painful for Italians to face.

Worst of all, he had humiliated the *Azzurri,* who should never have lost in Naples. It was the first time in the Mondiale that they had played away from their home turf in Rome, and they started out well enough. Schillaci scored his fifth goal of the tournament in the eighteenth minute, slotting home a rebound off a volley from Vialli, who had inexplicably replaced Baggio in the starting lineup. Argentina had lost to Italy in each of its last four meetings; most observers believed the defending champions would not have it in them to overcome any lead, and in the first half Italy seemed to be on its way to the final. Maradona's only inspired moment—with his back to the goal, poised at the edge of the penalty area, he juggled the ball up onto his right thigh, spun around, and volleyed it with his left foot —resulted in an easy save for Walter Zenga.

The Italians lost their nerve in the second half, however, abandoning their stylish runs on and off the ball in favor of a defensive, tentative approach. Their passing game unraveled, Maradona ruled the midfield, and minutes after Zenga eclipsed Peter Shilton's World Cup shutout record, the heretofore unflappable Italian goalkeeper made several mistakes in a row, the last of which—coming off his line without his usual authority—ended in Claudio Caniggia's heading home a cross from Maradona. The match was tied. Argentina had the run of play through extra time, helped in part by late injuries to Schillaci and defender Riccardo Ferri, who could not be replaced since Italy had already used its two substitutes. In the shoot-out Maradona scored the winning goal. The entire country collapsed. "Unfortunately for us," Vialli said after the match, "the dream has vanished."

"Zenga lost his center," the woman seated next to me at the reception was now saying. She was a Rolfer who had just returned from a massage seminar in Munich, and she thought the goalkeeper's mysterious breakdown had been fated. "He lost his center," she repeated. "It happens to all Italians. We're so emotional. Italy's so artistic," she added, "and so stupid."

"Who will win the consolation match?" I asked.

"England," she said matter-of-factly.

Everyone at the table agreed.

"What?" I said. "Won't Italy win?"

"No," Enrico interjected. "No way."

"Why?" I said.

He leaned back in his chair and sighed heavily. "Because they do not want to end in beauty," he explained.

"But why?" I persisted.

"Because they're shit," he muttered. "Their coach said they shouldn't even play this match!"

The timing for the reception could not have been worse. Who would ever have imagined that the *Azzurri* would have to play a consolation match? This night was supposed to be given over to celebrating Italy's impending, and unprecedented, fourth World Cup championship. But like the wedding, which had a consolatory air about it, and like the furtive, disorganized fireworks Antella's Communist party was setting off every night in honor of Communist Party Month in Italy, commemorating little more than the movement's demise, the *Azzurri* had to settle for the consolation match. They were playing for what was left of their honor.

No doubt Madonna was disappointed by this turn of events. The American singer had planned to attend the final if Italy made it that far. Her consolation prize? Roberto Baggio's jersey, which she wanted to wear during her current world tour. She had invited the Italian players (as well as the pope, according to Enrico) to her concert three days hence in Rome; the national strike would probably keep them from attending.

Yes, the timing was terrible. The reception ended suddenly, thirty minutes before the match. No one would admit that they were heading home to watch Italy play England, but Jackie assured me that despite their professed indifference to soccer now, none of these guests would miss any of the action. Even the bride and groom would not leave for their honeymoon until after the game.

We returned to Jackie's and Enrico's house to watch our last match together. It was a sad evening all around, not least because in the morning I would leave for Rome. My Italian dream was ending. So much had happened! The grass along the fence had sprouted in patches, thick tufts of green surrounded by hard-packed dirt; our battle with the ants had been declared a draw. The cisterns were at last in place—unsightly, leaking, and unable to collect water from the roof. Because the truckload of water delivered the other day had not been clean, we were back to boiling water before drinking it. Jackie was angry enough to sue the neighbors who had disrupted their spring, another sign that she was on the mend. In the fall she would give birth to a healthy baby girl, and the next time we met she would be fitter than she had been in years. Enrico would also look well, his law practice flourishing with new business generated by the European Community. Federico would be on his way to preschool. The world was about to change in dramatic fashion; our lives would be affected in ways we could not imagine.

Change was in the offing in the soccer community, too. Ronnie would keep winning at the University of Vermont, and Roy Hodgson would become the coach of Switzerland's national team. A number of American players would sign with European clubs, traveling abroad to gain the match experience necessary for their development. The most inspiring innocent abroad story would center around John Harkes, who in a year would become the first American to play in a cup final in London's fabled Wembley Stadium. A starting midfielder for Sheffield Wednesday, which in the championship match of the Rumbelows League Cup would pull off a stunning 1–0 upset of powerhouse Manchester United, Harkes would soon find glory in England's First Division. His would not be our only success story: Paul Caligiuri in Germany, John Doyle in Sweden, Tab Ramos and Peter Vermes in Spain—all would more than hold their own abroad, offering hope for America's soccer future.

Likewise, a turnover in leadership at the USSF would usher in sweeping changes in the national program. Bob Gansler would step aside as head coach, though not, as the rumor mill had suggested, in favor of Franz Beckenbauer. West Germany's coach would leave his national team to assume the reins of Marseilles, which would become one of Europe's top clubs. Instead, responsibility for shaping the Americans into viable contenders would fall to Veilbor ("Bora") Milutinovic, the former Yugoslav star who had orchestrated Costa Rica's triumphs in the Mondiale. Hugo Perez would rejoin the team; within a year the United States would win its first major tournament, the CONCACAF Gold Cup Final, defeating Trinidad & Tobago, Guatemala, Costa Rica, Mexico, and Honduras. Soccer would show signs of prospering in our country, despite the continuing absence of a genuine professional league. On its way to winning the 1992 Women's World Cup Championship the U.S. team, for example, would defeat Haiti 49–0—a score even an American-style football team would envy.

Meanwhile, Italy's First Division would still hold sway, though soccer's angel would grow impatient with traditional powers like AC Milan and Napoli, and threaten to migrate to Marseilles and elsewhere. Unaccountably, UEFA would readmit English clubs to European competition, "the relative good behavior of the English fans at the World Cup in Italy" cited as a reason for lifting the five-year ban. In an effort to boost scoring, the offside rule would change: "even is on," as the saying would go—that is, to be on side a player would now only have to be even with the next-to-last defender. The rule change would be welcomed throughout the international soccer community, which would turn its attention to the United States, where preparations were already under way for the 1994 World Cup. And Tom Landry's lobbying efforts would pay off: Dallas would be one of nine venues selected for the tournament. The sites would also include Detroit's Silverdome; for the first time in the World Cup, matches would be played indoors.

But that was all in the future when we sat down to watch Italy play England. Although Enrico believed this match would only deepen his despair, he was soon proved wrong. It was, as Italian coach Azeglio Vicini would later say, "one of the greatest third-place play-offs" in World Cup history. Hard-fought, clean, skilled, it was a match full of scoring opportunities, creative play, and passion. The pressure was off the *Azzurri,* and they responded in a free, imaginative spirit. Much of the excitement was provided by Schillaci, who at the outset was tied with Czechoslovakia's Thomas Skuhravy for the Mondiale scoring lead. Determined to conclude his Italia 90 story with another goal, in the first half Toto had several chances to win the scoring title, once missing a rebound right in front of the net. Each of his shots sent Enrico to his feet, pleading with the television set for "a little luck."

None was forthcoming, presaging perhaps Toto's infamous scoring drought next season. Italy's new hero would go without a goal for more than a hundred days in the following year, and the bigots he had silenced during the World Cup would start insulting him again. Indeed, in two years the Lombardy League, a political party advocating northern Italy's secession from the south, would replace the Italian Communist party as the voice of the future. The bridge that Schillaci had built between the rival factions of his country would crumble.

Now he was in his element, and though he did not score before intermission, twenty-five minutes into the second half he helped Robert Baggio exploit what one reporter called "the worst mistake of [Peter Shilton's] twenty-year career with the national team." Clearing a back pass, the English goalkeeper had not noticed Baggio behind him, and the Italian striker easily stole the ball from him, worked a one-two with Schillaci, and scored. It was an unhappy turn of events for Shilton, who was making his last international appearance. But the consequences of his error were obviated ten minutes later when David Platt tied the match with a brilliant header. Almost no noise came from England's end of the stadium; all but a handful of the team's supporters had gone home. Four minutes before the final whistle, Enrico got his wish. Schillaci was awarded a penalty kick, though my friend insisted that he had not seen any foul. Toto rarely took penalty shots, but there was no question that he would take this one. Soon he had his scoring title, and Italy had salvaged a measure of its honor. Gary Lineker, the scoring leader in the 1986 World Cup, hugged Schillaci. Italian and Englishmen exchanged flags. The *Az-*

zurri circled the field to the chant of "Champions! Champions!" throwing flowers to their fifty thousand delighted fans. Italy had ended in beauty after all.

There was more bad timing that night, and more beauty; during the consolation match, three of the world's greatest tenors, José Carreras, Plácido Domingo, and Luciano Pavarotti, joined an orchestra under the direction of Zubin Mehta for a concert in the Baths of Caracalla, a marvelous set of ruins dating back to the third century. Under a full moon, they presented a program of arias, songs, and medleys of popular tunes, as if to remind the audience of six thousand (including dignitaries such as Henry Kissinger), the billion viewers in thirty countries watching a live telecast of the concert, and the millions more who would purchase CDs and videos made there (the authorities, against all odds, had diverted all air and automobile traffic from the area) that Italy had more than one way to "end in beauty."

"This was a real opera world championship to set beside the soccer championships," said Carlo Fusagni, director of the state-run television network that broadcast the concert.

His comparison was apt. Soccer's drama, passion, pageantry, brilliance, orchestrated movements, and excitement bear more than a passing likeness to opera. In the Baths there was even room for the improvisational moment integral to soccer. After one encore, the tenors decided to sing another, an ensemble version of "Nessun dorma," the indescribably moving climax of Puccini's *Turandot,* an aria that always seems too short. Pavarotti had already sung it once (it was, in fact, his current hit on the charts), but now they would do it again, to everyone's delight. Mehta could not make himself heard above the crowd's applause, so he had to signal to the orchestra what piece they would play, tilting his head into his clasped hands, miming a person falling asleep. The crowd and the musicians smiled and laughed. The tenors quickly pointed to one another, determining on the spur of the moment who would sing which parts; even as Pavarotti sang the penultimate phrases, Carreras and Domingo were rapidly determining how to bring off the final notes. It was pure improvisation, and when the singers blended their voices in the end, repeating *"Vincero! Vincero!"* until the music died, it was not unlike three soccer players working a series of passes, a combination of moves that results in a goal. It was all too brief, and beautiful. *Depart, oh night! Set, stars! Set, stars! At dawn I shall win! I shall win! I shall win!*

In the morning I bid farewell to Jackie, Enrico, and Federico, then boarded a train to Rome, the first stage of my journey back to the States. My life was also about to change. By winter Lisa and I would be living in New Orleans, where she would be a member of the symphony; the first concert I would hear her play in that dark city would be Puccini's opera *La Bohème.* In the Orpheum Theater I would recall that Walt Whitman, father of American poetry, had found his poetic voice in New Orleans, inspired by opera, belly dancers, and the netherworld of the French Quarter. His work, a testament to gusto, would guide me through my experience of Louisiana and beyond. "I am the teacher of athletes," he wrote in *Song of Myself,* the originating poem in our tradition. "He that by me spreads a wider breast than my own proves the width of my own, / He most honors my style who learns under it to destroy the teacher." Soon it would be time for me to honor his teaching in the only way I knew—writing poetry.

This was all in the future when, the afternoon of July 8, I took my seat between Frank Elizalde and a West German couple who had paid scalpers more than $500 apiece for tickets. I had never heard such waves of sound, which grew and rippled and washed over the stands. The Argentinean players were nowhere to be seen when their national anthem began. "It could be a ploy," Frank said above the noise. "They'll do anything to unsettle their opponents. They did this in Argentina to upset the Dutch. The referee should give them two minutes, then call it a forfeit. Here they come."

At the sight of them the German fans drowned out their opponents' anthem. "This is not nice," said the German woman next to me.

"This kind of stuff makes you root for the underdog," Frank added, shaking his head, "even when the underdog is dog crap! That's poor sportsmanship on the part of the German fans."

Down on the field, during the coin toss, the referee, as he would later report, was saying to Maradona, "Diego, be calm. Great men, aces, have to overcome these things. Quality must dominate."

But quality was far from the Argentinean captain's mind. Four of his teammates had been suspended for this match, including Claudio Caniggia, who had scored the tying goal against Italy. In the words of Rob Hughes, Dr. Carlos Bilardo, Argentina's coach, had decided that "winning ugly" was his team's only hope. He had "sold out his principles trying to retain the World Cup at all costs," though it was true that for this coach those principles of skilled, fair play were a relatively recent acquisition. "Winning ugly is even deeper rooted in Bilardo's history," Hughes explained in the *International Herald Tribune.* "He played on the infamous Estudiantes de Plata side of the 1960s which was so systematic in its thuggery that European teams refused to meet it on the field."

Nevertheless, Bilardo, a gynecologist the rest of the year, had more recently become a spokesman for reason, presumably because of his medical training. Until, that is, Maradona and "the interfering president" of Argentina, Carlos Saúl Menem, had begun to usurp the coach's authority. They dictated personnel decisions, abused their privileges, pressured Bilardo to do anything necessary to bring the World Cup back to Buenos Aires. Thus from the opening minutes of the final it was clear that this would be a violent affair. As soon as a German touched the ball, he was hacked to the ground. Still it was Beckenbauer's side that dominated play. Argentina kept up its record pace of committing a foul every three minutes (also leading the tournament with twenty-four cautions overall). Yet it was Maradona, as Frank pointed out, who did all the complaining.

"Brutto," he muttered.

We were watching the end of Maradona's reign as King of Soccer. No doubt he had been fouled too often to ever regain his top physical form, and he was aging visibly on the field. He had already said this would be his last World Cup. What he did not know was how precious little time he had left. Within a year the man who had scored more goals in the Italian League than any foreign player in history would twice test positive for cocaine use. He would be implicated in a Naples drug and prostitution ring connected to the Mafia, have his passport seized (though the diplomatic passport Argentine President Menem had presented him as "a sporting ambassador" entitled him to diplomatic immunity and would allow him to flee), and then be banned from the game both by the Italian League and FIFA. Returning to Buenos Aires, where his ambassadorship would be revoked, he would be arrested for possession of cocaine. After he was released on $20,000 bail, his commercial endorsement contracts would be canceled or renegotiated; offers to play out his career in Japan for a fabulous sum of money would dry up; and his name and reputation would be tarnished beyond repair. Despite his many enemies, Maradona's downfall, at once swift and complete, would sadden millions of soccer fans.

What a difference four years made. In the last World Cup, Maradona had ruled the field against West Germany. Now the tables were turned. Argentina's captain took his country's only shot —a free kick that floated harmlessly over the goal. West Germany countered with sixteen shots, several nearly resulting in goals. "The gods are against us!" cried the German woman next to me after Brehme fed the ball to Klinsmann who was streaking into the penalty area, where the striker's shot was saved. But I doubted if she, or indeed anyone else in the stadium, believed that West Germany would lose. It was only a matter of time before one of Germany's chances turned into a goal—a Voeller run; Matthaeus stripping the ball from an Argentine at midfield, then dribbling brilliantly down the field; a free kick from Brehme; a diving header from Thomas Berthold.

"The trouble is the Argentineans play such a defensive game," said Frank. "If you beat one man, there's always another one right there. What they're waiting for is the counterattack. One a game is all they need. Patience. Ugly."

But Maradona and his teammates had no counterattacking opportunities in the first half, and at the start of the second Frank said, "They're realists, the Argentineans. They can't keep up with Germany. But if Germany scores, they'll have to open it up and play. I still think Germany will squeeze by," he added. "Maybe they'll call a penalty or something. The referee will never let this match go to a shoot-out."

In the opening minutes of the half the Germans had a flurry of shots on goal, any one of which might have gone in. Maradona's response? He fell to the ground faking an injury, drawing jeers and hisses from the crowd, giving his teammates a breather. Argentina adopted an even rougher approach. Less than twenty minutes after entering the match, Pedro Monzon became the first player ever expelled from a World Cup final, issued a red card for cleating Klinsmann. The foul gave the referee a chance to reassert his authority. Three minutes before the end of the match, Monzon's teammate Gustavo Dezotti was sent off as well for tackling Juergen Kohler. *Brutto.*

"A game like this justifies what a lot of Americans say about soccer," Frank sighed. "Much ado about nothing. This is the lousiest final I've ever seen."

The hacking continued unabated. Finally, in the eighty-fourth minute, Matthaeus took control of the ball at midfield and passed it to Voeller, who collided with Roberto Sensini in the penalty area, sprawled on the ground, and was awarded a penalty. Argentina's players ranted at the referee, drawing another yellow card. Frank was inclined to agree with their protests. "In my humble opinion, that was not a penalty," he said. "Voeller didn't have control of the ball. He was to the side." When Brehme converted the penalty, raising the noise level to a pitch only heavy metal rock bands or jet aircraft ever approach, Frank said, "I think the referee was looking for a penalty. He'd had enough of their shenanigans. Gamesmanship eventually backfires on you."

"Argentina didn't play," said the German woman as time ran out. "They made it a war."

"Tomorrow you'll read that Argentineans attacked the Mexican Embassy in Buenos Aires and tried to burn it down—anything to get back at the Mexican referee," said Frank, pointing at Maradona and his teammates circling the man in black. They screamed at him and waved their fists. Smoke bombs and debris landed on the field. The crowd cheered on and on.

"In the final analysis," Frank said, "Argentina screwed it up from the beginning to the end. Losing to Cameroon, then beating all the good teams—Brazil, Yugoslavia, Italy. And now this. That's luck and chance for you."

Luck and chance are integral parts of soccer, however, and I was grateful to have seen this final, marred though it had been by Argentina's refusal to abide by the spirit of fair play. Frank seemed to feel the same. "Look at Beckenbauer," he said, changing the subject. "He's a hero now. An hour ago, when his team couldn't put the ball in the net, he wasn't very popular in Germany. Now he could run for president!"

The awards ceremony began with women in white dresses marching onto the field with models of the Colosseum, the Forum, and other ruins propped on their heads. Thousands of spectators chanted, *"Italia! Italia!"* The Argentine fans rustled up a drum to beat in a funereal fashion. Smoke filled the stadium. The noise went on and on and on. Soon the German players would run their victory lap; Rome's streets would fill with honking cars and flag-waving fans. In reunified Germany men and women would dance and drink and sing until dawn. On the scoreboard was a simple message: CIAO USA! The World Cup was over, but there was time for one more revelation. A camera focused on Maradona, and on the video screen at the far end of the stadium we could see him crying. Suddenly the cheering of thousands turned into a clamor of boos, hisses, and laughter.

"The cruelty of the Germans," Frank said as we started for the gate, "knows no bounds."

• • • • • • •
SELECT
BIBLIOGRAPHY

Alison, M. *Soccer for Thinkers.* London: Pelham Books, 1967.

Batty, Eric G. *Coaching Modern Soccer.* London: Faber and Faber, 1980.

Bradley, Gordon, and Clive Toye. *Playing Soccer the Professional Way.* New York: Harper & Row, 1973.

Buford, Bill. *Among the Thugs.* New York: W. W. Norton & Company, 1992.

Caillois, Roger. *Man, Play and Games.* New York: Free Press, 1961.

Elias, Norbert, and Eric Dunning. *Quest for Excitement: Sport and Leisure in the Civilizing Process.* Oxford and New York: Basil Blackwell, 1986.

Fralick, Samuel. *Soccer.* New York: A. S. Barnes & Company, 1945.

Glanville, Brian. *A Book of Soccer.* New York: Oxford University Press, 1979.

Henshaw, Richard. *The Encyclopedia of World Soccer.* Washington, D.C.: New Republic Books, 1979.

Hill, Dave. *'Out of His Skin': The John Barnes Phenomenon.* London and Boston: Faber and Faber, 1989.

Hollander, Zandler, ed. *The American Encyclopedia of Soccer.* New York: Everest House Publishers, 1980.

Hornsby, Nick. *Fever Pitch.* London: Victor Gallancz, Ltd, 1992.

Huizinga, Johan. *Homo Ludens.* London: Routledge, 1949.

Lever, Janet. *Soccer Madness.* Chicago: University of Chicago Press, 1983.

Mandell, Richard D. *Sport: A Cultural History.* New York: Columbia University Press, 1984.

Morris, Desmond. *The Soccer Tribe.* London: Jonathan Cape, 1981.

Murphy, Patrick, Eric Dunning, and John Williams. *Football on Trial: Spectator Violence and Development in the Football World.* London and New York: Routledge & Kegan Paul, 1990.

Pelé, and R. L. Fish. *Pelé: My Life and the Beautiful Game.* New York: Doubleday, 1977.

Rollin, Jack. *The World Cup, 1930–1990: Sixty Glorious Years of Soccer's Premier Event.* New York: Facts on File, 1990.

Rote, Kyle. *Complete Book of Soccer.* New York: Simon and Schuster, 1978.

Vogelsinger, Hubert. *Winning Soccer Skills and Techniques.* West Nyack, New York: Parker Publishing Company, 1970.

Wagg, Stephen. *The Football World: A Contemporary Social History.* Brighton, Sussex: Harvester Press, 1984.

Walvin, James. *The People's Game: A Social History of British Football.* London: Allen Lane, 1975.